# CASE STUDIES
# IN CLINICAL AND
# SCHOOL PSYCHOLOGY

# CASE STUDIES
# IN CLINICAL AND
# SCHOOL PSYCHOLOGY

*By*

**RALPH F. BLANCO, Ph.D.**

*Diplomate in School Psychology*
*American Board of Professional Psychology*

*and*

**JOSEPH G. ROSENFELD, Ph.D.**

*Diplomate in Clinical Psychology*
*American Board of Professional Psychology*

*Temple University*
*Philadelphia, Pennsylvania*

**CHARLES C THOMAS** • **PUBLISHER**
*Springfield* • *Illinois* • *U.S.A.*

*Published and Distributed Throughout the World by*

CHARLES C THOMAS ● PUBLISHER

Bannerstone House

301-327 East Lawrence Avenue, Springfield, Illinois, U.S.A.

© *1978, by* CHARLES C THOMAS ● PUBLISHER

ISBN 0-398-03807-4

Library of Congress Catalog Card Number: 78-5914

*With* THOMAS BOOKS *careful attention is given to all details of
manufacturing and design. It is the Publisher's desire to present books that
are satisfactory as to their physical qualities and artistic possibilities and
appropriate for their particular use.* THOMAS BOOKS *will be true to those
laws of quality that assure a good name and good will.*

*Printed in the United States of America*
R-00-2

*Library of Congress Cataloging in Publication Data*

Blanco, Ralph F

   Case studies in clinical and school psychology.

   Bibliography: p.
   Includes index.
   1. Mentally ill children--Cases, clinical reports,
statistics.  2. Mentally handicapped children--Cases,
clinical reports, statistics.  3. Physically handicapped children--Cases, clinical reports, statistics.
I. Rosenfeld, Joseph G., joint author.  II. Title.
[DNLM:  1. Child behavior disorders--Case studies.
2. Learning disorders--In infancy and childhood--Case
studies.    WS350.6    B641c]
RJ499.B56    618.9'28'909    78-5914
ISBN 0-398-03807-4

To our wives, Lillian and Barbara
and children
Jeffrey, Janet, and Karen;
Andrea, Stephen, and Allen

# ACKNOWLEDGMENTS

MANY persons have assisted in the production of this book, particularly our clients, their parents, teachers and related professionals, all too numerous to record individually. Many of our talented students stimulated us with their persistent interest in the completion of the book and commented on its potential uses. Our able typist, Mrs. Anne Madden, translated our scribbled writing and garbled tapes with skill and comprehension.

Our resourceful publisher, Payne Thomas, supported our efforts to begin, encouraged us often, patiently waited, and finally edited our material personally.

We are most grateful to all these kind people.

R.F.B.
J.G.R.

# CONTENTS

# CASE STUDIES
# IN CLINICAL AND
# SCHOOL PSYCHOLOGY

# CHAPTER I

# INTRODUCTION

THE authors view the fields of clinical-child psychology and school psychology as closely related specialties. Although the dual professions maintain somewhat different emphases in the locale of services and treatment strategies, the focus of both specialities is on the child, the significant persons in the child's life, and the social system of interaction. Often the battleground for the child's conflicts and problems is in the school as well as the home.

There remain in both specialties (1) the constant need to "bridge the gap between theory and practice", and (2) an insufficiency of comprehensive case studies for training. To reduce these discrepancies, the authors have summarized their theoretical and research orientations when introducing each chapter and have accentuated case study and practice aspects so that several purposes may be served:

1. A psychology student, either graduate or undergraduate, may critically view what future professional work will be like and perhaps develop a heightened sense of anticipation.

2. The advanced student, while attending to the clinical material in the Workbook Sections, may sharpen diagnostic skills and practice creating prescriptions for change. Also, a detailed, item-by-item analysis of the test responses can be executed when experience is needed in interpretation of tests and the integration of data.

3. For the student struggling to learn about psychological and educational theory, practice, and research who wonders where this effort will take him or her, the case study book provides an experience, one step from actual practice, about the real world of applied psychology. The student may read, consider, and discuss how the authors

handled or supervised the management of an array of child-oriented problems. The cases are sometimes complicated and sometimes commonplace, yet typical of those needing resolution by clinical and school psychologists.

4. For the experienced practitioner, the material might expand his or her repertoire of intervention strategies as revealed by the hundreds offered in the presented cases. The clinical dynamics and attempted resolutions may be of interest during in-service training of interns or field practitioners, especially when the inevitable differences arise between the authors' viewpoint and the reader's. Certainly, reasonable people may disagree.

In dealing with the variety of problems in this book, it is clear that an eclectic or multi-theoretical orientation has been adopted for guidance and then adapted to the individual case. Strategies have been developed from dynamic psychology, behavioral psychology, medical considerations, educational perspectives and, in some cases, interdisciplinary practices. With the current, imperfect state of knowledge, a broad-spectrum orientation rather than a unitary theoretical approach to child problems is essential to both clinical and school psychologists.

The authors — the first a Diplomate in School Psychology and the second a Diplomate in Clinical Psychology, ABPP — feel that versatility and adaptability in utilizing theory and research are essential to good field practice and university teaching. They have, therefore, selected a variety of cases and situations that are not atypical in school and clinical practice and yet demand professional flexibility. In some cases, several thoretical orientations were actually merged into the remediation, resulting in positive outcomes.

The cases have been selected to represent not only interesting pathologies in various home and school settings, but also to demonstrate differing diagnostic and consulting problems in their respective milieus. For example, in just the dimensions of intelligence alone, the cases range from approximately 10 IQ to 166 IQ. The diagnostic and therapeutic problems include sensory handicap, emotional disturbance, behavior problems, learning disabilities, mental retardation, giftedness, and a multiple handicap. The living conditions range from the urban ghetto to wealthy estates. The learning environments include public and parochial schools as well as residential treatment facilities, all places where the authors have been employed for many years. Thus, the perspectives include not only the problems of the children but also the conditions psychologists must surmount in practice.

This case study book also represents a cross-sectional view of dual professions at a moment in time. It reveals how the professions currently attend to child pathology and remedial strategies. The need for appropriate prescriptions and models of professional behavior had been addressed by the authors previously (Blanco, 1972; Rosenfeld & Blanco, 1974). The material presented here, however, is in some contrast to older works that provided single-theory orientations, e.g. the essentially psychoanalytic interpretations of Kessler (1966), the ego psychology of Palmer (1970), and the behavioral focus of Ullmann and Krasner (1965).

The diagnostic model, as well as the behavioral model, is promulgated in this book in the steadfast belief that "diagnosis is not dead" when done competently as an essential basis to efficacious remediation. The authors, recognizing that many cases require careful differential diagnosis, note this to be especially true with regard to implementing the federal and state laws for evaluating handicapped children. Once a psychological diagnosis is made, the proper therapeutic and remedial strategies, some of which may be strictly behavioral, can be most effectively utilized. Individual Educational Programs (IEPs), derived from psychological and educational observations, arise from a developmental, diagnostic-prescriptive model.

While follow-up has been done on each of the cases, extensive follow-up was not possible due to the confidentiality of the material, mobility of the families, notoriety of certain cases, etc. All case materials are well disguised in terms of identities, sibling and family names, and schools while maintaining the integrity of the clinical material.

### The Workbook Sections

Two discrete opportunities are available to students by assignment from their clinical instructor or supervisor.

First, in three of the cases with relatively clear-cut diagnoses, the prescriptive recommendations are not given immediately at the end of each case. Instead, they are listed in the Appendix. The readers may write specific recommendations as they deem appropriate for the cases in question and discuss them with colleagues in class. The instructor may offer criticisms in regard to applicability, concreteness, theoretical consistency, etc. Further discussion will ensue when the students' contributions are compared to those of the authors as actually used on those cases. In a fourth case, dealing with the underachievement of a junior high boy, no such recommendations are offered, leaving this opportunity without a base for comparisons. This situation certainly occurs in daily practice.

The second Workbook section contains considerable raw data from various projective, cognitive and perceptual tests which can be used as a basis for clinical exercises. Assignments here might be to conceptualize, in writing, the personality structure of the child in question as well as his or her strengths limitations from a psychoeducational vantage point.

### Overview

The book contains a total of fifteen cases with varying pathologies. After the introduction, Chapter II includes the longest case and offers a mixed diagnosis, rich with clinical data; Chapter III deals with varieties of emotional and behavior problems and their respective interventions for change. Chapter IV illustrates the struggles of two mildly retarded children and the reactions of their parents; Chapter V notes some learning disabilities common to children; one gifted case is summarized in Chapter VI and provides a fruitful outcome; Chapter VII denotes cases involving sensory impairment and multiple handicap.

Cases of childhood psychosis (Bettelheim, 1950, 1955), autism (Des Lauriers, & Carlson, 1969), and depression (Schulterbrandt

& Raskin, 1977) were omitted from the book since they have been extensively documented elsewhere. More cases, lengthier sections on theory and research, or additional strategies with exotic twists could have been provided if the authors were to write an encyclopedic volume rather than a basic text for students and colleagues.

The authors hope that this book will provide provocative material for learning, a stimulus to further inquiry and research, and a demonstration of thorough psychological practices to aid deeply troubled children.

# CHAPTER II

# A MIXED DIAGNOSIS IN A TYPE I FAMILY: THE BOY WITH THE GUN

**B** ECAUSE of the richness of the personal data and the uniqueness of the pathologies involved in this case, pertinent socio-psychological perspectives will be summarized prior to the presentation of clinical information. The atypical details are offered to document the history of an unusual event in the life of one family and one school psychologist. Assuredly, not all school-related cases are so complex or perhaps even so compelling; nevertheless, any psychologist should anticipate that the problems encountered in the lives of children will, at times, place unexpected stress upon those concerned.

In this special circumstance, several disciplines were actively involved in their respective ways. Significantly, but not surprisingly, none had outstanding success. The experienced professional eventually realizes that few problems have total and permanent solutions. Thus, the textbooks that purport to aid in the training of young professionals should clearly reflect this fact of life and give a realistic view of authentic problems in clinical and school settings.

This detailed case history illustrates the interrelationships of clinical data, events, and personalities in an unusual community to provide a vivid basis for professional learning. The reader, given a summarized version of what transpired, may develop different impressions about case management. Since so much of the service aspect of applied psychology deals with the *art* rather than the *science* of clinical judgment, it is expected that opinions will differ between experienced clinicians as well as between novice professionals. These differences are not the bane of psychology, but rather the stimuli for revitalization and advancement in the profession itself. Conceivably, for the case in point, different approaches may have prevented the eruption of violence occurring two years after the first clinical work was done.

Lastly, the material provides (1) a procedural model for field work in school psychology, and (2) a humane perspective of parents struggling to help their son survive an array of interrelated problems.

## The Role of the Psychologist

Before the school psychologist on the case could offer direct services for the complicated problems at first purported to be "slight underachievement," it was necessary that he appreciate the values of the special community where the child lived, the origins of those values, and the belief system of the parents. Without a grasp of the powerful sociological forces that stimulated certain life styles, molded ambitions, and created family roles, the psychologist may have inadvertently directed the case toward infertile resolutions. He needed to construct strategies for remediation that were basically congruent with the values of the parents to enhance the success potential of the case. To be a helpful school psychologist, it was also necessary to appreciate the responsiveness and the resistance of the school personnel to the style of the community. The psychologist's contact with the case has covered an eight-year span.

## The Locale

It was a privileged, unique community on the distant edge of a large city. Private architects had sprinkled luxurious homes around a dredged, spring-fed pond that provided fishing excitement and water sports for the often talented, handsome children of the owners. Other residents lived in summer homes ringing the lush green of exclusive country clubs. Like the owners of the 2- and 5-acre estates, their offspring were groomed for future leadership roles. In this striving, somewhat brittle atmosphere, the children were conflicted by the dual messages from parents: Enjoy the relaxed, monied life of parental indulgence, yet prepare for the battles to come in the adult world of business, commerce, and the professions. The parents had set examples of the American Dream in action; they had manipulated the culture to provide well for themselves; they had "made it" and so would their children. The adults had accepted and succeeded at the All American Myth: You can achieve anything you want, as long as you try hard enough.

As with all myths, a nugget of golden truth remained at its core if not assayed too professionally. Thus, one could achieve very well if one "tried hard enough," but this singular vision ignored the mandated correlates congruent with high drive: superior intelligence, physical and emotional stamina, some luck, and a self-monitored urge to improve constantly in every way. Finally, the capstone of these qualities was the need for competition.

The men in this community were often first-rate talents — captains of the largest commercial aircraft on the most prestigious runs, officers of influential companies, well-ranked academicians, all neighbored by a scattering of the *nouveau riche*, unsure of their new status. An enterprising and imaginative engineer, for example, with one creative patent received a half million dollars in royalties per year, yet he and his family became alcoholic. By contrast, some wives in the area lived comfortably and sanely on interest derived from their wisely invested, inherited capital.

Taking the local train to the city, the executive class continued the taxing effort of enriching their companies and, presumably, their own lives. Mostly college men or at least those of unusual ability and drive, they enjoyed the struggle for business success. Such competition was basically unfair to more mediocre men. To the executives it was relatively easy to follow the Work Ethic of concentrating hard, being reliable — perfectionistic was even better — and manipulating people to achieve whatever goals needed to be reached. Achievement was great fun for them and, as these dynamic men keenly appreciated, society was generous and rewarding. If the wife was lonely or a bit ignored by being an executive's mate, well, that had to be accepted as a normal, minor consequence, a sacrifice to be repaid with the annual trip to the Caribbean. A two-week tour of Europe or a trip to Vail's ski slopes were acceptable rewards for the sixty-hour work week.

Many of the men were modestly self-congratulatory by the time they had passed the middle-management level of executive talent, having been escalated into the top administrative ranks. Country club membership was now available, since some companies paid their initiation fees under the guise of "business expenses." Yet no one man fit a stereotype, each being too individual to amass all the characteristics of a sociological pigeonhole.

The wives, not stereotyped any more than their husbands, were a chic group; generally slim and incredibly neat, they specialized in supporting their husbands at work and adoring them at home while being expert in coordinating schedules for school, music lessons, social life, and planned fun. Often well educated and alert, many women accepted their roles without major misgivings. Most concentrated on holding the household together and rising to the demands of their husbands' careers.

Not all women were pleased with their condition, however, for there often remained a powerful suspicion that they were being used. They felt manipulated by their husbands to forward business careers and used by their children with endless demands for chauffeur services to club meetings, parties, and orthodontic appointments.

Subliminal to the surface satisfaction was also the quiet desperation of the achieving man and the unsatisfied woman, each alienated from the other. The typical man wished to be perceived as the "solid oak" of his company and family in that order, while the woman was assigned the role of "partner" who could handle "her end of the bargain," a business term suitable for the market place but not the home. The women respected the husbands for their achievements, but rarely for their tenderness as lovers or their dedication as fathers. Such men, in their intense focus upon the external world of objects, deals, profit, and loss, found less comfort in the affective life, the world of mercurial feelings and of deep sentiments. To them the emotional life was too imprecise to handle and was thus rejectable.

In a self-deprecating way, the families joked that they lived in the "Alka Seltzer® Commune." Yet they loved it, for inherent in this residency was the privilege of being in the top 1 or 2 percent of a materialistic society, no mean accomplishment. It required great self-discipline and clever planning. Nothing should be allowed to go wrong.

### The Type I Family

What has been described here is a cross-sectional view of the Type I Family (Blanco, 1977) (theory and a case illustration of the Type II Family follow in Chapter III). In this discussion of the Type I unit, the characters in the family are artificially reduced to a near-stereotype for simplification purposes and rapid identification.

Within this group, there is a combination of recognizable characteristics that reflects the life-style of a striving, yet alienated family having various pathologies manifested in one or more offspring, frequently revealed through underachievement and passive-aggressive behavior. Never pure in form and subject to endless embellishment, the Type I Family is a dynamic relationship that needs to be appreciated by professional persons assisting the disturbed child of such a family. Easy to condemn from a distance, sometimes ridiculed in novels and television for stereotypic behaviors and trite attitudes, the family members have real problems, which are both punishing and intense.

Their concerns have distressed administrators of the local school districts and upset the tranquility of their staff. Such professional people are sometimes intolerant of the life-style of the parents and dislike the pressured expectation that their students must succeed at almost any price. The adaptable school personnel attempt to cater to the high expectations of the parents and the internalized strivings of their bright children.

Yet the parents are, of course, the community taxpayers who dominate the local Board of Education and transmit their demands to school administrators. Many parents clearly want carbon copies of themselves with relatively little room for individuality unless there is reflected some greater accomplishment.

In a psychoanalytic sense, a Type I Family reflects an updated Oedipal relationship. This becomes apparent when one considers the wife's dual roles with her husband and then her son. She has adjusted to her powerful and assertive male, learning to withdraw from him when he is enraged and has shut her out of his business concerns. She is at best a weekend mistress, since his real marriage is to his business. Since he is clearly a perfectionist, she can never quite meet all his demands.

Both are disappointed in each other as mates, as he finds it difficult to be genuinely gentle, lacking as he is in compassion and subtle feeling. She, in turn, cannot respond ardently because he lacks the very qualities that she needs to evoke her full emotional response. In her need for more emotional acceptance and gratification, she turns to her son and engulfs him with her loving overproteciton. Since the child, a rival for the mother's affection, eventually becomes the recipient of the father's rejection, the youngster inevitably turns to the safer and gentler of his parents. She comforts him when has faltered and angered his father for offering his childlike, less-than-excellent results in sports and school.

The mother feels that she has been a disappointment to her demanding husband. In her guilt she resolves to give him a perfect child, her gift of appeasement. In fact the father orders her in subtle ways to insure that all their children achieve. She accepts this assignment much like a junior executive. Mentally her husband grades her on a scale from *A* through *F*.

Perhaps predictably, the boy in such a family will often not become the "super child" in whom the parents are deeply invested. By the time he is only a few years old, he has recognized (1) the high aspiration signalled by his father, (2) the threatening countenance of the man when disappointed, and (3) his own need for individuality. The boy does not want to be molded as a carbon copy to satisfy parental demands but needs instead to be an individual relatively free from parental domination even at the expense of failure and its resulting condemnation. Thus, as learning opportunities appear in school and competitive areas, he avoids them in a self-defeating, parent-infuriating manner. He becomes a classic, passive-aggressive underachiever as a subtle way of retaliating against parental aspirations and tight controls.

The mother, seeing this pattern of school problems develop, feels even more guilty than before since she has "failed" to carry out her husband's executive mandate. Simultaneously, her feelings move sympathetically toward the boy in his apparent ineptitudes and passivity. She binds the child to her by their mutual despair and fear and places herself between the man and his son. The father may interpret this as a rejection of himself and then jealously resent her open affection for the boy. The latter is clearly in a rivalrous relationship, and the Oedipal dynamics are now in full swing. The lad enjoys the mother's comforting and quiet understanding, yet he also feels the need to be separate from her.

What has occurred is that she has sent the boy two distinct and contradictory messages: (1) "Grow up to be a competitor like your father," and (2) "Stay as my baby as I cannot let you go." The conflict resulting from these opposite thrusts is inevitable and debilitating.

Contrary to some expectations, the child does not hate his father or his mother; he admires and respects the man as a competent and often generous man. The father is recognized as a person who models ideal behavior in professional life, a shade of the Renaissance man. The boy sees the man as a moneymaker, a cut above ordinary men, as an athlete, and as a provider of sports equipment and fun vacations.

Nor has the daughter escaped the demands for scholastic accomplishments. Although she is not named "Junior," as is often the fate of her brother, she knows that she is expected to "shape up" on several dimensions. Secretly she has vowed to play the role, to keep quiescent her resentments, and to find a man someday who will be the antithesis of her father. Not all daughters in the Type I Family so react of course. Some adopt the drives of a family patriarch and seek accomplishments of their own, or select men who match their father's style, talents, and beliefs. Should such a man later disappoint her in marriage or professional accomplishment, she may become crushingly critical of him by using her father as a standard for comparison.

Another daughter may openly rebel with hysterical pyrotechnics or by running away, becoming pregnant, turning delinquent, or addicted. She may or may not achieve in school, but she certainly makes it known that she is in control of her own life whether her parents like it or not. For all the surface anguish the father feels at this daughter's rebellion, he still admires her strength, as it matches his in a lopsided way. The father secretly reinforces her for her "tough" stand.

Neither son nor daughter deeply admire the mother; rather, they feel sorry for her. Self-deprecating, uncertain of her status, but mindful of her obligations, the mother is a second-rate citizen designated to be attractive, helpful, and pleasing.

The standard prescription for this type of pathology with mild disturbance would be: Family and/or individual psychotherapy. On the other hand, several behavioral strategies might well encompass an assertive training program for the lad and his mother, tutoring for his sluggish academics, and perhaps desensitization for all concerned to reduce anxiety levels. Private school attendance might well be in store for the boy as well as a multitude of "tune-up" interventions to develop more harmonious social relationships during the years ahead.

An important and special development in the son's makeup is his secret admiration and simultaneous resentment toward other boys who "have everything going for them." He tends to envy age-mate adolescents who achieve well, are good-looking and athletic, and who are socially compatible with the community's values. Such talented children win the junior golf tournaments at the club, hold elected offices at school, and earn the obvious and financially rewarding respect of their parents. Often the Type I boy feels deeply resentful about his well-executing counterpart who is everything that he is not. Such was the case of The Boy With The Gun.

### The Referral

Into this unique community came a talented and insightful superintendent here given the name of Doctor Alan Martin, fresh out of his doctorate from a major university. Although initially disappointed that the domain of his first superintendency encompassed only one kindergarten-through-eighth-grade school building, he settled down to develop an educational program suited to the needs of this demanding community. Graciously accepted into the homes of people like himself (he later became superintendent of two of the country's largest school districts), he not surprisingly discovered that problems existed with certain students under his purview. After the known retarded and handicapped were referred to and accounted for by his local school psychologist, the next level of academic inefficiency was uncovered. This came through the superintendent's analysis of group test results for intelligence and achievement and through staff conferences. His attention focused on Ned Steer, a twelve-year-old who revealed an erratic pattern of achievement test scores but a cluster of average IQ scores. Teachers claimed that the boy was a "slight underachiever in the sixth grade."

Early in Doctor Martin's tenure the mother of Ned had entreated him to have the local school psychologist evaluate her child, who "wasn't working up to his level of ability." This presented a problem, for a glance at his cumulative folder for test score patterns revealed immediately that the boy had, in fact, achieved at the average level consonant with measured intelligence. The resolution seemed simple enough: The school psychologist would examine the boy on individual intelligence tests, and if Ned were discovered again to be average, then the parents were to be encouraged to accept his scholastic mediocrity. If, however, a discrepancy between measured intelligence and achievement appeared, a more penetrating investigation was in order. Both parents agreed to the referral.

### School Background

Prior to seeing the parents but after receiving their verbal permission to begin the psychological evaluation, the school psychologist inspected the school records. He spoke with Doctor

Martin about his knowledge of the family and the functioning of Ned in school. A generous quantity of test scores was available:

*Group Intelligence Test Results*

1. Science Research Associates, Primary Mental Abilities:

   First Grade:          94 IQ

   Second Grade:       88 IQ

*Group Achievement Test Results*

1. California Achievement Tests:

| Grade Norm | Reading | Language | Arithmetic |
|---|---|---|---|
| 2.9 g.p. | 2.9 | 3.2 | 2.2 |

2. Science Research Associates, Achievement Tests:

| Grade Norm | Reading | Language | Arithmetic |
|---|---|---|---|
| 4.1 g.p. | 4.3 | 3.4 | 3.3 |
| 5.1 | 3.6 | 3.8 | 3.9 |
| 6.1 | 8.0 | 6.4 | 5.6 |

Ned's marks in school subjects in the sixth grade were as follows:

| Reading | D | Language | C- | Arithmetic | D |
|---|---|---|---|---|---|
| Spelling | D+ | Social Studies | C- | Science | B |

Further, Ned's instructional levels in reading and arithmetic were estimated to be at the "fourth and fifth grades," respectively. It was significant that the typical student in this school scored 118 IQ on the SRA Primary Mental Abilities Test and measured, on related achievement tests, typically about two grade levels above the national norms irrespective of grade level. Thus, Ned was initially viewed by the school psychologist as a boy of low-average intelligence based on his scores of 94 and 88 IQ compared to the typical high-average child of the community. In one respect, he could be considered a gross overachiever in reading with his 8.0 grade placement when using as a predictive yardstick his apparently mediocre intelligence. His mid-sixth grade scores in language and arithmetic were well below peer averages but adequate for his estimated intelligence.

Further inspection indicated a rather slow rate of learning. The only written comments were, "He has difficulty in concentration; he needs direction and prompting, as he is not accurate." Most subject grades in five years in school scattered around *C*s, *D*s, and *F*s.

The superintendent gave his succinct impressions of the parents to the psychologist:

> My wife and I had dinner at the Steers' home a week ago without Ned being present. They unloaded a tremendous amount of information to us. They seemed confused about the boy and asked for our help. Here's the upshot. Ned is essentially infantile and immature in his behavior at home and school. Specifically, he stills sucks his thumb in school and does low mediocre work. He's regarded by my staff sympathetically but as one who is a "sad sack." Ned looks rather stupid and dull; he's basically unkempt. The child doesn't know when to stop when he gets excited or when he is having fun. He just overdoes things, gets carried away, and can't put on the brakes. I've known the parents less than a year and they're really lovely people. He's the vice-presicent of (a nationally known company) making an astronomical salary while his wife stays at home hovering over Ned. Luckily they're pro-psychology and trust that we can get to the core of the problems. Basically they can't grasp why the boy can't do better work in school and why he seems so awkward

socially. The whole problem is very upsetting to them, as their daughter, who is now about twenty-two, was an excellent student at (an Ivy League University); she went on to have a very comfortable marriage with a talented nice guy, as I recall. He is in the trucking business with a masters degree in accounting. He's a rugged, athletic fellow who made a big hit with his in-laws, the Steers. In fact, Ned is crazy about his brother-in-law, and they trapshoot and fish together whenever this super guy comes to visit.

It's pretty clear that the parents want Ned to be as outstanding as his sister and brother-in-law and feel that they have given him loads of opportunities, but he fouls up each one of them. It's a damn shame he's so self-defeating.

The mother is from an ordinary background I think but got some college work in and managed to attract the father, who apparently is a first-rate talent. You know, high school valedictorian, a genius at engineering, very masculine, and a fine trapshooter as well. The trouble is, he was so devoted to his company that he lost touch with his family to some degree. Yes, he got rapid promotions and found the financial rewards were simply incredible.

The family lives just off the lake in a lovely home. All the latest conveniences are at her disposal, believe me. Two good signs: Actually Ned does play a pretty good clarinet and trapshoots rather well. Friends? Forget it: He's been rejected by most of the kids in the neighborhood. He lives near the three talented Johnson brothers — very popular teenagers — but they can't stand him and have made life miserable for him.

The psychologist then interviewed several of Ned's teachers. All were eager to aid in the evaluation and felt sorry for the boy, perceiving him as a self-doubting, socially imcompetent student who was "occasionally" very motivated to learn but "poorly coordinated." Several noted that he was capable of furious temper outbursts. These explosions were easily diverted, so they said, by the calming influence of a nearby adult. As noted by others, Ned had trouble "putting on the brakes" to his emotions. One teacher complained prejudicially about "rich kids."

Teachers had independently sought to praise him in class, in fact, to protect him from scorn and ridicule. They testified that he was, at best, tolerated by children and at worst, used as a scapegoat. Reading and math teachers were confused by his constant letter and number reversals, his disorders in sentence structure and his "chicken scratch" handwriting (the indices frequently seen in a learning disabled child).

### Contact with the Parents

Both parents decided to meet with the school psychologist prior to his testing and evaluation to determine if they could trust him with their private apprehensions and the background of their son's problems.

A call to the parents by the school psychologist gave reassurance that his keen interest was present and that a comprehensive psychoeducational evaluation was planned, pending Ned's cooperation. The parents, not surprisingly, first requested a personal interview with the psychologist to "give the full picture." A two-hour conference was scheduled. Over the telephone the mother's essential concerns focused upon the underachievement in school and "social ineptitude of my son." She had some "private" concerns about Ned, which she promised to elaborate upon during the meeting.

On the day of the conference a very well groomed, attractive, middle-aged couple arrived and were greeted warmly by the superintendent who, in turn, brought them to the office of the psychologist. Here was a private nook supplied with comfortable chairs, two small desks, a professional library, and hot coffee. Once introduced, the psychologist seated the parents for a conference without the administrator. The father took command at once in his executive style:

*Father:* I've been a busy man, Doctor, perhaps too busy to attend to my boy, but now before it's too late I want to find out what's happened to him. Ned's really a sweet guy but not turning out right. He's confused, angry, and he does dumb things that get him into trouble.

*Psychologist:* What sort of things do you feel aren't going well for him? You're certainly very concerned in wanting to help him.

*Father:* Right! God, if I could only manage my son like I manage the business we wouldn't need to seek your help at all. Look, my wife and I have lots of observations on Ned. We've discussed these privately a hundred times. Tell me when you've got the picture because I don't want to repeat material that you might understand quickly. Honestly, I really want you to give us your very best help, we're up against it. Alan Martin (the superintendent) also wants a resolution to this wasted effort on my son's part.

*Psychologist:* I'm going to be just as helpful as I possibly can, Mr. and Mrs. Steer. I'm very curious about Ned, his problems, what he does well, and where he's going. You are both anxious enough to ask me to pitch in to help and so have a lot of school people I've talked with.

*Mother:* Then you've spoken with Doctor Martin? I'm so glad! He's been to our house with his wife, but I guess we belabored the social hour with Ned's problems. He got interested enough to alert you. Doctor, my husband and I are so upset (a few tears begin and a tissue is offered. Coffee is poured and the mother calms down enough to continue although she remains quite scattered in her remarks, which covered a span of many years). Where shall I start? He was a nice baby. No, he was really grumpy too, always liked black as a color when he was four or five years old, learned to skip and ride a bike late. Do you think he's retarded? Ned was fussy about school and still is to this day. Fortunately, his music goes well, second clarinet, and we're so proud of his musical ability.

*Psychologist:* Well, there are a lot of things you want to say that sound very interesting. I want to hear the whole story — right from the beginning. There's no rush and we've plenty of time today. If we don't finish, I'll meet you again, perhaps separately, to get even a more personal perspective. As I've mentioned over the telephone, if you want me to continue the evaluation with testing, then you can also tell Ned about our meeting today and express to him the very same concerns you're telling me. Please tell him that we have talked today and that I'll soon be seeing him for some testing. I've got a feeling that Ned and I will hit it off pretty well.

*Father:* Yes, I feel that too. He likes anybody who shows a genuine interest in him. I think he'll go the limit with you in trying. You know, Doctor, I confess that I was a bit anxious in meeting you. You never know what kind of a guy a psychologist is going to be — a real creep or a real person. If I read you right, you're telling me that you're going to go the whole way with us — interviews, testing, the works.

*Mother:* (Interrupting) What I'd like to know after you're done is this: What are we going to do for this boy? He's not happy and neither are we. I want the best for him. If I've done things wrong, I want to know what they are (mother begins crying again). We can't let him stumble into adolescence and adult life like this (deep sobbing). He is so rejected by the neighborhood kids he's just plain miserable.

*Psychologist:* To answer your husband first, Mrs. Steer, yes, I'm going to pursue these problems fully, but I need to have a clear impression about Ned, and here is where you folks will be a tremendous help to me. I sense a basic need to be honest and to be thorough. Believe me, I'll be careful with your boy, and I certainly will do my best to respect your feelings. I see that you're both upset and baffled on the direction to take in his life. At this moment I don't have a set of solutions partly because I don't know all the problems yet. It's going to take me a few hours of work to see them clearly in my own head. I've gotten an educational perspective from the staff, which I want to share with you now (this is then described in detail to the parents.) I still need to enlarge the story with your points of view and, of course, the child's vantage point as well. Why don't we settle back with a fresh cup of coffee while I listen to you tell me about Ned in detail. Mrs. Steer, what were your first recollections about him at birth? (A developmental history is started.) I understand for instance that a sister preceded him. How did you feel about having a boy for the second birth?

*Mother:* Oh Doctor, you hit it right!

*Psychologist:* How do you mean?

*Mother:* That question brought to mind that my husband and I were absolutely thrilled at his birth. We wanted a son so very much. I think men, or at least certain men, need a son, and Ned was so beautiful and big and blond. It was heaven (cries again and husband picks up the story).

*Father:* As you can see, my wife's heart is aching over this whole thing and so is mine only I've practiced self-control over the years. A beautiful baby boy and now twelve years later a miserable, almost friendless child who can't get a grasp on learning. What a damn shame. We've discussed it so much and asked ourselves that corny but oh-so-true line, where did we go wrong? (A clear bid for reassurance)

*Psychologist:* You feel that, in some unknown way, you're responsible for his immaturity. Is that the idea?

*Father:* Yes, You're on target completely. All the time I spent in the company, all those extra meetings and road trips, those special training programs I had. These distractions, fascinating as they were, took me away a lot. The boy and his mother leaned on each other in my absence. I guess I wasn't around when they needed me. He seemed to be a jumpy baby, irritable and didn't smile a lot like our daughter, Janie (father's face lights up at her name), my married one, when she was a baby.

*Psychologist:* You felt that your attention to business was a contributing factor to the closeness shared by the mother and son. Mr. Steer, since your wife spent so much time with Ned when he was a baby, why don't I direct most of my initial inquiries about birth and development to her and you can feel free to add your observations as we go along. I've got quite a series of questions about when he started to stand up, walk, talk, etc., which will give me a good lead about his rate of development and when some of these problems arose. Mrs. Steer, how do you feel about starting at the beginning so that we can lay out all the events in a row? Maybe a pattern will form.

*Mother:* Yes, let's get organized that way. I just couldn't hold back my feelings earlier but I'm ready now. I'm such a sentimental person. You know, you seem so willing to pursue everything. I'm beginning to feel that we're going to get somewhere (turning to her husband), maybe we can help Ned before he really has big trouble (back to psychologist). Doctor, we can start with the fact that there was a normal birth in terms of the number of hours, but he was born with a cord around his neck. The obstetrician indicated that this was not uncommon and he saw no difficulty in breathing, not a blue baby or anything like that. But soon after he was born the nurses and I noticed that he was very sensitive to noises and would scream all day. He became colicky for four months, and I started to get really jumpy about his health. My pediatrician wasn't alarmed, however, and she reassured me with comments like, "He'll be fine later on," and, "He'll snap out of it." The one thing she did notice at two years was that his neck was a bit awkward, like a vertebra was out of alignment. She had no solution to this, and only this past summer, when Ned was twelve, did we find a good chiropractor who put it back again, and Ned seemed to relax a lot. Could a neck problem be responsible for his irritability, I asked myself? Well, no one knew for sure then or now. (The mother continues with minor prompting in regard to other developmental details.) He didn't sit up until eight months of age, and the poor kid just laid there and rolled around in the crib. I often think he was hurt in the labor process but I don't know for sure. My obstetrician didn't think so. Anyway he stood up suddenly at eight and one-half months and walked at fourteen months. Boy were we ever relieved!

*Father:* I was nuts about Ned; I showed him off to everyone. He was a boy who would have everything: the finest schools, the best business contacts when he was grown, the best in athletic equipment and opportunities. I had all these nutty dreams that he was going to be a super kid, my kid. I wanted to be a first-rate dad to him like I tried to be with my girl. She thrived on it — great at tennis, excellent student, and an amazingly good-natured girl. People would remark how grown-up she was. When she met her present husband we were ecstatic. Ned didn't turn out that way, as you're learning. He wanted things immediately, was very impatient and jumpy at noises. At one and one-half or two years of age he was completely fascinated by noisy lawn mowers and

would watch them all morning and all afternoon, how do
you figure that out?

*Psychologist:* I don't have a pat explanation for these things
but I'm writing them down to recall them later. In most cases
a pattern or two emerges, which will give us a good sense of
direction.

*Father:* Just getting the facts before deciding. That's my style
too, Doctor. It sounds easy but I know that it isn't.

*Psychologist:* I feel that there are leads or clues to follow that
will give us a hint of possible causes. It's still too early in our
first discussion for me to get the full picture, but if you're
patient with me maybe I can pull it together through all
your observations. Go ahead, Mrs. Steer.

*Mother:* As he grew up he had a rather short temper and got
angry when toys wouldn't work. He would cry easily. Ned
just seemed to get into one mess after the other, and I had to
rescue him.

*Psychologist:* How do you mean?

*Mother:* Well, whenever he had a homework assignment, even
in the early grades, he wouldn't know how to get started so
I'd organize the work, get his supplies and kind of stay
around him until it was done. Even with projects he was all
thumbs, so rather than see him fail again, I usually did it for
him.

*Father:* Yes, I've always objected, as she well knows, but I've
learned that she has a great need to protect him. She felt
somehow that he was special or handicapped in some way
and, now of course, we know that to be true. I used to go out
of my way to make sure that he was successful at things as he
got older. You know, taking him to a stocked trout pond for
his first fishing experience, making the base for a good snow
fort or buying him a good gun for our shooting together to
optimize his success.

*Psychologist:* Do I sense correctly that both of you did a lot for
Ned, perhaps too much as you're both saying, but I note also
that you both felt that very early he had special needs.

*Mother:* Yes, that's it — special needs. And with my make-up, I
catered to him. I felt so sorry about his physical awkward-

ness, for example. I had him evaluated by our pediatrician, but she said something like, "He's within normal limits." This was supposed to be reassuring to me, but I felt that the subtle problems were being ignored again. Then there were struggles with friends; often as I watched him play, he would hurt the feelings of other children, be very egocentric, forget or twist the rules of the game until the other kids kicked him out. He was so much the opposite of my husband, who frankly is good at everything (she smiles in adoration).

*Father:* Hold on, I don't mind having a fan in the crowd but that comment is a distortion of the facts; there are plenty of things I don't do well.

*Mother:* Not really. You've got a great business head and your company knows it. You're an excellent athlete and a scholarship student. That's why I love you. You're just a terrific guy.

*Psychologist:* (Jokingly) Do we have Renaissance man here today? Cultured, energetic, a lover and swordsman, a connoisseur of art, etc.?

*Father:* (Thrilled and amused at the view) Ha, Ha, Ha. The two of you have made my day. I'm forgetting that we came here to talk about Ned.

*Psychologist:* Well, we are talking about his parents, their own style of life, and how Ned has adjusted to certain quiet expectations. How they have responded with all good intentions to his struggles is also evident.

*Father:* Yes, there is a pattern that emerges and once it's pointed out it looks pretty simple. True, my son has deeply disappointed me but it compels me into action. I can't stand seeing these problems go unresolved. Where will he go after a lousy and disappointing school career? What kind of dumb things will he do next? Where are the thrills of accomplishments in his young life that tell him he's on the ball? I think he's not having a good time. Doctor, you'll probably see that in your talk with him or do you just do tests?

*Psychologists:* Both. But what are these dumb things that you refer to?

*Father:* For example, he earns a little money around the house and spends it right away on nonsense. Never saves and then complains loudly when he has no money. Another item: when he shoots poorly at the firing range, he blames this on the weather not himself. Another: his homework area and room are a mess and he can never find a pencil, his shoes, or anything. Doctor, he won't make a list of the things that he has to do and then forgets so much. He disregards almost all his responsibilities in spite of reminders from us, encouragements, and rewards. It's like he doesn't learn anything. Then he gets mad when he leaves his toys or books somewhere and can't find them.

*Mother*: Socially he's very unsure of himself and operates like a much younger child with no confidence. Do you know that after he has trouble in school, a fight or does poorly on subjects, he just watches TV for days or draws monster cartoons.

*Psychologist*: I'll talk with him about these things and how he feels. Maybe he'll draw something for me.

*Mother*: I seem to recall everything better now. What do you make of this? At two or three he was always fascinated by these loud lawn mowers that my husband mentioned. He watched them go up and down, up and down. I tell you, it's perplexing.

*Psychologist*: Well, he certainly has some intense fascinations or some minor obsessions, but I won't fit that into anything else just yet. What else was difficult to explain? Where else was he different from other children?

*Mother*: Instant demand, that was Ned. He wanted things immediately. And sleep, my God, did he need sleep? Another thing: he couldn't stand change, can you follow that?

*Father*: Whenever we all would go someplace he would want to come home right away while the rest of us were having the time of our lives. He seemed to relax when he got back, definitely relieved. Same thing with moving the furniture in the house. At five or six years he'd be very upset if we moved the furniture, and then he would try to push it back to the old position. He would even go after our old furniture, which we discarded. Kind of weird to me. That's what neighborhood kids call him, "Weirdo."

*Mother:* On the good side, he was always crazy about his Dad and very affectionate to him and to me as well. There was lots of wrestling and fooling around with Ned and his Dad. Yes, the two of them were like bear cubs wrestling and laughing, but they don't really laugh much any more (very sadly spoken). You know, even lately when we got a new Lincoln® convertible, Ned still wanted the old one and said that we shouldn't have sold it. He just can't seem to accept change.

*Psychologist:* It rattles him when things are different, and it reveals behaviors that are difficult to explain.

*Father:* Yes, there are lots of confused messages. That's what gets us so anxious. He's just not predictable except that his school and social life are going downhill.

*Mother:* You remember that talk you gave, Doctor, at the PTA meeting last month? I was there and I heard your description of an underachiever. You hit it right; that's our Ned because we see flashes of real intelligence. He's got a clever sense of humor and reads our behavior very well, knows when we're disappointed and concerned. His ability to grasp geography is excellent, but that isn't taught this year, darnit. Music too. I think he's got ability and is sensitive to good music (the mother is very anxious to tell all these good points). In kindergarten he hardly paid attention but showed off to get a lot of attention for himself. The teacher was so kind and reassuring, but the boy "didn't grow out of it" like he was supposed to. Ned was distant with other kids, "preoccupied" is my ten dollar word for it, and didn't display the normal concern for others in kindness or sympathy if someone got hurt. But if an animal was hurt, stop the world! He had to rush in to help the poor thing.

*Father:* The other children teased him a lot about his coordination: I don't think he ever won a race or competed well in anything, so he just withdrew. That's not what we had in mind. I'd like the kid to be a little more hardnosed and competitive. I know the fun of competition in business and athletics even at the country club now. If you come out reasonably well, it's a helluva boost to your confidence. Somehow he never gets those boosts.

*Mother:* Dear, since we're honest with the psychologist I'd feel better telling him that in all of your heavy workload you had your own problems. Should we get into that?

*Father:* Of course. The other side of my coin is that when I hit forty years of age a while back I was really "zonked out."

*Psychologist:* "Zonked out?"

*Father:* I went into a first-class depression about my life even when business was going great. Couldn't attach any real meaning to life and didn't feel I had any control over how things were happening to me. A psychiatrist diagnosed me correctly as severely depressed. I was the most miserable person you ever want to see, and it scared the hell out of my wife and friends. I talked a lot about ending it all. I was committed rather briefly at (a private psychiatric hospital) and gradually got my sense of worth and values restored. My psychiatrist was a super guy; zeroed in on my concerns and let me take a peek at what had led up to my own depressions. I picked myself up gradually, found my colleagues at work very supportive. I guess they felt it could also happen to them. Now I feel fine. It's easy to connect my recollections of that depression with the fear that my Ned will be depressed someday, and he has only had a fraction of my good fortunes.

*Mother:* It was a bad time for all of us, and I think little Ned felt left out of his Dad's life for that year or so. There are so many things that have added to the fire that I hardly know what led to what. Gosh, we've given you such a rush of ideas and complaints today. The time has really flown (mother sighs very deeply). I do feel better talking to you (begins to smile). I think we're taking a big step in coming here today. Funny, it's painless and more like relief. Do you want to see us again or my husband?

*Psychologist:* Yes, it's been an experience for me too today in this past hour and a half. You've both given me such a rich background of incidents and observations about Ned and yourselves that it's making my job easier. With some parents they take quite awhile to warm up, but we didn't have any real problem here today.

*Mother:* You send out little reassurances, and parents need these so much.

*Psychologist:* Mrs. Steer, how about another hour or so early next week to get the complete developmental and medical history and these "other details" you feel I should know about Ned's behavior. And may I call your pediatrician? (Arrangements are made, medical references and telephone numbers are jotted down.) Let's get together after I see your wife, Mr. Steer. I'd like to know more about your activities with Ned. (The interview ends with warm expressions of regard on both sides.)

### Clinical Observations of Ned

Ned appeared at the psychologist's office accompanied by the school nurse, who had summated her hearing and vision records on him and reported normal test results in these areas. So began the diagnostic-prescriptive phase of the case. The violent reaction was to start suddenly two years later.

Ned, a blond-haired, muscular boy of average height for twelve years, appeared tense and fidgety throughout the testing and interviews. He grimaced rather than smiled and made quick, jerky physical movements rather than graceful ones as he seated himself. Speech came in staccato bursts. Uncertainty underlined his responses to simple questions about friends, school, hobbies, etc.

Too eager to please, polite, and acutely self-conscious, Ned hesitantly entered into the new relationship with the friendly and inquisitive school psychologist. Rapport developed slowly, the tempo congruent with the recognition that Ned was a fearful, self-deprecating boy who anticipated failure in his social contacts. It was clear, though masked, that he was bright and that his anxiety could easily block fluency and precision of thought. There was an "organic" quality in his behavioral style.

The nature of the referral was explained as well as the possibility that considerable interviewing and testing might ensue. Ned agreed to cooperate, adding hesitantly that he was aware

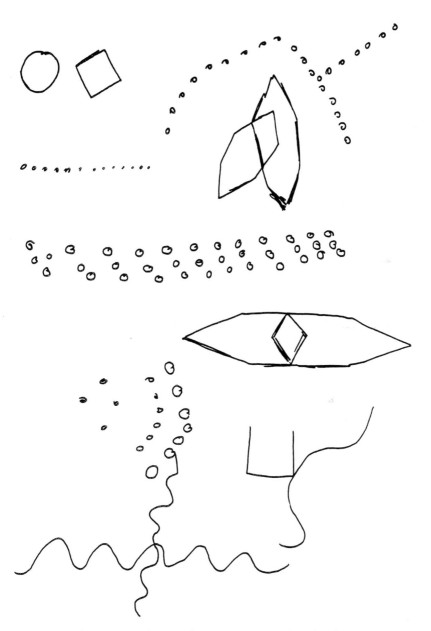

Figure 1. Designs executed by Ned Steer on the Bender-Visual-Motor-Gestalt Test.

that he struggled mightily with school and yet seemed to accomplish little, except in certain areas such as music and geography. He noted introspectively that he was often unhappy about his life and sighed significantly when reflecting about the depth of his relative helplessness.

The school psychologist, thinking to open the testing on a nonverbal note, offered the Bender-Visual-Motor-Gestalt Test. Ned executed the previous designs.

An interpretation of the results suggests that visual-motor and/or visual-perception problems are present by virtue of (a) separation of the designs in Card A, (b) various "scoreable" errors (via the Koppitz scoring system, 1964) such as producing circles for dots on Cards 1, 3, and 5, (c) some loss of gestalten on Cards 3 and 5, and (d) a small overlap problem of designs 3 and 6. The "reworking" or sketching around the six-sided figures of Cards 7 and 8 is more frequently attributed to anxiety manifestations than to visual perceptual problems. The "organic" quality is seen in the reproductions. Although the organization of the figures is not grossly defective, it is still inadequate for Ned's age level, and in a general way correlates with the low-average scores in his Performance section on the WISC (noted later). Although it is probably incorrect to state flatly that there are major visual perceptual problems in the reproduction, his work on Card A leaves this open to doubt.

After more informal interviewing with Ned about vacation preferences and activities during private hours on the weekends, the psychologist asked him to Draw-A-Man. The result are shown in Figure 2.

A psychological interpretation of the Frankensteinian apparition drawn by Ned is that it is a reflection of his self concept: weird, defective in the extreme, without (leg) support, helpless and sad, as well as grotesque and frightening. The dripping blood and the blood-shot eyes (as identified by Ned), the fissures in the skull, stomach, and especially the heart suggest mortal wounds and irreparable damage to the personality. Ned evidently viewed himself as hideous, unlovable, and pathetic, perhaps a "Thing" already attacked by others and beyond rehabilitation. The psychologist, admittedly rather stunned, failed to obtain a full interrogation of Ned about his drawing. When

Figure 2. Result of the Draw-A-Man test.

asked about his production, Ned merely said that he "enjoyed" drawing such people and fantasized that he was the creator of a comic strip printed in newspapers throughout the country, a hint of his powerful need for recognition and approval. He was undoubtedly stimulated by such strange caricatures and persevered in the theme on the next drawing.

Ned was requested to draw a "tree" and, seizing his pencil eagerly, revealed gleeful interest in another weird scene as he drew the following picture:

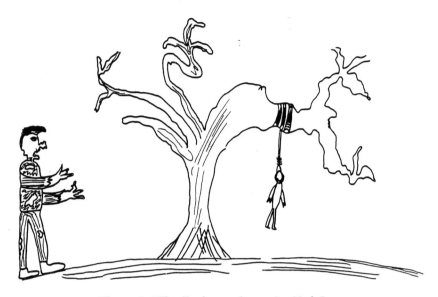

Figure 3. "Tree" picture drawn by Ned Steer

An interpretation of the "tree" and its accompanying details suggests his obsessive focus on the weird, distorted fantasy about monsters and death. Perhaps he (or a significant person in his life) is already dead or dying by hanging while a potentially devouring (or cannibalistic), half-dead creature rushes to attack (or save) the hanging body. The gnarled tree is lifeless and hopeless, matching in structure the hideous "thing" approaching from the left. The left tilt of the hanging body, a macabre detail, might be perceived as a pendulum swing of the body. The supporting tree limb was so sturdy as to be unbreakable, and thus left no chance of a "reprieve" for the hanging body. The picture reveals, from a psychodynamic orientation, an outlet for the impulses of the Id. Ned's fantasy life was indeed dramatic and death oriented, an almost prophetic scene of later developments in the case.

The school psychologist, finding rapport to be good, switched to the administration of the Wechsler Intelligence Scale for Children (the WISC-R had not yet been printed). Clinical interpretation follows concerning the extremely wide discrepancy of 38 IQ points between the Verbal IQ and the Performance IQ on Ned's testing. Ned's WISC and WRAT Test results were as follows:

| *Wechsler* | | *Wide Range Achievement Tests* | |
|---|---|---|---|
| Verbal IQ | 125 | Approx. Word Rec. | High 7th Gr. |
| Performance IQ | 87 | Approx. Arith. | High 5th Gr. |
| Full Scale IQ | 115 | | |

### Second Test Administration

During the second session of the evaluation and finding Ned eager to talk about himself, the psychologist gently interviewed about family relationships:

*Psychologists*: What do you like about your Dad?

*Ned*: He's good at hunting and business. Maybe I'll be the same size as he is someday. He's nice. I like him because he gives me things and helps me with school work when I'm stuck.

*Psychologist*: Well then, Ned, how are you different from your Dad?

*Ned*: We have a different mind level, that is, he's smarter, college and all that business experience. He's strict though. I won't spank my own children someday. Yet he says that it teaches you to behave. My Dad and I spend lots of time together in fishing and shooting. I really appreciate those things. (Further inquiries are made by the psychologist about the above responses and noted.)

*Psychologist*: And your Mom?

*Ned*: Yeah, well, she cooks for us, helps me with homework, sees the teachers when I'm stuck, and is interested in what I say and do. My folks love me and do lots of things for me. You know, I've really disappointed them sometimes, I can see it in their faces. Like when I break a window or get into trouble at school. My Mom does too much for me, too many things. Even in homework, she knows all the answers and wants me to do good; I don't know. My ability? I'm about average in ability. Just look at my grades. She gets me out of trouble when I should get out all by myself, like when I broke a vase and wanted to pay for it myself. It wasn't that expensive, maybe four or five dollars, but no, she paid and thought everything was solved. I was still stuck with the bad feeling that I should have paid. She's always smoothing things over. How can I ever learn to get out of these problems myself?; she even does my thinking for me.

(Considerable discussion followed his understandable complaints about his mother's overprotection, and the fact that Ned himself did not feel he was growing up with a sense of responsibility.)

Following more clinical interviewing, the Michigan Picture Stories, a projective test, was administered. An interpretation of his lengthy responses was that he was an overly dependent, emotionally disturbed boy with a shattered self-concept. Retaliatory and aggressive feelings were present to counteract parental domination of the father and peer rejection. Many immature themes, some again featuring grotesque characters, revealed a great need for nurturance and recognition. Finally, confusion on identity and subtle signs of prepsychotic ideation were noted.

To provide supplementary clinical data, selected responses from Ned's Sentence Completion Test are listed below. He revealed a sense of guilt and personal inadequacy, feelings of rejection, some infantile vocabulary, and a suspicion of defectiveness in his own mental and emotional functioning.

Other people: "want me to be different."
My mother: "paddles me good when I'm a bad boy; makes me feel low and worthless like a bad, bad boy."
Girls my own age think: "I'm nuts and I think the same of them."
I can't: "play baseball well, I have a bottom rating."
I can't understand: "what makes me not do well in arithmetic and why I'm not like Fred Johnson" (a neighborhood boy whom Ned deeply resented).

My mind: "should work better, it works slow, okay on paper
but not in the head."

I can't make myself: "do the work right when I'm tense."

My temper: "goes way out of control."

My father is: "very nice when you're nice to him if you do
what you're supposed to do. If you don't, it's just the opposite."

The clinical diagnosis of Ned was of an unhappy, self-
deprecating, apprehensive, somewhat inhibited boy with
learning disabilities and the strong possibility of neurological
problems. He was emotionally disturbed by being depressed
and harboring aggressive feelings about peer groups and parents. Ned perceived parental support to be partially present but
believed that he fell quite short of his father's standards. Yet, he
resented the safe haven of maternal indulgence. In short, he was
in detrimental psychological conflict.

After a parent feedback interview, the psychological report
was distributed to the superintendent and the staff. It was followed immediately by consultation sessions by the psychologist
to work out the school-related prescriptions.

### Supplementary Analysis

The following subtest results and interpretations are presented here to offer additional case information: The scaled
scores on the WISC, presumably indicative of strengths and
deficiencies in areas assessed by the subtests, are noted below.

| *Verbal Subtests* | | *Performance Subtests* | |
|---|---|---|---|
| *Scaled Scores* | | *Scaled Scores* | |
| Information | 16 | Picture Completion | 8 |
| Comprehension | 13 | Picture Arrangement | 10 |
| Arithmetic | 9 | Block Design | 8 |

| Similarities | 16 | Object Assembly | 8 |
|---|---|---|---|
| Vocabulary | <u>16</u> | Coding | <u>7</u> |
| Total | 70 | | 41 |

The Scale scores in the Verbal section of the WISC reveal superior to very superior mental ability, with the exception of the Arithmetic subtest where he was unable to manipulate quantitative concepts at more than an average rate, perhaps a manifestation of test anxiety. Ned's language level was quite high, more like that of a bright teenager.

In the Performance areas of the WISC, the motor deficiencies observed in general coordination and with the Bender apparently held him to a slow speed. However, speed was not his only problem, as he was poor in organizing the materials in the latter two subtests. Ned lacked insight about the relationships of concrete materials and used inefficient hand movements to accomplish his goals, e.g. twirling two blocks simultaneously. Furthermore, he conceptualized poorly in the middle of the two subtests showing confusion, for example, on the "Face" assembly task.

A 38 IQ discrepancy between Verbal and Performance areas often, but not always, reveals marked deficiency in visual-motor and/or visual-perception skills. This discrepancy is reflective of Clement's (1962) Pattern I — high Verbal with low Performance scores — and is suggestive of neurological dysfunction. Ned's marginal Bender designs did not unequivocally verify visual perception handicaps but still suggest "organicity." Recalling that Ned maintained above average reading skills (7th to 8th grade level), visual perceptual problems either were not that seriously interfering with reading or were overcome by adequate compensation in earlier years. Yet, his reading level was still lower than general expectancy (perhaps 9th grade level) for his Verbal mental age of approximately fourteen years. Obviously, many other variables affected his reading proficiency beyond Verbal mental age and, in this case, many point to an organic condition and personality factors, i.e. stress reactions, anxiety, passive-aggressive resistance, low self-esteem and drive to achieve.

## Parent Feedback Conference

Following the psychological testing and diagnostic interviews, an extensive parent conference was held. In this case the Steers were quite fascinated with the clinical findings, disputed only one interpretation, and revealed genuine anxiety about (1) neurological problems, (2) emotional disturbance, and (3) marked underachievement for superior verbal intelligence.

What could be done? Who was to blame? How did this happen and why did it happen to them? Where had the school teachers failed? Weren't the parents really blameworthy, etc.? All these questions poured from the parents. Each question was taken and refined separately, thought about, discussed, and reconsidered at a later appointment.

Additional recommendations were offered to the parents at a later conference with the school psychologist. In an abbreviated listing, these were as follows:

1. Lowering their expectations for academic mastery and accepting the limitations often inherent in a pronounced learning disability. (The parents would not consider the recommendation for a residential placement for learning disabled children. Most public schools at that time had not yet started such special education classes except for those containing the retarded, blind, or deaf.)
2. Learning to reinforce his appropriate behaviors regarding homework, care of his room, courtesies toward others, verbalizing "good points" about himself, etc.
3. Hiring a personable tutor to assist Ned twice weekly with his math and spelling deficiencies in a supportive and structured experience.
4. Refocusing on his needs for attention and approval from them.
5. Setting up a simple behavior modification plan to reward certain changes in behavior with extra opportunities to

attend sports events with his father, a plan which met
with instant acceptance by both.

6. Permitting Ned to solve most of his own daily problems
   and subduing their disappointments when Ned's solutions
   were not perfectly congruent with their own.
7. Considering referral for family therapy plus individual
   therapy for Ned's pronounced emotional problems.
8. Accepting a referral for a pediatric-neurological evaluation to rule out minimal cerebral dysfunction. The acceptance of both referrals was stressed as having primary
   importance.

As is typical in the Type I Family, the parents, having
viewed themselves as quite independent, were reluctant to seek
"outside help," e.g. therapists, and tried instead to adapt the
above prescriptions to resolve the problems at home. Many
such parents wish to execute the new ideas before admitting the
need for therapy and will admit it only if they are unsuccessful
with these less penetrating (and less costly) adjustments. Many
families of this variety are quite skillful in adapting to relatively minor problems. The concern of the professional in offering such advice to parents is that they will focus on these
relatively minor but sensible prescriptions and perhaps ignore
the primary recommendations. There is a greater likelihood of
more rapid change for the child, however, if parents, school
personnel, and related professionals adopt, in unison, the
major and minor recommendations and act upon them to effec-
tuate major environmental change. Especially with school-
related problems, it is quite unreasonable to expect that the
psychotherapist should assume that entire burden for stimulating change in the child without the support of the systems
that influence the patient the other hours and days of the week.

Within a day or two the Steers had arranged Ned's appointment with the local pediatrician. Wisely the physician requested that the psychological report be sent to her first.
Finding evidence of neurological impairment such as his tight
hamstrings, general awkwardness, and specific delays in development, she referred him to a neurologist. The pediatrician
informed the school psychologists privately that she chastised
herself for not "picking up" earlier on Ned's subtle indices and

complained about having too many patients to service carefully.

Two months later, the neurologists sent his report to the referring pediatrician and school psychologist.

Dear Doctor (Pediatrician):
Re: Ned Steer, Sixth Grade, June.

On June 14th, I had the opportunity of examining your patient, Ned Steer. As you know, he was born of a thirty-five-year-old woman after a very long and hard eighteen-hour labor. . . . (The other motor details were noted earlier in this chapter.) The parents feel that he has "matured considerably" lately, in contrast to what has been written in his recent psychological report.

Although in general good health, neurological examination revealed some "soft" neurological findings such as grimacing, hyperhidrosis, tongue apraxia, incoordination of fine succession movements, slight tremor, very poor sense of finger order, some hamstring tightness, and hyperactive knee and ankle jerk. Also, I felt that there might be some tendency towards ambidexterity, as generally he tends to be right-handed but left-sighted.

It was my impression that we were indeed dealing with an organically brain-injured child, with the neurological examination thus bearing out the clinical impressions gathered on the psychological tests performed by the school psychologist. Since there are also emotional conflicts present, I urged that the parents proceed with their resolution through a therapist of their choice.

I placed Ned on Librium®, 10 mg., to be increased as needed to 20 mg., in the hope of reducing some of his anxieties and tensions. Perhaps medication will eventually permit him to demonstrate skills more efficiently in the Performance IQ area, although these may never reach his Verbal capabilities, which are rather remarkable. The parents were to contact me again about Ned in a couple of months.

M.D. (Neurologist)

## Further Parent Contact

In a July discussion with the parents, the school psychologist learned that their earlier anxiety levels had reduced since hearing feedback from him and, later, the neurologist. They accepted, however, only one of the diagnoses offered by the psychologist — the possibility of minimal cerebral dysfunction with attendant learning disabilities — and struggled against the second, emotional disturbance with aggressive components. They were now able to identify certain portions of Ned's "peculiar" behavior in childhood as being derived from his mild organic condition. Now that the neurologist had seen a physical relaxation taking place in the boy immediately after prescribed medication (assuming this was not a placebo), the parents felt that "Ned is well on the road to recovery" in all spheres: social, educational, and personal.

The psychologist raised the serious question about Ned's emotional instability. Both parents again rejected the specific recommendation derived from that diagnosis: some variety of therapy. They felt instead that since he was "organic," and that much of personality was based in constitutional factors possibly aided by medication, his personality problems would gradually disappear. They felt further that "a lot of his emotional difficulties were aggravated by being discussed so much." They instead stood firm with a "wait and see" attitude. The psychologist disagreed strongly with their decision, claiming that intense, unresolved problems remained relating to Ned's self-concept, his passive-aggressive style, resentment of pressures, and hatred of the peers who rejected him. All of these concerns lay dormant and subject to provocation under stress. This effort at persuasion also failed, as the parents retained their determination to "let Ned's problems run their course" and hope that medication would have a more generalized effect.

### Medical Follow-up

A number of months passed, uneventfully, in Ned's life except to note that he was promoted to the seventh grade. The mother, conscientious about medical problems and anxious to determine if others verified the positive changes she perceived in her son, brought him to the neurologist for a reevaluation. He sent the following letter to the local pediatrician:

Dear Doctor (Pediatrician):
    Re: Ned Steer, Seventh Grade, December.
    Today for the first time in some six months, I had a chance to see Ned Steer and found him very much more composed. He seemed more relaxed, and on neurological examination he exhibited no tremors; he seemed fairly well coordinated, and he had no difficulties with tandem gait. There was good tongue motility.
    I had a long discussion with Mrs. Steer concerning Ned's occasional stuttering and occasional thumb sucking. I also learned from her that he definitely seems better on the Librium 20 mg. After my discussion with the mother, I again thought it worthwhile for Ned to receive supportive psychotherapy and suggested that they contact the school psychologist, whom Ned seems to like. Possibly he can give the therapy or suggest someone who could.

                                                    M.D. (Neurologist)

Mrs. Steer stated in a parent conference that there was a gradual but distinct improvement alleged to be in muscular coordination, self-confidence, the ability to hold friendships, willingness to participate socially and, lastly, a slight improvement in his grades at school.

Mrs. Steer appeared to be less overprotective and let Ned handle his own responsibilities for school and some additional ones in the home. The father was described again as a rather perfectionistic, driving individual who has made some accomodations toward his son since he realized that his son was not "retarded." The mother wished that she could deny that any emotional problems still existed, but the psychologist again documented their presence.

The recommendation for therapy was again given, along with a list of several capable clinicians in the area. The mother took this list but indicated that she would probably hold off in contacting one unless further problems developed.

Another year transpired without special incident in the Steer family. Ned's school career reflected some increased efficiencies in terms of grades. Informal contacts with the mother, often at school to aid the music program, determined that the parents were "satisfied" with his slow progress. She tensed noticeably when the psychologist inquired about the boy's social and personal adjustments, but admitted that he was "still edgy; he always downgrades himself and resents our help."

Neither parent accepted the psychologist's invitation to discuss the matters more fully.

Many months later, the neurologist reevaluated Ned:

> Dear Doctor (Pediatrician):
>     Re: Ned Steer, Eighth Grade, July.
>
>     Today I saw Ned, whom I had not examined since nineteen months ago when I wrote to you. I was very pleased to see how tall and mature he had grown. He told me with a great deal of pleasure that he just graduated from the eighth grade and discussed his music lessons, working with weights, and his hopes of going out for the high school football team.
>
>     I also learned from Mrs. Steer that she had some talks with the school psychologist, who felt that psychotherapy was still needed. I think this is a very wise decision to pursue this direction, and I supported therapy in conversation with Mrs. Steer.
>
>     Ned's neurological examination today was essentially within normal limits. I found him much less tight. There was no tremor. Coordination even for fine successive movements was excellent. Tongue motility was excellent. Deep tendon reflexes were all physiologic. I felt that Ned could now come completely off of Librium but be reinstated if there should be some need for it. I expect to see Ned a year from now.
>
>                                             M.D. (Neurologist)

### The Tranquil Interlude

No significant information reached the school psychologist about Ned Steer while he finished the eighth grade. He then started the ninth grade in the local high school. The counseling staff and teachers there had been alerted to the presence of his personality problems via the psychologist's report and a personal telephone call by the school psychologist to the high school principal and another superintendent. "Special adjustments" were made in his academic schedule by counselors, but these were not specified in the boy's cumulative folder. Presumably these dealt with enrolling him in less stressful academic subjects and assigning him to the more sympathetic high school teachers.

Informal contacts with the mother indicated, "Ned is doing a little better each day, Doctor. He gets tense anticipating more problems in high school, but we think that he'll be okay. His grades are practically all Cs except gym."

## The Gun

Suddenly, in Ned's ninth grade year, events took a drastic turn that brought to mind in bold relief all the predictions of professional workers and the worst apprehensions of the parents. In spite of his facade of normality and the parents' denial of emotional problems in their son, significant pressures had been exerted on Ned since his entrance into the large high school. Although the curriculum was apparently suitable for his abilities, his emotional defenses were becoming untenable. The social acceptance so desperately sought by him in high school did not develop. In fact he received the social rejection of the student body generally in spite of efforts on the part of the counseling staff. Ned was still socially awkward. He developed some eccentricities by being verbally aggressive to other children in his bid for attention. Most of his classmates from the previous elementary-junior high school were disgusted with his old temper tantrums, his disorganization, and his social ineptitudes: interrupting others, ridiculing their successes, and degrading their efforts to achieve in school. He attempted to enlist the friendship of new children who had not known him, but his present behaviors alienated them quickly.

Ned's last effort at gaining attention focused on the "motor-cycle gang" of the high school, the most rowdy and rejected group made up of mini-sociopaths and other rebellious youth. This group likewise ridiculed him and excluded him from their nefarious, delinquent activities.

Friendless and angry, depressed and yet demanding status among peers, he unfortunately sought an argument with the football team's star halfback, a junior of robust build and "gifted" reflexes. The original stimuli for the fight are long forgotten, but the subsequent events are not.

In the hall of the local high school, Ned started an altercation by threatening to "beat up" the larger and older boy. He ridiculed the halfback, who sized up the aggressive ninth grader as "weird." The athlete made an about-face to walk away from an unequal fight. Ned trailed after him by stepping on the older boy's heels and muttering prophetic curses. The stronger boy urged separation and an end to the dispute, but Ned would not accept the "cowardice" of the athlete.

After more verbal provocations, Ned again challenged his selected opponent to fight "behind the school where the teachers can't see us." The place was agreed upon, and immediately after school the two boys, with several classmates watching, began to fight in earnest. Within the first two minutes Ned had been beaten to the ground three or four times, and his face was bloody. His threats to the older boy proved harmless, and he was thoroughly humiliated in unequal combat of his own choice.

Of primary consequence in the fight was the riveted attention of Fred Johnson, one of the three brothers in Ned's neighborhood. This handsome, able, and high achieving boy had been a subtle provocateur to Ned all his life, and the resentment toward Fred was deep and volatile. Ned had heard about the virtues of Fred, all those he himself lacked. While lying on the ground, beaten and dazed, Ned looked up at the small crowd and saw Fred "smiling down" at Ned's wretched condition, and he silently vowed to kill Fred, but not the athlete who had beaten him in the fight.

Wiping the blood off his face and seeing the puffiness develop under one eye, Ned cleaned up in the boys' lavatory and still managed to catch the early bus home. He had a mission to complete: shoot Fred for "smiling down" on him in his agony and retaliate for all the "digs" and rejections he had received that were suddenly no longer tolerable. Ned ignored the bus-riding children who asked about his bleeding as he concentrated solely on the act to follow. He knew that Fred, delayed by his leadership activities in school, would catch the next bus about fifteen minutes later to their neighborhood. He swore, "I'll get him at his house."

Still furious and hurting from the body and facial blows received, Ned was pleased to find that his own home was empty — his father was in the city and his mother was at a card party as he recalled. He threw open the door, raced to his father's locked gun rack, and selected from an array of rifles, shotguns, and hand-guns a .22 caliber, six-shot pistol, which he had used many times at a local gun club. In his rush to kill Fred, he grabbed quickly at the first full box of .22 shells available in the nearby workbench drawer. All ammunition was kept there under lock and key, but of course Ned knew where the key was. In his haste, however, Ned neglected to observe that he had taken a box of .22 caliber birdshot — tiny pinhead pellets — rather than the standard lead-headed, long-shelled bullets. Nevertheless, he rammed the first look-alike bullets into the gun, ranted and raved about his fight, the world, Fred, and death, etc., for a few moments, knowing that Fred's bus would arrive shortly several blocks away.

Impatient to shoot, he left his home to stride urgently toward his intended victim. He saw the yellow school bus stop near Fred's house dropping off several school children in the distance. In another few moments Ned arrived there breathless, blind to reason, and consumed by anger, ready to kill. Ned stabbed the doorbell several times on the front door while he pointed the gun waist high, finger on the trigger, ready to shoot Fred.

In place of Fred, however, came his next younger brother, Bobby, age thirteen, who had come home on the first bus with Ned. Bobby opened the door a few inches to see who rang so insistently and was greeted by three shots at the thick, wooden panels of the front door. Ned was enraged that the blast caught no one, so he threw his shoulder against the rapidly closing door while the brother screamed in fright and ran into the hallway. Bobby raced out a side porch, leaped over the rail, and screamed for help, "Ned's gone crazy, he's shooting me, help!"

Recognizing but not caring that he had fired at the wrong person, Ned raced into the hallway and up the flight of stairs to look for Fred in his bedroom. Fred, in leaving the bus only moments before, had stopped to chat with a girlfriend about a forthcoming term paper. He later recalled hearing no noises or screaming only two blocks away. Now that Ned had reached the bedroom, and finding it vacant, he emptied the remaining three bullets into Fred's neatly made bed. He quickly reloaded and fired a chamberful into mirrors, a TV, and a new stereo set, then reloaded again more slowly. By this time Fred had come into the kitchen back door. He later recalled hearing "a set of shots" upstairs but, not comprehending, noisily sat down at the kitchen table to look over his homework assignments, knocking a book to the floor. He then heard a shout from upstairs, "Fred, is that you? I'm going to get you. I'm going to blow off your goddamn head." Fred, stupified by the remarks, got up to peek up the stairs and saw Ned coming down, stretching out his arm with the gun about to shoot.

Fred raced backward toward the kitchen and burst through the back screen door just as two shots broke the door frame over his left shoulder. He ran into the woods nearby and waited, not pursued.

At this exact moment, the third and youngest brother, age eleven, got out of the family car in the basement garage with his mother, who had just picked him up from the elementary school about a mile away. This boy, Steven, had two thick books in his hands as he mounted the garage steps toward the hallway. He entered the house followed by his mother, the school psychologist's secretary, who was on her half-day off. Both were extremely alarmed at the shooting they heard above the garage, the glass breaking, etc., that Ned now engaged in during his next rage for having missed his intended victim. The family TV and expensive vases were now in ruins. As Steven reached the top step and turned toward the kitchen while holding the two books at groin level, Ned whirled from 4 feet away and fired two shots, hitting both books dead center.

Since they were birdshot and stopped by two inches of bond paper, no damage occurred to the boy's genitals. The mother reached the main floor simultaneously and was almost knocked over as Ned raced past her to run upstairs to Fred's bedroom again, to reload a final time.

Seeing the house in ruins and having witnessed the firing at her son, she ran to the telephone and immediately called her employer, the school psychologist who had worked with the Steer family in the nearby elementary school. "Ned Steer is shooting my children, for God sake, come here and stop him," she screamed on the telephone. The psychologist, not understanding any of what had transpired, ran immediately from his office and while passing the superintendent's office yelled, "There's a shooting at the Johnson's house, call the police." His car started instantly, and the wheels spun in the parking lot in his dash toward the home. What has happened? Who has been hit? What do I do when I get there? The speedometer read 75 miles per hour as the school psychologist whipped off the highway and onto the lane leading to the lake home.

Just as the psychologist jammed on the brakes in front of his secretary's home, while expecting the worst, a local repair man servicing a TV next door was finally alerted and had come at Bobby's insistence after the first attack. The man walked into the home just as Ned had raced upstairs for the third time: he followed the mother's pointed finger gesturing toward the stairs. She was too breathless and incoherent to speak. The man quietly climbed the stairs, peeked in the first bedroom, and looked into the barrel of the loaded gun held by a wild-eyed, sweating, chest-heaving boy. As the psychologist ran into the living room downstairs, the repair man walked up to Ned and said, "I think there's been enough shooting for today. Give me the gun." And Ned gave it up quietly.

Mrs. Johnson, the mother of the three brothers, finally relieved after seeing the gun unloaded and now in adult hands, wept quietly on her sofa, her sons still stunned at the confrontations with violence. Ned, escorted downstairs by the psychologist, sat sullen and disoriented on a sofa waiting for the hysterical reactions of parents to cease and the official inquiries to begin with the police. He was now mute. The psychologist called Mr. and Mrs. Steer as well as the father of the three intended victims. Each was given a brief, subdued description of the events and was requested to come to the home. The police and juvenile authorities were notified by the psychologist. The local superintendent was notified of the near-tragedies and offered immediate assistance in terms of school records, testimonial, and support for the respective families and Ned.

The event shook the community from its facade of tranquility and upended the life of the Steers forever. No longer could emotional disturbance be denied in their son; no longer could therapy or special intervention be sidestepped in view of the impact of attempted homicide. The Steers were emotionally devastated and were filled with compassion for Ned and, simultaneously, the horror of what might have been. Of course they felt terrible about the shootings and damage and profusely apologized to the other parents and their three sons.

The rehabilitative efforts moved rapidly toward a climax. Ned was taken by the police to the Juvenile Bureau of the county authorities. Removed to the detention home, he soon had a preliminary hearing before the juvenile court judge. All interested adults were present, including the school psychologist, while the Steers were also represented by an attorney. The other parents sought only to recover damages (several hundred dollars) and to insure that thorough rehabilitative efforts would be mandated to prevent an explosive reoccurrence.

The judge heard a summary of the circumstances from his probation officer and the Steers attorney and asked Ned to testify to the authenticity of the descriptions. He listened to both sets of parents and called for testimony from the school psychologist. The latter's psychological report and all school records had been sent previously, with the parents' consent.

The psychologist, with the agreement of Ned, his family, their attorney, and the various school officials recommended the following:

1. Reevaluation by another neurologist.
2. Team evaluation by a neuropsychiatrist and a clinical psychologist.

3. Residential treatment for emotional disturbance.

The judge agreed to these recommendations, but indicated that since these forthcoming professional visits would entail a number of sessions, Ned was "free to go home" until the next court hearing in about five weeks. The school psychologist, with the silent thanks of the parents of the three brothers, objected vigorously against this decision, to the surprise of the judge. Since Ned had not been successful in his aggressive attack on the three brothers, reasoned the school psychologist, would he not become aggressive and punitive against himself? He asserted further that Ned was to be viewed as a potentially suicidal child in need of twenty-four-hour supervision beyond that capable of his parents. The judge reversed his previous decision and kept Ned in constant observation in the detention home until the case was adjudicated pending psychiatric examination.

That week, in consultation with the parents, the school psychologist recommended one of several certified child psychiatrists in the metropolitan area. He revealed an immediate interest in the case, having followed it briefly in the newspaper. Ned was evaluated psychiatrically in tandem with a clinical psychologist with considerable experience in court cases. Both professionals had access to all previous psychological material, school and medical records, and held clinical interviews with Ned and his parents.

The clinical psychologist provided an analysis of the boy's personality functioning in these excerpts:

> Ned reveals himself to be severely disturbed emotionally and presently using a defense of constriction to avoid emotional involvement. There appears to be a long-standing history of feelings of inadequacy. He is frustrated by his incompetence socially and by his failure to gain acceptance and recognition by others, particularly by his peers. He sees his parents as rigidly overprotective without giving him emotional warmth. A lack of relationship with the father has hindered his development toward a mature identification. As frustration mounts he becomes more and more angry, and defenses of passivity and constriction break down, resulting in impulsive

outbursts.

Apparently he has never felt any significant success. The origin of this may lie partly in the incoordination and perceptual problem resulting from the hypothesized neurological deficit. The parents, too, may have set standards that he could not reach. He appears to have developed a schizoid personality, with an ego that cannot adequately function in the face of tension and pressure. Ned ruminates on his inadequacies and is almost obsessively preoccupied with them.

His great anxiety about himself has had a definite effect on his intellectual efficiency. He is not now psychotic and has the facility for adequate reality testing. It is felt that Ned needs a therapeutic environment and placement in a residential treatment center.

Clinical Psychologist

The psychiatrist submitted the following report:

Dear Doctor (School Psychologist):

I am of the opinion that Ned had suffered early organic brain dysfunction resulting in faulty maladaptive growth and impedence in intellectual and emotional development.

Neurologic examination discloses the dull demeanor of the epileptic (no history of seizures), slow methodic speech, marked awkwardness in motor dexterity, and brisk asymmetric reflexes. EEG is decidedly abnormal (see copy); PKU test and skull X-ray normal. Dilantin®-phenobarb precipitated an abnormal degree of thalamic irritability and was promptly discontinued.

Ned has never before been in difficulty with society, evidently secure within the protective care of dedicated parents who were able to set limits and controls. His inner growing conviction of ineptness and failure on the peer and academic levels brought him to an explosive state on the recent occasion of the gross stress reaction described in the history. His despised self-image became unbearably painful when he finally failed to find acceptance even among others having severe problems, either aggressive or underachieved. I believe Ned is one who does not make excessive or unreasonable demands, nor has he ever been hostilely antiauthoritarian. Actually, I believe he will savor every little bit of personal attention, gratefully and maturationally. He may adjust rapidly and amicably in a residential treatment program that will help him erect a durable, realistic identity.

Formal Diagnosis: Chronic brain syndrome with behavioral reaction; acute transient situational acting-out in response to gross adolescent stress. The EEG may warrant an attempt at medication and the study of its effects upon his behavior, attitudes, and learning process.

I am most optimistic about Ned's ability to relate effectively and to flourish more maturely in an institutional program. His parents are most eager to collaborate in supporting his needs.

M.D. (Neuro-psychiatrist)

### The Treatment Plan

Upon receipt of the above reports, the judge pronounced that Ned was a delinquent child by virtue of assault and attempted homicide. He recommended that Ned be sent "until rehabilitated" to a residential treatment home satisfactory to the parents, the school psychologist, and the court. Full adjustments for property damage were made to the Johnsons.

Ned asked to be heard by the judge right after he finished the recommendations, "Your Honor, I've done an awful thing and I'm sorry. I think that I can learn to control myself. I promise to go wherever I'm sent." The parents wept.

An outstanding residential school accepted Ned for long-term care. It was anticipated by the clinical staff that this out-of-state institution would keep Ned possibly for the remainder of his high school career, three years at a cost of (currently) $17,000 per year. He would receive several simultaneous services at the school: psychotherapy, special education, behavior therapy, music training, physical therapy, and cottage living with an adolescent peer group.

The parents have kept in touch over the years, sharing with the school psychologist an occasional note from Ned's residential home:

Dear Mr. & Mrs. Steer:
This has been our second year with Ned, and I have some

good news to report today. Our awards banquet was held, and many staff viewed with pride as Ned received the following awards:

Most Improved — Math II; Most Outstanding — Power Mechanics; Most Outstanding — Math I; Most Improved — Fishing Club.

We are delighted to inform you that once again Ned has captured the only award given for the "Most Improved Boy of the Year." Needless to say, he was very proud and we are of him. He has also made continuous academic progress.

Parent Coordinator

## Final Follow-Up

More recently, a letter from the mother was received by the school psychologist eight years after the original referral for service:

Ned continues with problems, but he is making an honest effort in working at them and did manage to stay out of the mental hospital this year. He had five short weeks of college life (pretty good grades, too), but got himself deeply involved in college theater, lost sleep, couldn't take the pressures, and had to quit. Then came a period of depression, but of his own doing he entered group therapy at the Mental Health Center here four days a week plus some juggling of medicine by his doctor. He's feeling a lot better again. His big interest is jazz music, some classical. He joined Alcoholics Anonymous last year, really surprised us with that; he scared himself when he realized that liquor would run away with him.

So we live one day at a time; life could be much worse. I'm happy to see that more progress is being made in helping minimal brain damaged children; too late to help my Ned, but the many Ned's of today can receive more help and probably won't have the trauma our boy had. We know you and Temple University are right in there pitching for the kids. Any more books in the planning? I may write one myself someday — I've learned so much, the hard way.

Mrs. Steer

(No further follow-up information is available.)

# CHAPTER III

# EMOTIONAL DISTURBANCE AND BEHAVIOR PROBLEMS

W HEN a parent asks, "Why isn't my child learning in school?" The psychologist needs to consider a wide array of contributing possibilities from mental retardation, brain damage, medical problems, perceptual impairment, sensory limitations, emotional disturbance, to poor educational practices. The diagnosis of emotional disturbance as the primary cause is frequently made by default, i.e. first ruling out the other possibilities. However, emotional disturbance can and frequently does provide an overlay exacerbating the original problems. For example, if a child is perceptually impaired and has difficulty learning, he may be taunted by his peers, feel frustrated because it takes him longer to learn, fear and dislike the school program, and eventually develop a poor sense of self-esteem. Thus his inability to learn will be further hampered by the concomitant emotional problem.

The disturbed child may show a variety of symptoms including inattention, over- or underactivity, strong feelings of anxiety, rejection, or guilt. The child may cry excessively or be overly timid. One may be overly aggressive or may manifest blatant delinquent behavior. Another may reveal psychosomatic problems, eneuresis or encopresis, or have sleep disturbances. Problems may vary from temporary adjustment problems, revealed in anxiety, conflict, or confusion when moving to a new home or school, anger at the birth of a sibling, tension during divorce proceedings, or depression due to a death in the family, to a pronounced neurotic disturbance, a behavior or personality disorder, or an actual psychosis.

The psychoeducational diagnostician approaches these problems by a careful review of data from developmental, medical, school, family, and social histories. The cognitive features are evaluated, the social performance in school observed, and the achievements measured. The child's emotional life is assessed by clinical interview and a series of projective and objective tests appropriate to the situation. The psychologist then needs to determine (1) the scope of the deviant behaviors, (2) the many causes of the problems, (3) what sustains the symptomatic behavior, (4) the child's assets, value system, and motivations, and finally, (5) what prescriptive strategies might alleviate these conditions. The therapeutic approaches for emotional problems may include individual psychotherapy, family therapy, behavior modification, therapeutic tutoring, milieu (residential) therapy, or some combination.

The therapeutic approach in three of the cases in this chapter depicts an application of rational-emotive psychotherapy, the theory created by Ellis (1962, 1974). Essentially, this concept holds that reason and emotion are closely linked and that many emotional problems develop and are sustained by the individual's own interpretation or misinterpretation of social situations. Problems are maintained essentially by what the individual tells himself or herself through personal values and belief systems. The therapist must assist the patient in recognizing irrational thoughts and ideas that are debilitating. The patient is helped to think through and assess situations more rationally and to take productive action in solving his or her own problems. As circumstances dictate, behavior therapies, hypnosis, and other adjunctive techniques are utilized where appropriate.

While the formal diagnostic categories of emotional disturbance are listed in the *Diagnostic and Statistical Manual* of the American Psychiatric Association (1968) or focused for children in *Psychopathological Disorders in Childhood* (Group for the Advancement of Psychiatry, 1966), some state departments of education define their own categories more broadly. It is thus incumbent upon the educationally attuned clinical or school psychologist to use these latter official categories for school placement. An example of one is the definition taken from the Pennsylvania Special Education Standards. This defines emotional disturbance as "a severe major affective psychosis which is characterized by a single disorder of mood, either extreme elation or depression that dominates the mental life of the person and is responsible for whatever loss of contact . . . with the environment" (Manchester, 1977, p. 3).

Another category offers the parameters for the socially and emotionally disturbed. This is defined as follows:

> a condition exhibiting one or more of the following characteristics over a long period of time and to a marked degree: inability to learn which cannot be explained by intellectual, sensory or health factors; inability to build or maintain satisfactory interpersonal relationships with peers and teachers; inappropriate types of behavior or feelings; a general pervasive mood of unhappiness or depression; or a tendency to develop physical symptoms, pains or fears associated with personal or school problems. A person shall be assigned to a program for the socially and emotionally disturbed when the evaluation and individualized education program indicate that such a program is appropriate. . . . (Manchester, 1977, p. 4)

Thus it is seen that, at least in the schools of one state, the term *emotional disturbance* relates only to an affective psychosis. A different term, *socially and emotionally disturbed*, refers instead to most other neurotic, personality, and behavior disorders.

Assessing the kind and severity of emotional disturbance in children and later treating or modifying these can be the most difficult and challenging aspects of the practitioner's work. When the child and family improve and suffering is relieved, the psychologist may feel a genuine sense of satisfaction.

The following cases illustrate some of the varied dimensions of emotional disturbance and document an equally diverse set of treatment strategies in the office, home, and school.

## ACTIVITY-ORIENTED GROUP THERAPY IN A RESIDENTIAL FACILITY

The orientation of the experience will follow the principles of rational emotive therapy, with some behavior therapy concepts being applied. Essentially, an attempt will be made to help disturbed adolescents in a residential treatment facility to see how they create problems for themselves by what they do and think. An effort is made in the therapy sessions to help them look critically at what they are doing and to change their behavior because it benefits them and gets them what they say they want.

The group is made up of John and Bobby, age thirteen, and Ronny, Steve, and Eddie, age fourteen. The five members of the group had been selected by the clinical staff of the institution prior to the arrival of the therapist. The selection criteria were simply that the boys were hostile, had difficulty in classes, and were close in age. The therapist's first contact with each of the children was at the first group therapy session. These students were all aggressive and presented extreme management problems to their teachers. The boys frequently fought with the other students, became uncooperative in class, and refused to do many of the class assignments despite the low pupil-teacher ratios and the individualized lessons. The following excerpts give the flavor of the first session, which takes place in a tastefully decorated staff lounge. The residence supervisor is present and makes the introduction of the boys to the therapist.

*Resident supervisor* (Mr. Y.): Boys, I would like to introduce you to Doctor Rosenfeld. He's going to be your therapist and help you with your problems. Doctor Rosenfeld, this is John, Bobby, Ronny, Steve, and Eddie. These guys think the staff and most of the kids don't like them. You can tell Doctor Rosenfeld all about it. I expect all of you guys to talk together and behave. I'll see you later in the afternoon (supervisor exits).

*Therapist*: Hello, I'm pleased to meet you. . . .

*Eddie*: Wait a minute, Mr. Y. says you're gonna help us. Is that true?

*Therapist*: Yes, we're all going to be together at least once a week for an hour or longer and we all might be able to help each other.

*Bobby*: You really want to know my problems?

*John*: Don't believe it, he ain't gonna help us; he'll be just like all the other grownups.

*Ronny*: Give the guy a chance to talk.

*Steve*: (Interrupting Ronny) You really want to help us?

*Therapist*: Yes.

*John*: (Interrupting) Yeah, well what are you going to do good for us?

*Ronny*: Yeah, what?

*Eddie*: You know the bastard ain't gonna do anything good.

*Ronny*: Give him a chance to talk.

*Bobby*: Nah, let's tell him how he can help us!

*John*: What do you want him to do, Bobby?

*Bobby*: Take us in your car, drive us into town so we can buy candy and stuff. Well, will you do it?

*Steve*: Yeah, will you do it?

*Bobby*: You know the bastard won't. Well, will you?

*Ronny*: Give him a chance to talk.

*Eddie*: What for, he's only gonna say no!

*John*: Yeah, that's my problem, Doc, I need candy. I really need it.

*Eddie*: Don't give us any shit about bringing it to us, we want to buy it in town.

*Bobby*: You gonna take us now or not?

*Therapist*: I really hear your message. You'd all like to go to town and buy candy. (The students obviously want instant gratification. They are apparently unaware that a therapist cannot take them off the school grounds without clearing first with the administration, getting parental permission, having forms signed, and then making sure that the school's liability insurance would cover this type of extramural activity. Besides, at the moment, the therapist does not want to be driving to town with five wild teenagers in his car.)

*Therapist*: I think we might consider this for another meeting later on.

*Bobby*: (Screaming) No, now! You bastard, retard you. That's what you are, a retard.

*Steve*: (Walking over to a bookcase in the room, takes one book) Should I throw this book at him, guys?

*Bobby*: Let's kill the bastard, he's not gonna help us!

*Ronny*: Give him a chance to talk, you guys are just screaming.

*John*: You can see he don't like us either. He ain't gonna take us to town.

*Eddie*: Yeah, I knew he wouldn't like us. Let's kill him (approaching the therapist menacingly).

*Therapist*: You guys are worried about my liking you. Notice, I just about said "hello" before you decided what I should be doing. You started to curse at me and now you're saying you want to kill me. Gee, if you treat people this way, you know it's going to be hard to like somebody who wants to curse at you and kill you.

*Ronny*: He's right.

*Bobby*: Bullshit, he just don't like us. We ought to really kill him (making a fist and walking menacingly towards the therapist).

*Eddie*: Yeah, let's kill him. (He also makes a fist and joins Bobby. Other group members are a little hesitant but begin to join Bobby and Eddie as if to attack the therapist.)

*Therapist*: (Speaking rapidly) I haven't had time to tell you one of my rules when I do group therapy. No one is allowed to hurt the therapist or any other member of the group. Let me be clear, I defend myself if I'm attacked. Look carefully, I'm bigger and heavier than you. If you come at me it must be because you want me to hurt you. I know I don't really want to hurt you. (Bobby is the closest to the therapist and looks like he's about to throw a punch.) Bobby looks like the first kid who wants to be hurt. Bobby, why do you want me to hurt you? (Bobby is puzzled by the question and surprised that the therapist is truly prepared to defend himself. He drops his fist and steps back. The others do the same.) Maybe we can discuss what just happened.

*Bobby*: (Shouting) It happened because you won't take us to town right now!

*Eddie*: Yeah!

*John*, *Ronny*, and *Steve*: (Together) Take us to town today!

*Bobby*: He's a retard bastard, we should kill him.

*Eddie*: Hey, Bobby, get the lamp.

*Bobby*: (Unscrewing the bulb) I'll take the lamp and hit him with it, you take the bulb, break it and cut him with the glass. (The group seems to get renewed courage with the acquisition of weapons. Bobby raises the lamp as if to hit the therapist. Eddie has the bulb. The others have their fists up to attack. Ronny is the most reluctant but joins the group in the assault.)

*Therapist*: I have warned you. I'm not going to let you hurt me. You guys must want me not to like you. You really want me to hurt you.

*Eddie*: Kill him!

*Therapist*: I don't want to hurt you but I'm going to defend myself. I don't know if you can tell but that's an expensive lamp. If you break it, I'll tell Mr. Y. I know that he keeps your spending money and I'll see to it that you pay for anything you break. If you break that lamp, it'll be a long time before you have any money left to buy candy. If you break that bulb, you'll pay for that too. It will be your own fault if you don't have enough money to buy what you want.

(At this point Bobby has the lamp raised almost to striking position, stops in his tracks, attempting to reason out what has been said. Perhaps he's even looking for an excuse to get gracefully out of the position into which he has maneuvered himself.)

*Bobby*: The fucking bastard would probably tell Mr. Y. He'd use our money for a new lamp. Eddie, you'd better give me back the bulb. (Screwing back the bulb and returning the lamp to its place) It ain't worth paying money to kill him.

*Eddie*; I'd rather have the money for shopping in town.

*John*: Yeah, me too.

(What follows in the remainder of the session is mainly continued cursing at the therapist except for a closing remark.)

*Ronny*: Well, Bobby, Doc's not afraid of you or Eddie.

*Bobby*: Oh yeah, we'll see.

(The boys, exiting, are told that they will meet again with the same therapist next week. None protest the forthcoming meeting.)

The next session takes place a week later. The therapy room was changed from the comfortable lounge with its soft chairs, expensive lamps, books, and magazines to a less stimulating, more bland room. However, the behavior displayed was still anger and verbal abuse. Bobby and Eddie attempt to threaten the therapist but no physical assault occurs. By the third session the administration informed the therapist that the liability coverage of the school will not allow for the use of his personal vehicle, but they authorize a hike with the boys off the school grounds.

The third session begins with the therapist informing them that he has considered their request to go off school grounds to buy candy. They are told that the school rules do not allow the therapist to use his personal car, but that they all may walk to town if they promise to stay together. The boys respond affirmatively, seem satisfied, and point out the location of the closest store.

The therapist tells them that part of group therapy has to do with talking together, and it does not have to be in one room. They are invited to discuss their problems as they walk. Interestingly, the group stays together. While John has a tendency to wander off, Bobby quickly brings him back in line. Mr. Y has given each member of the group enough of their money to purchase two candy bars. They complain that the amount is insufficient. The therapist tells them that if they stay together and continue the discussions as they walk, and if they return to the therapy room for ten minutes of additional discussion, he will buy each boy two candy bars of his choice. They believe that that is a "good deal."

The hike to town and the return to school were uncomplicated. Some talked about their families and others talked about how they were treated by the teachers, other students, and staff members. When they returned to the therapy room they sat down together and stated that they enjoyed the walk into town. However, Bobby informed the group that the therapist, being a doctor, must therefore have lots of money. The discussion rapidly shifted to how a karate chop to the therapist's neck could disable him, and they could then steal his wallet. They discussed the merits of this together while seated calmly. This represented their first success in calm intercommunication.

They were duly rewarded with two candy bars for peacefully talking together (not for the content of the talk). John informed the therapist that he was a "sucker" for spending his own money on them.

As the sessions progressed, the boys began to communicate peacefully for greater periods of time. In the meantime, the therapist was able to describe his goals to them. They were told that it was the therapist's job to help them to get more "normal and smarter." He forcefully indicated that when they fought the therapist they were in fact fighting to be considered as "crazy and retarded." The students in the first session had clearly indicated the negative valence of the term "retard" or retarded. The therapist attempted to sell his point of view emotionally by aligning it with the more positive terms "smarter and normal," the ideal of all these students. It was frequently pointed out when the group was most hostile that to attack the therapist who was fighting to make them "smarter and normal" was for them to be fighting instead to be "crazy and retarded." This "hard-sell" approach was successful. Combined with the fact that the therapist was also a provider of concrete positive reinforcement, understanding, and reflection of feelings, the students eventually developed a positive relationship with the therapist.

Within ten sessions the group agreed that the hike to the candy store where their own money could be spent could take place every other week. The therapist agreed that he would pay one candy bar for their coming to the session and one additional candy bar for peacefully communicating together. Communicating was defined as discussing some common problem or playing a game cooperatively. The following excerpts are taken from the eleventh session:

*Ronny*: Let's play a game today, I don't have anything to discuss.

*John*: Good idea, let's play.

*Therapist*: Do all of you want to play a game?

*Eddie*: Yeah.

*Bobby*: Yeah, let's play Monopoly®.

*Steve*: Good idea, I got a Monopoly game, my parents gave it to me for my birthday.

*John*: Okay.

*Therapist*: Do all of you know how to play Monopoly? That's a pretty hard game. (All respond that they know how to play.) Okay, we do have a time limit. The one with the most money at the end of our time wins.

*Bobby*: We know.

*Steve*: I'll be the banker and give out the money. (He distributes the money equitably.)

The game progresses normally, each person moves around the board, buying properties, etc. Steve seems to be able to handle the changing of money from the purchase of property although he occasionally asks the therapist for help. Shortly the following interchange occurs:

*John*: Hey, Eddie, you landed on my property, hah.

*Eddie*: Yeah, I can see. I landed on your property, so what.

*John*: The rent is eighteen dollars.

*Eddie*; No it isn't.

*John*: Yes it is.

*Eddie*: (Angrily) No it isn't!

*John*: Look, here's the card. You see it says rent $18.

*Eddie*: (Looking at the card) Well, even if it says so I ain't gonna pay you.

*John*: Come on, Eddie, you're supposed to pay me.

*Eddie*: Well, I ain't gonna do it. Just try to collect! (Becoming more menacing and grabbing John's collar) I'll beat the shit out of you if you tell me again I gotta pay!

*John*: (Obviously frightened) Okay, okay, so I won't collect. I don't like this game anyway. I don't know if I really want to play.

*Bobby*: Oh come on now, are you afraid I'll win? I'm having fun. (All but John want to continue playing. No one spontaneously comments about Eddie's threatening behavior.)

*Therapist*: Let's stop for a moment to take a look at what happened. Eddie was just screaming and really scared John.

*John*: Who me? I wasn't scared.

*Ronny*: The hell you weren't.

*John*: Well, maybe I was. Eddie's bigger and stronger than me.

*Therapist*: What were you screaming for, Ed?

*Eddie*: He cheats!

*Therapist*: Well, I was watching this one. You landed on his property and were supposed to pay the rent.

*Eddie*: (Agitated) I don't have to and you can't make me!

*Therapist*: Look, Ed, last week you complained that lots of kids both here and at home don't like to play with you. Now I can see why. Who wants to play with somebody who won't follow the rules of the game?

*Eddie*: You ain't gonna make me pay!

*Therapist*: That's not the point. Nobody has to make you pay. You decided you wanted to play this game and that's the way it's played. If you land on somebody's property you pay him rent. John is entitled to eighteen dollars rent. He doesn't really want to have to fight to collect it. I wonder what you're telling yourself to get you so angry. John really didn't do anything for you to have a good reason to beat him up.

*Eddie:* (Pausing for a moment and then speaking softly) Well, shit . . . I don't know how to make eighteen dollars. I can't do numbers. (Looking around at all the other students) I didn't want these guys to know that.

*Therapist:* Oh?

*Eddie:* Yeah, I don't want people to think I'm a dumb retard.

*Therapist:* I see, it's better to have people think you're tough rather than dumb.

*Eddie:* Well, nobody calls a tough kid names.

*Therapist:* I'll bet that's why you act up in class, too. If you make a big commotion everytime the teacher calls on you, she stops calling on you and then nobody knows that you don't know the answer.

*Eddie:* Well, yeah.

*Therapist:* Look, the teacher is teaching you arithmetic and if you don't listen and act up who loses out?

*Eddie:* The teacher.

*Therapist:* Let me put it another way. Suppose the teacher is teaching you how to count money and she is successful, who benefits?

*Bobby:* The teacher.

*John:* Yeah, she feels good. I don't like teachers that feel good.

*Therapist:* I see. If you're dumb about counting money and you feel stupid because you can't count money and the teacher is able to show you how to make change and count, I see, you believe only she benefits.

*John* and *Bobby:* (Together) Right!

*Therapist:* Wrong! The teacher gets paid whether you learn or not. Look, let's say I don't know anything about fixing cars. Suppose my car breaks down and I have to call somebody to fix it and suppose he says, "You're stupid, you don't know how to fix cars." Is the mechanic making a true statement?

*Eddie:* I'd punch the bastard if he said that to me.

*Therapist:* Wait a second. I know Eddie would want to beat him up. He would be angry. I wouldn't become angry because I know I'm not stupid about everything, but the mechanic is telling the truth about my not knowing how to fix cars. Let's say that I really am stupid about fixing cars. If I don't want to be stupid about fixing cars what should I do?

*Ronny:* Have someone teach you how to fix cars.

*Bobby:* Go to a school that teaches you how to fix cars. My brother did that.

*Therapist:* Right! So if I'm stupid and I don't want to be stupid, I should do something about it that will make me smarter about fixing cars. Learning more is the way we cure stupidity. If I'm dumb or stupid about something and I don't want to be dumb or stupid, then I have to learn something more about it to become "unstupid" or smarter.

*Ronny:* That sounds right.

*Therapist:* If I had beaten the mechanic up like Eddie suggested, would that have made me smarter?

*Bobby:* No, and your car would have just stayed stuck.

*Eddie:* Oh, I get it, I should let the teacher teach me to count so I don't stay dumb.

*Therapist:* Right! If she is successful, you get smarter and don't stay dumb.

*Steve:* Besides, Eddie, if you told us you didn't know how to make eighteen dollars I would have told you it was a ten, a five, and three ones. You have it right there (pointing to the money). Look, man, it's no big deal if you don't know something.

*Bobby:* Yeah, Eddie, we'd have helped you.

*Therapist:* Okay, guys, remember if you don't know something you have to let us know. We're all willing to help if we know you need it.

Eddie pays the eighteen dollars and continues in the game. John stops complaining. Eddie seems relieved that they know he can't count and are willing to help him.

In future sessions various games are played. The students are helped to understand that they have a responsibility for their own behavior and they have to do something to learn. This is heavily reinforced at each session. They are shown how they have previously set up their own roadblocks to knowledge and to their own popularity. While their aggressive behavior was never completely eliminated, it diminished significantly.

After a few weeks, the teachers reported that the boys became more amenable to instruction in class. In therapy, attendance and discussion were always reinforced by one candy bar, with an extra candy bar for cooperative, nonassaultive interaction. The sessions continued on a once-weekly basis for about eighteen months. All the boys were considered by the staff to be significantly improved. Eventually three of them were discharged to their home and local school districts. One continued at the school largely because his home area had no facilities for his continued educational and vocational training. One returned home and went to work. Since the students functioned in a therapeutic milieu, it would be difficult to isolate the precise benefits of this group therapy experience from other social and educational experiences, but many staff members felt that it played a significant role in the boys' personal and academic improvement.

## SCHOOL PHOBIA

Basic to many phobic circumstances in children is an unmitigating anxiety state, a fear reaction that dominates thinking, interferes with school performance and social adjustment, and upsets even the physiological systems. Such anxiety also results in muscle tension and thus inhibits a relaxation response, a clue to the treatment of choice (McDonald & Sheperd, 1976).

It has been estimated by Kessler (1966) and Woldfogel et al. (1957) that less than 2 percent of school children, about evenly divided between the sexes, are *school phobic*, a term imprecise for measurement purposes, yet a useful label for professionals to identify diagnostically a group of children having the common reactions. In Kelly's (1973) astute review of the theory and research related to school phobic conditions, he noted three interpretations for the phenomenon: (1) psychodynamic, (2) behavioral, and (3) power struggle. In the first circumstance arising from an analytic orientation, the child with great dependency needs for the mother also has underlying fear and hostility toward her. The mother, likewise, has repressed her hostility, this having arisen from the child's incessant demands upon her. The child unconsciously develops death wishes against the mother but, fearing that these may become true, reacts instead with gastrointestinal disorders, stomach pains, headaches, pain in mobile places, and a variety of excuses for staying away from school so that he can "keep an eye" on his mother. He begins to equate anxiety with leaving home as part of a neurotic fear. Not surprisingly, when the child remains home, bedridden or not, he recovers instantly, sometimes even playing outside in the yard away from his mother. The absence from school produces a near-panic state in the parents, who are concerned about truancy laws and who wonder why their child "is not like the others." As is so often the case in a disturbed relationship, the parent has sent both a conscious and an unconscious set of messages to the child: go to school and behave like all others; stay home so that I may control you. Under these trying conditions, the child reacts in an infantile, regressed style. The treatment of choice from this orientation is psychotherapy for the child and the parents or family therapy.

In the behavioral interpretation (Patterson, 1965), the child's anxiety state is produced by maladaptive learning where the child, fearing the mother's loss because of his great dependency, is conditioned verbally to the concept of "school." To keep anxiety down he avoids school strenuously. In essence, the child has learned inappropriate habit patterns. In reference to treatment considerations, desensitization procedures are considered to be mandatory. Thus, behavior therapy focuses primarily upon relaxation and deconditioning as well as on minimizing parent and school variables that bring about the phobic reaction, e.g. the parents are not to reinforce or reward his dependency at home while he remains in a "sick condition." Other ramifications in a behavioral intervention consist of the therapist talking with the child about pleasant school conditions, leaving the mother gradually, reflecting calmly about walking to school, using visual imagery procedures, practicing role-playing experiences of walking to school, drawing pictures of school and classroom, gradually increasing the child's adaptive responses through relaxation and the decreasing absence of stress. The child is to be attending school as often as possible or at least receive tutoring so that achievement deficiencies do not occur to add a further basis to the child's concerns.

In brief, the third condition involves a power struggle where the child may have been worshipped and adored at home, resulting in his unrealistic perception of himself and his abilities. As the young child begins in school to compare himself to peers and perceives the teacher's more realistic view of him and his worth, he finds his previous feelings of omnipotence shattered from this conflict condition. He seeks solace, at all costs, in the overprotection of parents who regard him as exceptionally valuable and potentially powerful. This "overvalued" self-opinion must be changed by way of psychotherapeutic sessions for the child and for his parents.

Given these interesting theoretical possibilities, how does the diagnostic syndrome appear in an actual case, and what are the prescriptive interventions that modify or extinguish its all-encompassing impact?

Since psychologists will likely encounter pronounced anxiety states in school children at all grade levels, it is well to recognize, first, that there is a considerable amount of clinical information known about this condition. Second, it may be comforting to professionals as well as their clients and parents that an array of treatments is available for school phobic reactions.

The behavioral literature testifies to the relative effectiveness of behavioral therapies, although psychodynamic works abound with similar claims for long-range successes. While the latter does not stress relaxation, tension reduction, or training procedures as the former approach, it values instead the effectiveness of "insight" and corrective approaches of child management on the part of parents.

Marine (1968-1969), in particular, has referred to four levels of school phobia, varying from mildly neurotic to psychotic, and has offered treatment considerations for each level. Also, Blanco (1972) has listed thirty-seven prescriptive approaches to school phobic states, which appear to be derived from three theoretical frames of reference: behavioral, psychodynamic, and need-motivation.

In some instances investigators and clinicians without strong theoretical bias, writing on this interesting phenomenon, have insisted that practitioners eclectically select treatment strategies, i.e. those that best suit their *client's* precise circumstances. The variables in many school phobic cases include (1) the teaching staff and its flexibility, (2) the family dynamics and the parents' willingness to make changes in certain parent behaviors, and (3) the theoretical orientation of the practitioner. Given reasonably good cooperation of the school staff, the parents and occasionally the child's peers, a great deal can be done by a psychologist to alleviate the child's powerful anxiety state and redirect the client's energies constructively toward school attendance.

As a case in point, Kathy K., a bright junior high girl, was referred by her seventh grade counselor to a school psychologist. The counselor reported that since school had begun a few weeks earlier Kathy had become teary eyed and tense, having complained to the school nurse about stomach aches, head pains, and anxiety. A mounting list of absences was viewed with alarm by the teachers and the counselor, who recognized Kathy as a talented child now performing well below her capabilities. The diagnosis of school phobia was simple enough. The referral noted that she seemed "preoccupied" and "day-dreaming" in class, "unhappy" and "a loner" with no social interests. Inquiries by teachers and the counselor had produced only minimal responses from the girl. On days of attendance, she was often seen to be calling her mother from the school's public telephone. On two previous occasions, classmates reported that after she got to school via the school bus, she turned around "crying" only to walk home alone about two miles away. The counselor had telephoned the mother, who claimed to be "very irritated" by her daughter's behavior while admitting that "reasoning with her" was not at all effective.

In pursuing the case with parent permission, an inquiry was made about Kathy's health. Mrs. K. reported that the family doctor found Kathy to be in excellent health, but since she was viewed as "shy and anxious," he had prescribed small amounts of tranquilizers. Within two weeks he discontinued these as being ineffective.

As frequently predicted in such cases, Kathy was relatively relaxed and in no distress when she stayed home on school days. She occupied her time by helping her mother, reading, and watching television. The counselor reported her parents to be "at wit's end" and definitely concerned enough to permit a psychological evaluation. The psychologist, in contacting Kathy's previous elementary principal, learned that Kathy had manifested the identical pattern although at a lesser intensity when younger. Interestingly, Kathy's elementary school was directly across the street from her home, where her mother was readily accessible when she previously showed fear reactions. Kathy's new school, its associations, and its significant distance from the mother apparently provoked the present and marked reaction. The psychologist reviewed the etiological conditions and planned a comprehensive evaluation and a multi-therapeutic attack on Kathy's problems.

### School Information

School records revealed IQ scores of 124 and 139 on the Otis-

Lennon Mental Ability Test, testifying to superior to very superior intellectual potential. Yet it appeared that Kathy had been an underachiever since entering school. Although teachers through the years had reported her to be "cooperative" and a fairly conscientious worker, Kathy had been a *B* and *C* student at best, earning only slightly above grade level scores on most standardized achievement tests.

Lacking in confidence, timid, and reticent, Kathy was poor in attendance. Kathy appeared sad, futilely fighting tears, and unable to sustain the normal school day without being excused from classes to call home. Peer relationships were minimal; Kathy had no friends and did not seek other companionship. When a principal called the mother about the problem, Mrs. K. recently said that she would no longer pick up Kathy by car as "it doesn't do any good anymore."

### Family Information (Interview with Parents)

The members of the family include Mr. K., age thirty-seven, Mrs. K., age thirty-six, Kathy, and two boys, ages nine and four.

Mr. K., a sports enthusiast, is a bright, shallow, talkative individual who is currently employed as a statistician, junior grade. He reported that he was a poor student through high school, to his father's dismay, but later was admitted to and graduated from a small, noncompetitive college although never fulfilling his own ambition of becoming a doctor. Valuing high achievement but unable to realize this himself, he is attempting to meet this need through Kathy's school and vocational career. By attempting to "prevent Kathy from making the same mistake," he cannot tolerate any imperfection in the girl, and he places high expectations and pressure on his daughter. His sons, he claims, "Will be athletes some day!" He also expresses the view that a child "should serve the parents" while the child's individual needs, desires, and unique qualities are regarded by him as quite secondary in focus.

Mrs. K., a high school graduate, appears as a self-centered, anxious, uncertain, and mildly depressed suburban housewife. A "less attractive fraternal twin" in a family of six children, she recalled that her childhood, particularly her adolescence, was unhappy and unfulfilling, as she lacked attention, social experiences, and achievement. Like her husband, she also seeks to meet her own needs of social acceptance and achievement through her daughter. As Kathy is unable to live up to these demanding expectations, Mrs. K. in certain ways rejects the girl. In this case, such rejection takes the form of criticism or stringent demands. Ironically, the mother's behavior fosters Kathy's feelings of inadequacy and fear, the very things Mrs. K. cannot tolerate.

Although Mr. K.'s career and sports interests take him away from the home a significant amount of time, he is quite opinionated regarding child rearing and family life and is the dominant member in the family. Although his wife resents his absence and control, she submits to the situation, yet feels angry and despondent. Kathy's anxiety and fearfulness regarding separation may, in part, be a reflection of the mother's similar feelings when her husband is absent.

Kathy's relationships with siblings, particularly her nine-year-old brother, appear poor. Being a rather aggressive, confident, and athletic boy, he receives parental attention and praise. As Kathy resents him, she sometimes hits him very hard when she is irritated. The boy, in turn, is reported to be "merciless" when he taunts her for being absent and having "fake pains." Kathy often has spoken of her desire to be left peacefully alone, as she cannot tolerate such ridicule.

## Test Administered

*Stanford-Binet, L-M:*

CA 11 Years, 10 Months

MA 14 Years, 3 Months

IQ 128

*Personality Area:*

Tasks of Emotional Development

Sentence Completion

House-Tree-Person

### Behavioral Description and Personality Functioning

Kathy is an attractive, petite, eleven-year-old with short brown hair and large brown eyes. Although anxious, insecure, and soft-spoken, Kathy related surprisingly well to the examiner by articulating her feelings concerning school, family, and herself. At the threshold of adolescence, Kathy would like to assume increased independence, yet she is unable to assert herself. Rather, she has presently become more dependent on her parents, particularly the mother, due to fear and anxiety experienced while in school and away from home. Preoccupied by this conflict, Kathy is despondent, confused, and unable to concentrate much on academic work or peer relationships during the school day. On the weekends near her mother she is domestic, helpful, and somewhat more relaxed. Her stomach aches cease until the inevitable school day approaches.

Kathy, although respectful of her mother, also sees her as a controlling and critical woman who has high expectations concerning social and school achievement. Due to such standards and Kathy's present inability to meet these, she feels inferior and inadequate. Much ambivalence is present concerning the mother. On one hand, Kathy feels that Mrs. K.'s intentions are rooted in love and concern, but on the other hand, the girl feels rejected by the woman and angry at the pressure. Feeling that it is "not proper" to aggress against her mother, Kathy cannot manifest anger directly. Her anger is expressed by less-than-outstanding achievement and other passive-aggressive behavior. Aggression is also manifested in the form of forbidden wishes, which are projected or displaced. For example, Kathy revealed in the Tasks of Emotional Development that danger might befall adult females. Similar themes were revealed in other projective responses. These hostile wishes against the mother are considered too dangerous to discuss. Thus, Kathy may defend herself by increased dependency (remaining home to reassure that death wishes against mother are not coming true), while displacing the anger against her parents on to her younger brothers. She craves more attention from her father, who openly shows his affection toward the mother and brothers. Thus, she may feel as a rival with her mother and be self-condemning for these repressed thoughts, leading to her depressive moods.

Kathy views her father as a domineering individual who demands accomplishment. She identified with the father in this respect and would consciously like to succeed. However, she again feels inadequate and angry, believing that even ardent efforts would not reap the gains necessary to satisfy the father.

Undoubtedly, the conflicts described above, rooted in family dynamics, are fundamental to school difficulties. Since her status and self-esteem depend on her school success and since she is unable to achieve as she is capable and would like, the school situation remains a negative experience. Also, anxiety related to separation from the mother, which becomes unbearable during the school day, hinders her further from fulfilling her needs.

## Physician's Report

Her pediatrician called back the psychologist to report that Kathy is "in fine health; she must have some psychosomatic complaints that I can't help her with," and that "neither tranquilizers nor placebos" have helped.

## Diagnostic Summary

Kathy is an eleven-year-old girl with a school phobic reaction. Anxiety, due to separation from the home, the mother in particular, and related factors, is preventing the girl from concentrating well on academic subjects and from developing good peer relationships. Optimal school achievement is hindered further by lack of confidence and passive-aggressive behavior rooted in family struggles. As the school staff correctly observed, Kathy is currently depressed, insecure, and very unhappy as well as frequently absent without verified physical causes. She apparently has no perceptual or intellectual deficits; in fact, she has at least superior intelligence.

### Workbook Exercise: Prescriptions

The reader may consider the previous data and clinical information and use this Workbook opportunity to devise some reasonable strategies to minimize Kathy's problems. It is suggested that the recommendations be listed separately for (1) school personnel and (2) parents. After the two listings have been completed, it is further suggested that the book, *Prescriptions for Children with Learning and Adjustment Problems* (Blanco, 1972), be consulted to obtain supplementary remedial strategies, as listed under the appropriate diagnosis or problem area. These are to be attuned individually to each problem in the case. A final consideration, after class presentation and discussion of the treatment options, would be to refer to the Appendix, p. 215, to determine the nature of the actual prescriptions used on her behalf as a comparison.

### Summary of Follow-up (8 Weeks Later)

This particular case had excellent outcomes. By the third week, Kathy was smiling more and said that she was "less tense." She began to use her school time more constructively and revealed very infrequent crying. The parents refused to visit the mental health clinic but carried out "about half" of the recommendations listed for them in writing and discussed in consultation with the school psychologist. They were less demanding of her achievement and, reportedly, were more affectionate and responsive to her and less "fault-finding." Kathy, at the fifth week, went to an all-girl party and said she enjoyed it. She no longer insisted on calling home but still needed to be met by the mother, though at greater and greater distances. By the eighth week the initial school phobic reaction had largely disappeared. ("I'm just not scared so much for the first time in my life".) Desensitization sessions ceased and were replaced by counseling about study habits and her feelings about parental standards.

## Final Note

About ten weeks after the behavior therapy and related prescriptive interventions started, and Kathy was no longer an overly anxious person, the referring counselor saw the psychologist in the hall and spoke of "the fact that Kathy seems all calmed down now." He naively noted, "Well, that's how some of these school phobics are — they just snap out of it sometimes without any help at all." He was taken aside by the psychologist for an update on the effectiveness of simultaneously applied interventions.

### INDIVIDUAL AND FAMILY THERAPY

Name: Walter W.    Age: 15 Years, 7 Months    Grade: Tenth

## Reason for Referral

A volatile youngster who was suspended three times this year for fighting and disruption in class, Walter has also threatened the teacher. He cannot tolerate the touch of any adult. His mother and stepfather see him as "a nervous child" who bites his nails, is always in motion, and is subject to extreme temper tantrums when he does not get his own way.

## Background Information

BIOLOGICAL FATHER: Mr. Williams was born in 1933 in El Paso, Texas. A parochial school graduate who felt that "the nuns settled me down" in school, he later served with the U.S. Air Force as a technician for four years. He was the youngest of two sons in an intact family of working parents. He was described by his present wife as being "carefree and quite self-centered."

After a very stressful marriage, Mrs. Williams left her husband when Walter was eleven months old. Mr. Williams wanted a divorce, claiming that he was not ready for the responsibility of marriage and fatherhood. For a brief time later, he provided sporadic financial support but never visited his son. Shortly after the divorce became final, he was killed in a car accident, leaving Walter with Social Security and veteran's financial benefits, the father's insurance being placed in a trust fund for Walter.

MOTHER: Renamed at her second marriage, Mrs. Jones, thirty-six years old and the only girl of five children, was born in rural Pennsylvania. She dropped out in the tenth grade of school because she felt strong feelings of inferiority in keeping up socially and academically with her peers. She reported having problems with both concentration and reading comprehension in school. In terms of a medical heritage, tuberculosis and heart conditions were present on her side of the family. She recalled that her paternal grandmother was quite "odd" in being very hostile toward males in general. Whenever she would have an argument with her husband she would call the police to have him arrested.

Mrs. Jones resented her first husband, Walter's father, for his irresponsibilities and his parents as well for their indulgent and overprotective behavior toward their own son. Failing to communicate or relate well with others, Mrs. Jones became very close to her son Walter, feeling that she was the only person who could genuinely love him. More recently Mrs. Jones has been quite active as a Den Mother since her second marriage and has also been a teaching aide in school. Before and between marriages she was a factory worker.

STEPFATHER: Mr. John Jones, also born in Pennsylvania, is currently forty-three years of age. Feeling that he had a poor memory for learning, he dropped out of school in the eleventh grade but later earned his high school equivalency diploma while serving in the Air Force. He is currently a civilian aircraft mechanic with an airline. He has felt a tremendous frustration over his difficult relationship with Walter and has often conveyed these feelings to his wife. He reported that although they share authority on peaceful concerns at home, when there is a real disagreement "she always wins," especially where Walter is concerned. Although Mr. Jones felt estranged from Walter, he was quite knowledgeable about the boy's early development, his likes, and his friends, and revealed a genuine interest in the boy. He expressed guilt about never adopting him, explaining that the income from Social Security helped to defray the mortgage payments on their homes. When Mr. Jones did make an attempt later to adopt Walter, the boy refused and said that he wished to retain his own name.

HALF-SIBLINGS: Larry, two years younger, is a capable student who is occasionally disruptive in school. He is well regarded by his parents and consequently receives much positive attention. His sister, Mary, age eleven, presents no problems for her parents. Closest to Walter, she has offered to help him with his reading problems but, without being offended, he has been unable to accept it from her, yet he likes her kindness. The youngest child, Alan, age six, is somewhat pampered by all. His school adjustment is excellent.

### Developmental History

Walter was a product of his mother's second pregnancy, a miscarriage having occurred two years earlier. His delivery was normal and full term. The mother recalled that he was "a good baby" and that she was delighted to be deluged with attention from her close relatives, the son being the only remarkable event in her life.

Breast fed for one month, Walter took the bottle up almost until kindergarten. To change his thumb sucking, he was also given a pacifier. He finally gave up both the pacifier and the bottle in response to parental predictions of his being laughed at by other children in kindergarten. At age seven months Walter was reported to have had pneumonia and an unspecified high fever but no convulsions. After the marital stress became very evident, Walter was taken into his mother's bed until he was two, when she remarried.

Walter walked at ten months yet was said to have been poorly coordinated until the age of twelve. Since he could not tie his shoes at age eight, his mother bought him buckle shoes, but this was an indication that she rarely trained him to be independent. Speech was markedly delayed with the first words coming at age three and sentences just prior to kindergarten. The mother blamed this on his use of a pacifier, but more significantly, she anticipated all his needs in her effort to love and indulge him.

Toilet training at age one was a source of problem only to the father. The mother claimed she was never upset by Walter's soiling (until age 4) or by his enuresis (until age 10). Walter's stepfather would spank him, then put him on the potty and make him stay there, whereas the mother kept him in diapers.

### Psychological Background

Currently Walter is "a pokey eater," according to his parents, and he is still subject to extreme temper tantrums if any attempt is made to discipline him. When seven, he was taken to a child guidance clinic. The reports there indicated that he was viewed as a seriously emotionally disturbed child who was incapable of establishing close relationships. Further, he was reported to be quite withdrawn and eccentric and sometimes irrational. The staff recommended that in view of his disturbances he should be receiving residential treatment, but the mother rejected this idea instantly. Instead, he was placed on a mild tranquilizer for a brief period of time and was seen in group therapy. The parents were counseled toward child management concepts and the need to help him become more independent, but did not keep most of their appointments. After a short time in the boy's group therapy, Walter was reported to have been verbally too aggressive and was then seen individually.

After a year he seemed to be sufficiently calm and was then transferred to twice-a-week group therapy. In treatment for two and one-half years, he then had learned to control his impulses more effectively. Although the clinic recommended that his parents continue in treatment, they did not follow through. Neurological examinations and EEGs were administered and yielded no significant abnormality. All treatment at the clinic was terminated at the parents' request by the time Walter was twelve years old although the staff sought to continue his program.

## Social Development

Walter's first two years of life were spent in the protection of his mother, who felt insecure and rejected. Since her marriage to Mr. Jones, however, there have been camping trips, visits to historical places, and vacations with all the children at the shore. By age twelve, Walter refused to accompany them on such excursions and did not become active in any community or youth groups or school activities. He learned to play guitar moderately well despite his initial refusal to follow his music teacher's instructions on fundamentals.

Currently, at age fifteen, he likes to play guitar with a newly formed rock group. He is tolerated there mainly because he lets them use his musical instruments. Walter is not on any regular allowance. If he needs money for any special activity he has certain chores that he can do to earn money, and he picks up a little bit for occasional music gigs. Walter has occasionally obtained several short jobs as a stock clerk and as a car washer, but as soon as anyone criticizes his work he immediately quits in a petulant rage.

## Educational History

Walter started school at five and one-half years of age, had an uneventful kindergarten and no problems in separating from his mother or home. In the first grade, however, he became disruptive and impulsive in talking out in class. Although a school psychologist classified him as emotionally disturbed, the only class available in that school district was for the educable mentally retarded, where he was illegally placed with the parents' consent. At a later date when classes for the emotionally disturbed were established, he was placed there from the third through the eighth grade. He has been in regular classes since the ninth grade except for a brief and unsuccessful stay with his grandmother in another state. She complained that he would not obey her and subsequently sent him home to the mother.

### General Appearance

Walter, a handsome boy 5 feet 10 inches tall with light red hair, looked older than his chronological age. He usually dressed in a neat pair of dungarees and sneakers, with his shirt unbuttoned, revealing his bare chest. Speech was clear; cooperation was good. Occasional nail-biting behavior was observed as a reflection of tension.

### Psychological Testing: Workbook Exercises

On the Wechsler Intelligence Scale for Children-Revised, Walter obtained a Verbal IQ of 84, a Performance IQ of 98, and Full Scale IQ of 89. Five years earlier he had scored slightly higher on the WISC.

Performance on the Bender-Gestalt Test was normal.

The following responses were given on the Tasks of Emotional Development (TED):

*Card 1:* It looks like a new kid. There's the friends or guys he wants to play with. He's not sure if he wants to go there. Well, it looks like he does. That's all it looks like to me. (How does he feel?) He's got butterflies (meaning he is nervous). That's all it looks like. (How does the story end?) He probably goes over and makes good friends. All stories end happily ever after. They don't want us kids to think bad things.

*Card 2:* Cookies, it looks like it might be a cookie jar. It looks like she wants him to sample something she made. She wants him to see how it tastes, whether it's any good or not. She wants to see if the old recipe works. It looks like he just came in. (How does the story end?) He gets his school books and goes down to the library. (How was the recipe?) Good, well I don't know.

*Card 3:* They're playing a game of tiddlywinks. No (laughs), that kid wants to fight. The other kid doesn't want to. He wants to talk it out. The other kid's like me, he just goes and sees if he wants to fight. (What are they fighting about?) Over a leaf on the bush (laughs at his own attempt to be facetious). The kid gets beat up. (Which one?) The one with his fist down.

*Card 4:* He came home from school. He's doing his homework because he has a history test tomorrow morning, Thursday at 8:45. (How does he feel?) Great, I guess. (What's the outcome?) A "D." He only studied for five minutes and the guy said, "Let's go out and play football or let's go to the keg (beer) party."

*Card 5:* He's tempted all right. He's going to take his Dad's money so he can go to the keg party with the other guys. He took his Dad's whole wallet and took it with him. His Dad put him in the Detention Center for two days. He learned his lesson. That's it. (How does he feel?) I don't know. He felt good because he donated to the party.

*Card 6:* Goodbye Mom. I'm going to Sunday School. I got to read verse 5, Luke 4 for the people. (Laughing) Something like that. That's it. He's leaving. (Really going to Sunday School?) No, he's going to the corner to hang out, but he told his Mom he's going to Sunday School. (Why did he tell his Mom that?) It was a joke.

*Card 7:* Mom's washing dishes. Dad is fixing the cabinet door. He walks in and he asks if he can make a fast buck to take his girlfriend to the movies. His Dad gave him the money. Him and his girlfriend went out. They didn't go to the movies. He went to the circus or something with a six-pack (of beer). (How did he make a fast buck?) Sweeping the cellar floor.

*Card 8:* He's looking at the baby. He's staring at the baby like the baby did something wrong. He's kind of teasing him. (Why does he want to tease the baby?) For fun. Then he takes his wife and baby out to McDonald's® and then food shopping. His car broke down along the way and he had a flat tire.

*Card 9:* Jimmy, hang up the phone. You've been on it for twenty minutes. I'm glad my Mom ain't like them, yep, yelling at me to hang up my clothes all the time. He's talking to Charlie down the street. His Mom wants to call her sister, Aunt Florence, because her son George was in a car accident. (What does he do?) Tells Jim to meet him halfway down the street and we'll all do the town. No, he plays football.

*Card 10:* His Dad came home from a business trip. He greets his wife. He's been away three months. He must have had a nice business trip. The son doesn't know what to do. He's just looking at him. "Pop, you're home." He brought him home a present. It's outside the door. It's a brand new ten-speed bike, a Schwinn Continental®. He doesn't get it until he earns it. He has to mow the lawn and help Mom with the garden and housework. Father surprises them. He drove home in a new Camaro®. He brought a present home for the guy's Mom. An urgent call came. His Aunt Jean is in the hospital. She's in the hospital with a broken leg. They brang her blue flowers in a yellow vase. They got home and had a steak dinner. Then an urgent call came from Gary, Indiana. Then he had to fly to New Mexico on a business trip. His family drove him to the airport and then he took United Airlines because he saw a pretty stewardess. They waved goodbye and waited until the airplane took off.

*Card 11:* The kid's getting yelled at because his room looks almost as messy as mine. The kid's upset because she's making him clean it. He cleaned it up and missed his band practice. That's all.

*Card 12:* Why is the dresser against the door? I think he don't want someone to come in. He's going on like me. He's running upstairs and blocking the door. Then he looks in the mirror and realizes what he looks like when he's doing it. He's staring at himself saying, "Gee, you're ugly" (laughs), "no."

*Card 13:* It looks like Billy Allen, a corny kid around our way. The same haircut and suit. He plays the flute. He's coming home walking on the sidewalk. No. He is coming home but his girlfriend's there. Looks like he's walking by some house and the girl is coming out to say "Hi" or "How's the keg party?" (How does the story end?) He went home and ate lunch.

In summary, the TED results indicate Walter's strong desire for peer acceptance; he wants to be "in" and "one of the guys." Contemptuous of adults in authority, he believes that they are stupid and easily fooled. He sees the environment as hostile, where people have to be forever vigilant and prepared to defend themselves. His level of frustration tolerance is low, and a major fight over a minor issue could ensue. The fact that his overly aggressive acts sometimes upset him gives one positive sign for therapeutic change; no remorse is felt when a societal or parental standard is violated. Motivation for change would likely be based on peer acceptance or doing things for "his own good."

The following is Walter's Rorschach record. The area designations will be based on those by Beck (1950). The record was administered in the standard fashion with the free association of all ten cards, followed by the inquiry. For reporting purposes the inquiry will follow each response below.

*Card 1:* (7 seconds) I don't know, it doesn't look like nothing. (47 seconds) A skull of something in the desert. A cow's skull. That's what it looks like. It has two front teeth, ears, and a small nose. (Most people see more than one thing, doesn't it remind you of anything else?) No, nothing else (115 seconds). (Inquiry): It's the whole thing. Here are the horns (D8). Here are the eyes (Dds30). Here is the nose (Dds26, connected together). Here are the teeth (Dd31). It's the shape that makes it look that way. (Desert) Well, that's where you would find a skull.

*Card 2:* (16 seconds) It looks like a spaceship blasting off (D4 + Ds5 + D3). (Inquiry): It's a ship okay. The fuel's coming out. It looks like it's blasting off because of the color. It's shaped like a ship. Two laughing faces (D1, on each side). (Inquiry): It just looks like the faces of two people laughing. It's shaped that way. (Total time 90 seconds)

*Card 3:* (14 seconds) It's an ant. That's all it looks like. (Total time 40 seconds) (Inquiry): It's just shaped like an ant, that's what it looks like (D1). Here are the eyes (D4) and here is the mouth (D8) and these are the legs (D5). It just looks like an ant.

*Card 4:* (15 seconds) It looks like a monster's leg. It's the whole thing. You're kind of beneath him and you're looking up at him. This is his head (D3). This is his tail (D1). These are his arms (D4) and these are his feet (D6). (Inquiry): It just looks like a monster. (Total time 45 seconds)

*Card 5:* (3 seconds) It's a bat. It's like you seen the bat fly away, the opposite way. (Total time 30 seconds) (Inquiry): It's the whole card and it looks like a flying bat.

*Card 6:* (16 seconds) A wolf's carcass. It's skinned and all. That's all I can see. (Total time 30 seconds) (Inquiry): It's the whole card. It's furry (responding to texture) and it looks like it's skinned because it's flat. Here is the head (D3) and here is the nose (D7).

*Card 7:* (31 seconds) It looks like a mole's face on both sides. There are little teeth and eyes. That's all I see. (Total time 60 seconds) (Inquiry): Here is the mole's face (D3). Here are the eyes (responding to some slightly darker shading spots). Here is the nose and here are the teeth. It could also look like men with hats on. Like little elves. This is the hat (Dd21).

*Card 8:* (10 seconds) There are two beavers. One on each side. Some kind of an animal. They're not charging but walking. It looks like it's strong. That's all I see. (Total time 65 seconds) (Inquiry): They are two beavers walking (D1). It could be a jackal too.

*Card 9:* (45 seconds) Looks like one of those big goofy guys with a smile, nose, and eyes. (Total time 65 seconds) (Inquiry): It's here (D1). Here is the nose (Dd 24), here is the eye (white space in the D1 area), and here is the double chin. It's the shape of it that makes it look that way.

*Card 10:* (10 seconds) Here's a guy with a moustache and a nose. (Inquiry): (The face is bound by the bottom half of both sides of D9). Here are the eyebrows (D6). Here are the eyes (D2). Here is the nose (D5) and here is the moustache (D4). There's a guy on top with an old German's hat (D11). Here's his eyes (pointing to the white space between D11 and D9). Here's his moustache (D3). This is his coat (top half of D9). Here's his chin (white space edging above D6). He's looking down. That's all it looks like to me. (Total time 55 seconds) (Inquiry): He's all crunched up in the coat. The coat is up, it's part around his face, kind of like his shoulders are up too.

The full analysis of this record is left as an exercise for the reader. The Rorschach does not show any great creativity on Walter's part nor does it indicate any detachment from reality. Fears of loneliness and abandonment are present. He desires to grow into an aggressive adult but struggles concomittantly to retain a more childlike, irresponsible existence. The need to grow into a responsible adult can be explored in the therapy sessions.

His drawing is significant. While it does show artistic ability, it quite evidently represents the anger and aggression he feels inside himself. The struggle to contain this aggression by adopting some standards of behavior may be represented by the cross.

## The Therapy

During the first therapy session alone, Walter indicated that he really wanted help because he was tired "of screwing up my life." The parents had previously described his temper tantrums where he smashed furniture, put his fist through a wall, and beat up his brother. Walter meekly confirmed this and indicated that one of his major goals would be to establish better self-control. He also stated that he resisted teachers and hated regimentation; specifically, he was "not going to let any teacher push me around."

One prior incident involved his behavior during the school's testing program where his teacher noted that he spoke momentarily to another boy. Reprimanding Walter, she asked him to change his seat, but he stubbornly refused. She then asked him to return his answer test blanks, but he adamantly resisted and vigorously cursed at the teacher. The principal's intervention was requested, but Walter continued to refuse to return the test papers, warning the administrator and his staff not to touch him or he would attack. In desperation at this unwarranted resistance, the principal called the police. While initially refusing the police officer, he eventually gave up when the officer threatened to "break his head." In view of this disruption and "incorrigible behavior" Walter was suspended and referred to the school's Child Study Team. Most teaching personnel were secretly hopeful for his permanent expulsion from school.

The following are excerpts from his second psychotherapeutic session, this time with the parents present:

Figure 4. Man drawn by Walter W.

*Walter:* The goddam teachers and principal think they run the school. The damn teacher had no right telling me to be quiet.

*Therapist:* Oh? Teachers aren't supposed to keep students quiet during a test?

*Walter:* Well, she shouldn't have told the principal. She didn't like me and had it in for me just like the rest of the teachers.

*Therapist:* I see, so you were really angry because you believe a teacher had it in for you and wasn't treating you fairly (reflecting but not interpreting).

*Walter:* You bet, that's exactly right.

*Therapist:* Okay, I see how you made yourself angry by deciding in your mind that the teacher was unfair. You also believe that teachers should *always* be fair or you're going to get damn mad if they are not.

*Walter:* Goddam right! They got to be fair when they deal with me. Nobody is gonna crap on me.

*Therapist:* You kind of make yourself angry whenever you're not treated exactly the way you think you ought to be treated. One of the things we have to look at is how you maneuver yourself into trouble and make yourself angry.

*Walter:* What? I maneuver myself into trouble and make myself angry? That's a crazy idea.

*Therapist:* Let's see, you were about to take a test and you started to talk. What's the teacher supposed to do when somebody talks during a test?

*Walter:* (More calmly now) Well, I guess she's supposed to tell you to keep quiet or put you somewhere where you don't talk.

*Therapist:* Okay, so according to you the teacher was really just doing her job. She didn't single you out before you talked. It was after you began talking that she asked you to change your seat.

*Walter:* (More meekly now as he reasons with the therapist) Well, I suppose so. I wasn't going to listen to that bitch. Why did she have to make such a big deal out of it?

*Therapist:* Because you made a big deal out of it first. Got it? Instead of moving, your actions informed the teacher that you weren't going to do what she asked you to do; in fact, you just about dared her to do something about it. Well, what could she do? Naturally she called the principal.

*Walter:* (Trying to think clearly) I see what you're driving at. Since I told the principal to go fuck himself and wouldn't give him the papers, he called the police. Wasn't he stupid to call the police over a lousy paper! (He is exasperated at the behavior of others, but not his own.)

*Therapist:* That could be. You kept challenging them to do something to you when you wouldn't follow the rules or directions. You invited a confrontation. You know, Walter, teachers and principals will accept challenges just like you do.

*Walter:* I guess that's only fair. But I didn't see it that way then. I was so mad I wasn't thinking too good.

*Therapist:* Okay, so as we go on in treatment we'll take a look at how you see things and how that leads you into making yourself angry. We'll also try to understand how others might react to your behavior.

(Toward the end of this session, the therapist asked the parents to leave briefly. They showed no reaction to Walter's foul language and did not interrupt the therapeutic session.)

*Therapist:* Walter, I know some teenagers have problems that they don't like to discuss in front of their parents. I wonder if you have any that you feel you'd like to tell me right away while your folks aren't here.

Walter immediately responded by relating that his thirteen-year-old girlfriend was about ten days late with her period and possibly pregnant. He was very anxious about what kind of legal trouble he would be in if he were responsible. While he felt that they were both in love, the girl's father resented their teenage friendship while being presumably ignorant of their sexual activities. Since she was "young" (at age 15, Walter did not consider himself "young"), he believed that he could be charged with statutory rape. He wanted to avoid a detention center, predicting that with the tough guys there he would "act tough and get into more trouble." Through the therapist's questioning, it was apparent that no medical advice had been sought about the possible pregnancy. His basic knowledge of sexual facts was indeed limited, and no contraceptive methods had been used. He knew of one birth control method, the condom, but was too embarrassed to make such a purchase either directly or through friends. He asked questions of the therapist about marriage and its feasibility for "a guy almost 16." The therapist recognized Walter's anxiety and became sympathetic as well as instructive. Since Walter was uncertain that the girl's periods were regular, he was informed of a reputable medical facility nearby where a confidential examination could be done. He seemed instantly reassured when he realized that the existence of his "crisis" had not, as yet, been truly established. He was made aware that a delay in a period of ten days in a thirteen-year-old girl was not confirmation of pregnancy. He was "sweating it out" until the girl was examined. Fortunately she was not pregnant, to the relief of all concerned.

In setting his long-range goals, Walter indicated that he would like to "settle down, have a wife, family, and a job along with a high school diploma." He thought that the latter would help him get a better job so that he would not be considered a "dummy." He confidentially admitted a genuine desire to stay out of trouble.

The therapist assured him that he would be helped to achieve these specific goals dealing with education and graduation, as well as a better control of his temper. (When a client is convinced that the therapist is going to help him get what he says he wants, i.e. to go in the same valued direction as the client, the latter is more apt to regard the therapist as a helping friend and also to respond with greater motivation to seek relief from his problems.)

Since Walter felt protective of his much younger siblings, he had no difficulty with them. However, with the teenage brother he had frequent fights or terrorized the boy's friends. If he lost at table tennis to such competitors, he would assault them and break furniture in his fury.

Therapeutic exploration revealed that he perceived almost every competitive task as one where his very self-esteem was at stake. To lose was totally demoralizing.

Extensive efforts were expended to help him appreciate that he did not have to be "perfect" or "great" in every sport or social event to compensate for his poor school performance. Further, he had been oblivious to the fact that none of his brother's friends were comfortable with him, since they would be assaulted if they won a game. Nor did his little game of wrestling his brother's friends until they said, "uncle," endear him to them. He only wished to crush his opponents and was truly ignorant of the negative impact of his own behavior.

After several therapy sessions with his brother present, he finally perceived the insightful message about his behavior, which was accompanied by a surprisingly rapid change for the better in Walter. He consciously tried to accept defeat gracefully; not surprisingly, the number of incidents of temper loss was considerably diminished. In fact, he liked the consequences of his change, since for the first time his brother's friends now asked him to join a game instead of rejecting him. As Walter further associated about these incidents, it became apparent to him that he needed to prove that he was "somebody special" because of much belittlement by neighborhood boys for previously being in the retarded class. His behavior revealed, "If I can't be smart, at least I can be tough."

In the family sessions, the mother believed that Walter developed this feeling of rejection and worthlessness because his stepfather never loved him. She admitted that she shielded Walter from the discipline of her current husband because of the man's sternness and resented how he heavily favored their other teenage son over Walter.

Reacting to this accusation, the father claimed that he had been prevented from taking an active part in the child's reasonable upbringing because the mother intervened so often. Since he married her when Walter was an infant, he felt awkward in handling small children. He went on to state, "My wife incorrectly decided very early that I didn't like Walter because he wasn't mine and that since no one would love him she would do it all herself. She never really gave me a chance with Walter; maybe it's too late for me."

Walter, however, testified that he never felt that his father didn't like him but rather believed that the man just never liked to do things with children. Walter stated, "I listened to my Dad. I know he could knock my block off and I know I can wrap my Mom around my little finger. But if I got into trouble I knew she'd be there to help. I'm not so sure about my Dad."

As the sessions progressed, the mother allowed the father to become more involved in Walter's management and help set standards of behavior. Behavioral restrictions and rewards were negotiated in the therapy sessions with Walter present regarding bedtime, household chores, weekend expectations, etc.

Yet Walter's weekend drinking was a problem. His community had no organized teenage activities with the exception of a Boy Scout program attuned to younger children. Instead, teenage boys and girls set up camp sites around the wooded area near town for "keg parties," beer-drinking at two dollars per person.

When intoxicated, Walter would frequently fight, especially if another boy glanced at his girl or even talked to her. He might also attack her if she recognized or spoke to another boy even if it were just to pass another beer. In general, however, he felt a sense of camaraderie with most of the other drinking adolescents.

The parents concurred that there was little planned activity for Walter. The neighbors viewed teenagers basically as a nuisance and discouraged their presence. The local police officer told the mother that he had attended keg parties when a teenager so that she should not worry about it with her son.

With this issue the therapist recognized his limitations in changing something quite as socially positive, possibly reinforcing, as the keg party. It was obvious that community involvement would be necessary to change the positive valence of this special social event. The therapist expressed his disapproval about an adolescent disobeying the law and suggested that it might be desirable for him to stop. However, the therapist also recognized that since Walter did not see this as a problem he probably would not follow such advice.

It was further indicated that there was, nonetheless, one aspect of Walter's drinking that definitely led to trouble: his intoxication and fighting. Since he (1) had been in a number of serious fights as a result of his drinking, (2) did not like the violent part of his own behavior, feeling that he wanted to change it, and (3) needed to use much effort in controlling his irrational outbursts, Walter decided that he should at least work on lessening the drinking. Yet he felt he needed to be "man enough to keep up with any other guy with a mug in my hand most of the night."

Recognizing Walter's need for a "macho" image, the therapist suggested that he could still have a mug in his hand but could control himself by drinking much more slowly with perhaps two beers that could last the night. At first Walter was skeptical and wondered if just two glasses were worth his two dollar contribution.

The next week Walter tried out the suggestion, reporting that he felt and acted better. As the weeks progressed, and although there were occasional periods of intoxication, the number and intensity diminished.

In school Walter disliked some of the basic rules. He related that since he liked excitement he had set off firecrackers there. Of course he resented any disciplinary action which came from "having fun." As long as the action is exciting, it must be "good," he figured.

To the school policy of receiving detention slips for cutting classes, he responded by defiance. Since he would not stay in school during regular hours, he certainly did not plan to stay after hours. The eventual result was suspension from school and continued strife with school authorities and his family.

Additional therapy sessions revealed some changes in his thinking:

*Walter:* I've been thinking about what we talked about last time. You said the therapist's job was to help people to get what they want. I told you I wanted a high school diploma and you thought that I had the ability to get it. You also said I was interfering with my own plans. Now I find that it's hard to keep up in school by getting myself suspended. I guess I got enough trouble keeping in school without getting kicked out, so I'd like to talk about my temper a little bit.

That's one of my problems.

*Therapist:* Okay, let's look at the way you make yourself angry. Before, we talked about how people make themselves angry because of what they think and how they handle situations.

*Walter:* Like the fight I had at a dance?

*Therapist:* Right.

*Walter:* Well, when I'm out with my girlfriend she's supposed to spend time with me and not look at the other guys.

*Therapist:* That's a good example. If you're out with Carol she is to look at no one but you. Not only shouldn't she look at anyone else, she shouldn't talk to anyone else. What's the reason for that?

*Walter:* Because that's the way I like.it!

*Therapist:* Oh, I see, if "King" Walter likes it that way, that's the way it has to be.

*Walter:* (Laughing) Kind of.

*Therapist:* So if she looks at someone else . . .

*Walter:* Then I get mad!

*Therapist:* So you make yourself mad.

*Walter:* Bullshit! She makes me mad.

*Therapist:* How? Does she cast a spell over you, hit you? All she did was look at somebody else. How did that hurt you?

*Walter:* She makes me feel like shit if she pays attention to other guys.

*Therapist:* I understand. You feel like shit when she pays attention to other guys, but what do you have to tell yourself to feel that bad? I bet one of the things you say is, "Carol has to do what I say and it's a terrible thing if she doesn't!"

*Walter:* Goddam right it's a terrible thing! What will all the other guys think if I can't even control my girlfriend?

*Therapist:* They'll think you have a girlfriend who doesn't let you control her.

*Walter:* (Hesitating a moment) They'll think I'm some sissy who can be pushed around.

*Therapist:* And if they thought that, that would be awful, terrible, a catastrophe. Boy, I can see why you make yourself angry. You've got a nutty belief that every time your girlfriend doesn't do exactly what you want or for that matter if anyone tries to cross you, it makes you feel like a sissy and not a man.

*Walter:* Right! But it's not nutty (angrily).

*Therapist:* Oh, do you become something because someone calls you that?

*Walter:* Well, I . . . guess not.

*Therapist:* Let me give you an example. Suppose someone says to me, "Doctor, you're a stupid jerk."

*Walter:* (Interrupting) I'd punch him in the mouth if he said that to me!

*Therapist:* I know you would but if I was interested in the guy's opinion, I know that he would be either right or wrong. Since I don't want to be a stupid jerk, I would ask him why he thinks that. If he gave me a good reason and told me about things I should know about and I didn't, like if I really did something dumb, then I need to do something to make me smarter. Then I really won't be a stupid jerk. Maybe I have to learn some new things. Punching a guy in the mouth won't give me the information I need.

*Walter:* What if he doesn't have a reason and just calls you a name?

*Therapist:* Well, then he's telling me that he, himself, has a big problem. He likes to call people names for no good reason. In short he's telling me he's a disturbed guy. As a psychologist I might want to give him therapy. Should I become angry because he's got a problem? If it were a friend I could either help him with the problem or choose not to be his friend. I might decide that I don't need friends who call me names all the time. The difference right now between you and me is that you make yourself angry about the name and I don't. I can give other people the right to be wrong and the right to act stupid, that is, to mistakenly call me stupid because of an incorrect reason. While I might try to correct their mistakes, I'm prepared to accept the fact that they might sometimes do or say something stupid. And I know that I don't become what they call me. The trouble you're having is that you believe that you do become what they call you.

*Walter:* (Hesitating and obviously trying to grasp the idea) I see, just because someone calls me a sissy or a jerk when I know I'm not one, I shouldn't get so upset about it?

*Therapist:* Right. When the teacher calls on you in class and you don't know the answer, does not knowing that one answer make you an idiot?

*Walter:* No, it just means that I don't know the answer to the question. You know, I never thought about it that way before. I think I know what you'll say next. If you want to answer the question the next time, you should learn the answer beforehand instead of feeling stupid, getting mad, and walking out of the teacher's room.

*Therapist:* Hey, that's good! If you want to get smarter you have to do something to get smarter, remember that.

*Walter:* Yeah, but I sure get angry at my girlfriend. She does a lot of things I don't like and I think she does it deliberately.

*Therapist:* You told me several times that your girlfriend bugs you but you're really in love with her. You're fifteen and your girlfriend's thirteen. You're both pretty young. Do you consider going out with other girls?

*Walter:* (Sadly) How many girls would really like me?

*Therapist:* You don't feel other girls would like you?

*Walter:* Well, I really don't know. I bet some wouldn't like me.

*Therapist:* You're a nice-looking guy, but I guess it's fair to say that some girls would like you and some would not.

*Walter:* Well, how do I know a girl would really like me before I go out with her?

*Therapist:* You want a guarantee that people will like you?

*Walter:* Damn right! I ain't gonna let no girl put me down!

*Therapist:* I see, you believe if any girl doesn't like you then you're put down and she's trying to make you feel worthless.

*Walter:* Goddam right and no girl is going to get away with that!

*Therapist:* Wow. Sounds like you have to be on your guard all the time to prove that you're somebody worthwhile.

*Walter:* Huh? Well, I guess so.

*Therapist:* Walt, if somebody doesn't like you then you become worthless?

*Walter:* (Hesitating for a few seconds) I see what you mean. I guess you really don't become worthless. Worthless doesn't come from being called worthless.

*Therapist:* Good, you got the idea: because someone doesn't like you, you don't automatically become worthless. How worthwhile a human being you are doesn't depend on who likes you. I know most of us would prefer people to like us. Walt, suppose someone you like and want to like you tells you that he hates your guts. What do you think you ought to do?

*Walter:* Well, I would probably bust him in the mouth but I know you're going to say that this is not right.

*Therapist:* That's pretty good, you're right. What do you think I'd tell you to do?

*Walter:* I don't really know. You said it was someone I wanted to like me?

*Therapist:* Right, but would busting him in the mouth help to get him to like you?

*Walter:* No, but it would if it were a girl who likes you to treat her rough.

*Therapist:* Maybe, but do most people, including you, like to be treated rough?

*Walter:* No, but what would you do?

*Therapist:* If he or she hated my guts and I cared about their opinion I'd ask why. If there were something about my behavior that that person disliked then maybe I could change it.

*Walter:* Well, what if someone said he didn't have any reasons, he just didn't like you?

*Therapist:* Well, if I believed what he said that would tell me there is something nutty about that person just like it did previously. It would mean that he had a real problem, that he formed opinions about people for no good reason. Maybe the guy's got a secret hang-up and only likes people who have blue eyes and drink beer or for some emotional reason he can't like other kinds of people. Should a person feel worthless because this kind of guy has a hang-up?

*Walter:* So if somebody gives you a good reason you should

listen to it and maybe do something about his complaint if it makes sense. But if he doesn't have a good reason I still think I should punch him out.

*Therapist:* Do you just enjoy punching people or do you do it just when you're angry?

*Walter:* (Annoyed) I'm no sicky. I don't do it for fun. I do it when they make me angry. Then they deserve it.

*Therapist:* Okay, what I'm going to try to do is prevent your anger from developing in the first place. I know that when people get so angry and feel they have to punch somebody, these people make themselves angry by what they think.

*Walter:* Hell no. What do you mean? It's simple: he said he didn't like me. That made me angry.

*Therapist:* How? He didn't hit you, stab you, or punch you. He just said some words. He wasn't a magician with secret powers. You merely thought something about what he said. Then you became angry based on what you thought.

*Walter:* (Pausing, trying to reason it out, and repeating the idea) I thought something that made me mad? You mean I should try to understand how I think and what I tell myself?

*Therapist:* Exactly. We sometimes have to study what we think and discover what nutty ideas we have. What we learned so far today is that you decide how someone is to behave and when they don't behave exactly the way you believe they ought to, you actually make yourself angry. You also said that if your girlfriend doesn't do what you desperately want her to do, you tell yourself that everybody will believe you're a sissy. You even believe that you might be one. What I'd like you to do over the week is to notice each time when you get angry and then just stop for a moment, try to think, and see if you can figure out what you told yourself to make yourself angry.

*Walter:* Okay, that sounds interesting. It's tough, but I'll try it.

## Later Therapy Sessions

Walter was seen for approximately 30 therapeutic sessions. Some were individual, others were sessions with all the family present, and some were sessions with just him and his parents. Besides setting standards of behavior for Walter, the parents' own inconsistencies in discipline were directly pointed out. There were times when the mother would punish behavior that she would later condone. Not surprisingly, some of the sessions were quite stormy.

As expectations were clarified and standards of behavior were negotiated, Walter protested and screamed most of the way toward a more mature outlook. Eventually he accepted the imposed limitations. For example, he was expected to be home for dinner and to spend at least one hour on homework (which he claimed he never had). The agreement was made that he return home no later than ten o'clock on weekdays and twelve-thirty on weekends. He adamantly refused to give up his keg parties, since these were the major social events of the week. Besides, the people who frequented these were his friends, and it was essential that he feel accepted as part of a group, as it defused his anger. He agreed to specific limitations on his drinking. As a result he would not become intoxicated either as often or to the same degree.

On the other hand, the sexual acting-out behavior had been subtly encouraged by the family. As the psychotherapy sessions progressed, Walter revealed that his brother Larry was calling his boyfriends to view some parent-owned pornographic films. While embarrassed, the parents admitted that they did show such films to their teenage children because they believed that "sex is fine and children of all ages should know about it." However, the emotional, affectional, and responsible aspects of sex were totally omitted from the films, and there were no family discussions of sexual behavior. The therapist pointed out also that their neighbors might not share their liberal attitudes or appreciate the local children viewing the erotic films at their home. They recognized that this could create some difficulty for them with their neighbors and possibly with the law. They began to supervise more carefully what their children were doing at home. Their film collection was put under lock and key, and the children never saw them again.

They had no negative view toward Walter's sexual escapades

with his girlfriend "unless he would someday come home with a floozy." The mother said that she would then kick them both out. The mother further related that if Walter's girlfriend got pregnant and wanted to have the baby and her own mother didn't like the idea, then the girl could come live with them. This particular idea terrified Walter. While some discussion developed in this area, the parents did not consider this to be a problem. In the meantime, the parents became involved in their own interrelationships. The father felt that his wife was neglectful of his feelings by being too involved with the children. In an effort to defend herself, she brought in the following list of complaints about her husband:

1. (a) He completely ignores my feelings and won't talk to me when I'm upset. (b) I am to be perfectly attuned to his feelings. (c) If I keep things to myself and I don't talk much, then I'm cold. If I talk, then I'm neurotic. (d) How can I care about his feelings if I have to hold back on my own feelings? And if I do want to share my feelings with him, I feel he isn't hearing what I'm saying. I feel stupid when I'm a little kid trying to get the attention of the most important person in my life. When I try to share my feelings he says I put stress on him. Of course it's easy for me to turn my love on the kids and maybe to turn to my girlfriend, who really hears me and can laugh or be sad with me.

2. All these years I held back and tried to handle Walter and all the problems because I knew how Jonesy felt about Walter and how it upset him. Then he told me I was all wrong. So I told him about all the problems. But by doing this, all I did was add fuel to Jonesy's negative convictions about Walter. Jonesy got so upset, he said that I wanted to give him a heart attack.

3. He has told me repeatedly that he didn't want kids and I pressured him to have more. Now he feels that they are my kids and I must not bother him. He doesn't feel he should spend his life doing things for the kids. Actually, he must start a life of his own and not expect us to live with him. Walter needs a father, a guiding person, but my husband wasn't man enough to do it.

4. I was told he didn't care about Walter and my feelings especially when it comes down to money. He knew I was upset, but he won't sit around and talk to me. Then he said, "You're cold."

5. I can't feel at ease anymore expressing my feelings and fears about the kids because I know how Jonesy believes, "You wanted them, why bother me?"

6. He doesn't give Walter attention, hardly says a word to him, and doesn't even like being in a room with Walter. Yet he does things for one brother but not for Walter.

7. He tells me how people get tuned in if you can feel how they feel and care. But the two most important people he should try to tune in on he doesn't — Walter and me.

Mrs. Jones summarized her feelings as follows:

> My only hope is that I can hold out until Walter is eighteen and that he will never bother us again. I also hope that Jonesy finds a woman who will give him the life he really wants.
>
> Yet something has to give. I'm turning into a sad person. I wish just once someone would say, "Don't worry, we're together, we're healthy, and we don't owe a dime." Instead I have to say it even though I don't believe it. I guess I'm trying to convince myself that everything is all right.
>
> Not once all this week did my husband ask, "What's the matter?" But just let a couple of neighborhood girls come in who are friendly with our kids and he's right there asking, "What's the matter girls? Can I help you?" He's right there to fix their bikes, "If you would have come sooner, I could have helped you." What about the bike that Walter wanted him to fix two or three weeks ago? He hasn't got to that yet.

### Follow-up

These matters were worked on with the parents and an effort made for each to explain what was wanted from each other and from themselves. Eventually their affective and sexual relationships began to improve, especially as both became able to express deeper feelings and dependenices to one another.

In the meantime, Walter had begun to improve in his academic work and to obey school rules. With the parents being more consistent about what they wanted and more supporting of each other, his tantrum behavior also diminished. There were no "skirmishes" with authorities. Walter finished his semester, accepting help from his teachers and tutors. As the summer months arrived and with the initial stress alleviated, the parents terminated treatment.

Follow-up a year and a half later determined that Walter had completed one more year of school with average grades but had decided not to obtain his high school diploma. He had taken a job in a building trade and was gainfully employed as an apprentice. Dating someone new, he was now saving money for a car and eventually his own apartment. His relationship with his family had continued to improve. He had not yet established any long-range goals, rather he focused more on immediate teenage pleasures.

While the sessions were terminated prematurely, the therapist was not in a position to insist on further treatment. The therapist believed that there is only readiness for additional gains when the clients are uncomfortable with their problems. The discomfort was no longer present in Walter's family.

Sometimes it is better to allow the client(s) to continue without the therapist. Here the therapist must trust the clients' judgment in regard to how much help they need. Occasionally therapists err in making the client too dependent on them. An essential criterion for insisting on further treatment is whether or not the client will potentially injure himself or herself or someone else. The client should be allowed to make his or her own mistakes, while the therapist should offer the possibility for additional treatment when and if desired by the client. By the end of the sessions, the parents acknowledged that they were also clients of the therapist just as much as their son although their initial referral included only Walter and his multitude of problems.

## THE TYPE II FAMILY

In contrast to the characteristics found in the Type I Family illustrated in Chapter I, the Type II Family (Blanco, 1977) has only the common feature of the underachieving child, while the parental life-styles are markedly different. In the Type II unit, it is the mother who is the dominant force and who is skilled at "taking charge," managing the budget, nagging the husband into action, and solving the family problems. Being self-confident, she passes on this characteristic to her daughters who, not surprisingly, identify with her and reveal their own high sense of worth in performing competently in school work, holding down part-time jobs, being reliable, etc.

By direct contrast, the father is noticeably passive, noncompetitive, and self-denigrating, a spectator rather than a participant in life. He has felt defeated since childhood and has often been a rejected son, an orphan perhaps, or one who never received his full measure of love, support, and guidance. Still sensing this void of love within him, he has sought a wife to fulfill this desperate need. In the process of finding a loving, maternal person, he bargains away his assertive rights in marriage by receiving affection and not involving himself in the family. The wife, seeking a controllable, passive, low-keyed mate, has previously rejected men who have challeneged her decision-making and who have stated their claim to either full or shared control of the family. They are discarded because they simply will not take orders from her. Assuredly they make her anxious and uncomfortable.

When the Type II people are courting, it appears that each sends out complementary signals to the other so that an unconscious "bargain" or "contract" is struck: he will let her be the dominant influence and decision maker in the family as long as she offers considerable affection to him. She insists upon "the last word" in the daily issues, yet promises him to be as affectionate as his needs require. He is too lacking in confidence to effect a change in his passive life-style and clings dependently to her and often to alcohol as well. Basically she has always resented men, viewing them as unreliable like her own father and ridiculing them generally as incompetent.

And so the marriage begins. She shortly discovers that he is not necessarily inept, but rather that he feels he is inept. One such man, a dropout from college with two years of training in accounting, was hired in a small company. On his own efforts he effectively redesigned its entire bookkeeping and payroll system, to his employer's amazement. Yet when interviewed by a social worker about who handled the family checkbook, he answered dejectedly, "I'm no good at math — my wife handles all those things for me."

Since he lacks a competitive spirit and a sustained drive for achievement, the Type II man does not rise significantly in employment level or salary. As an obvious consequence, the family stays at the low average or average income level, never to join the monied elite or to achieve self-actualization on any dimension. He is stalled, stagnated, or perhaps enslaved by his powerful need for her affection and acceptance. For him the battle for society's accolades never started, and his wife knows it. She feels sorry for him but does not admire him.

She also complains about his lassitude, his irresponsibility about home chores, his beer and TV watching, and the fact that she "must do everything" herself. Of course, this is exactly as she has wanted it. Yet, in martyred fashion, she proclaims her marriage burdens to all sympathetic relatives and neighbors, e.g. "I get no help from him." If, in fact, he does become assertive and enters into her domain of decision making, she retaliates by feigning sexual aloofness, a violation of their original "contract." He cannot tolerate this very long, and after drinking "with the boys" comes roaring home to beat her into submission. Although often too late to redirect the initial onslaughts, she eventually realizes that she has gone too far and learns to soften his rage by showing tenderness and thus soothing him into the quiet, satisfied husband she has always wanted.

Since the man feels inferior, he passes on these attitudes to his son, who strongly identifies with him. And since the women in the family generally feel men to be the "dumb Doras" of a matriarchal society, the father and son receive very few positive reinforcements for their genuine achievements whenever these infrequently appear. They are, instead, reinforced by "affectionate forgiveness" for their ineptitudes. The males are then bound together in their mild state of rejection and passivity.

It is not surprising that by the time the boy reaches school he is already the recipient of an aura of condemnation from the mother and his capable sisters, as well as the reservoir of self-defeating attitudes from his father. The obvious outcome is a depressing and serious underachievement by virtue of low motivation and a negative self-concept — a male tragedy of wasted abilities and unfulfilled goals.

The following case of Charles C. typifies in many ways the dynamics and minor pathologies found in the Type II family. The child was not expected, even at an early age, to accomplish much, and the behavioral consequencies of this expectation have made the parents rethink their contributions to Charles's problems.

## TYPE II UNDERACHIEVER: PASSIVE-AGGRESSIVE BEHAVIOR

Name: Charles C.    Age: 13 Years, 4 Months    Grade: Eighth

Mr. and Mrs. C. contacted the school psychologist to have their son evaluated because they felt that he was unmotivated in school and not working up to his ability. They questioned if an evaluation would identify some psychological "block" that Charles had toward learning. After interviews with the parents, it was also obvious that they were dissatisfied with the racially integrated school that Charles attended and hoped to find that his IQ was high enough to meet the 115 IQ entrance requirement at a certain high school for scholastically accelerated boys in their city.

### Family Background

The C. family consists of the parents, who have been married for twenty-four years, their twin sixteen-year-old daughters and thirteen-year-old son Charles. Mr. C., a passive and dependent man, is fifty years old and employed as a butcher in a supermarket. He has also been in the Naval Reserves for eighteen years. He was the third oldest in a family of four whose parents owned a produce business and some real estate holdings. His family was basically under the control of the mother, and discipline was rarely needed, especially since he was "a conforming child, a loner," as he termed himself. Mrs. C., the youngest of three children, was raised in "a nice home" and despite some financial difficulties, "never felt poor." She reported being favored by her father, who was "a job jumper. He was affectionate but drank a lot." Mrs. C. worked in a clerking position and then was promoted to a supervisory job when quite young, soon after graduating from an "academic" high school. All four of Charles's grandparents came to this country from a central European country.

Mrs. C.'s first two pregnancies ended in stillbirths. Charles's older sisters are in the eleventh grade and are interested in scholarships to certain local colleges, since their school grades have been quite good. They are fraternal sisters who look distinctly different and are unique in personality as well. Both are regarded as bright.

The C.'s define themselves as a middle-income family, but both of them are unhappy that they cannot afford to move from their present home in a recently integrated neighborhood to a more expensive area of the city. They are apprehensive about crime rates, the growing number of "strange faces" in the neighborhood, and a "deterioration" of discipline in Charles's local junior high.

### Developmental History

Mrs. C. was thirty-four years old when Charles was born. It was a breech birth with a difficult, although short, labor and apparently no known adverse effects on the mother or child. Charles's development was "slow" but not retarded, the milestones "not recalled" by the mother in an avoiding way. The parents described him as "basically healthy," "a lot of fun to 'baby'," noting also that "maybe we spoiled our only son a little."

Since the first grade he periodically complained of stomach

pains, which the parents assumed to be an excuse to stay home from school; however, last year an internist discoverd a slight deviation in the intestinal tract, which caused the pain. This was corrected by surgery last summer, and his complaints have minimized. The mother reported that he "loved" being sick in the hospital and forced everyone to cater to his slightest need (signs of dependency and skill in manipulating adults to gain his ends).

### Educational History

The C.'s report that since first grade Charles has been in average ability classes and that all of his teachers have always said that he could do better. He is a C student, presently in the eighth grade, and has been reported by teachers twice this year for "playing around and talking excessively in the classroom." He is not active in any clubs and has never earned money.

### Discussion of Parent Interview Information

Mr. and Mrs. C. willingly discussed Charles's school difficulties but were very defensive about their own involvement. They readily blamed the schools, the teachers, and the neighborhood for their son's lack of achievement, particularly the fact that Charles has never been in a classroom with high ability children "so that he could learn motivation from them." The parents believe that most of the teachers are in the schools "only to collect a paycheck" and have little interest in the students or in using new, more "creative" techniques (unspecified) to motivate them. They also feel that the school's failure to educate the children is due to the recent arrival of a minority group in the neighborhood and the negative effect this allegedly has had on the academic atmosphere and discipline in school.

Both parents believe that the job of education is the total responsibility of the school. Mrs. C. feels that perhaps she did not push Charles enough when he was younger to learn things, and her husband reluctantly feels that Charles's poor study habits and inability to concentrate on things that do not interest him might be the fault of "his home training." Feeling that their son lacks motivation and that he would do better if he had a "taste of success," the C.'s state that their only goal for Charles is to see him want to do well, admitting, however, that they would like to see him prepare for a professional career. They stress to him the importance of a college education in acquiring a good job and material possessions. Specifically, they want him to be a dentist.

Charles's primary interest, on the other hand, is in sports, and he spends much time both playing ball and going to sporting events with his father or friends. His memory is very good when it comes to sport statistics and, although small, his athletic ability is good. Other social activities include eating out with his friends and attending parties on the week-ends at the homes of other boys and girls his age. Although many of his friends have moved, his parents do not want him to lose social contact. The family is envious of their friends who have moved to "the safe suburbs."

Both parents agree that Charles is closer to his father, who is generally extremely lenient and loving with him. Mrs. C. however, sets the rules and enforces them on all her children. She "cracks down" on Charles for his laxity in following through with chores and homework and berates him for his indifference to responsibility, remarking frequently that "you're just like your father," in a disgusted tone. The father feebly defends Charles saying, "he'll eventually be earning a living" and that "childhood is over too soon." At remarks like these, Mrs. C. seems to regard her husband as her second son, incapable of mature judgment and adult expectations. At other times, she expects little from her son and gives him money rather freely for whatever he wants. Charles can be very stubborn and will sulk to get his own way. They cannot often tolerate his anger at them, so they give in to his demands sooner or later. Charles has apparently been faced with inconsistent expectations all his life.

### Behavioral Observations

Charles is a small, cherubic-looking boy who appears about

two years younger than his actual age of thirteen. He presented a neat appearance for each session, as he was dressed in a stylish safari suit selected by his mother.

Charles said he came to the clinic because his parents felt that he was not doing well enough in school, and he admitted that he rarely did homework but was capable of getting better grades. He remarked that he was concerned about his grades and wanted to do better but gave the impression that he felt this would occur without any effort on his part, revealing wishful fantasy if not magical hopes. He did not appear to be a "driven" or well-motivated boy but rather one who was casual and passive. Although generally cooperative with the examiner, Charles exhibited resistive and negative behavior when confronted with tasks that were the least bit difficult. He did attempt tasks that were presented to him when prodded and when he knew the examiner would not excuse him from performing. This minimal-effort style was seen as a good random sample of his general approach to problem solving.

Charles's work habits were good when he consented to do the work, and he was able to work quickly and accurately. His attention and concentration were adequate for his age level. He reacted to praise with pleasure and relief but became anxious and evasive in the face of more difficult tasks. Insight and autocriticism were good, as he was able to distinguish readily between success and failure.

### Test Results

| *Stanford-Binet L-M:* | *WISC-R:* | |
|---|---|---|
| CA  13 Years, 4 Months | Verbal | 102 IQ |
| MA  13 Years, 0 Months | Performance | 97 IQ |
| IQ  97 | Full-Scale | 99 IQ |

*Bender-Gestalt:*                    **WRAT:**

  Normal Visual Perception          Word Recog.:        6.2 Gd. Pl.

                                                Percentile:         10th for
                                                                      8th Gd.

*California Achieve. Tests:*         *Wepman Auditory Discrim.:*
(From School)
                                               Normal

  Reading Total:    6.4 Gd. Pl.

  Arithmetic Total: 5.7 Gd. Pl.

  Language Total: 5.9 Gd. Pl.

ITPA:    (Administered to check
        for possible learning
        disabilities)                    *Personality Tests:*

  No deficiencies compared          Thematic Apperception

  to norm                           Michigan Picture Stories

Interpretation of projective testing revealed that Charles sees his parents as affectionate and concerned people yet the mother as demanding and rejecting also. A very dependent boy, he has learned some contradictions: be responsible yet recognize that his parents and other will forgive his ineptitudes and solve his problems — social, academic, vocational, etc. Although socially adequate with his peers, none apparently academically motivated, he does not feel responsible for his own behavior and is quite narcissistic. (The connection between the C.'s child rearing practices and Charles' subsequent noncompetitive behavior is easy to discern, as the parents are uncomfortably aware.)

Charles has developed a generally negative attitude toward school and school work. Because his parents' expectations are also too high for his ability, he has not been able to please them, and he feels badly. He is particularly angry at this mother's demands for achievement, and he subtly and unconsciously retaliates against her by losing books, forgetting assignments, and acting like a helpless infant. One projective story revealed a child doing ridiculous, embarrassing antics before all the parents' relatives.

### Diagnostic Impressions

Charles, a boy of average intelligence, is a confused, passive-aggressive child lacking motivation to learn. He is not a learning disabled child, having no visual or auditory handicaps. He is an underachiever in reading and math and is under considerable pressure from his parents to achieve at a superior level and, perhaps, to live out their vocational expectations in the American Dream. He is unhappy in his role as a nonproducing son, but he is basically too dependent and unconvinced of his own abilities to resolve many of his own problems. Also, to keep him from being unhappy over his situation and to avoid implicating themselves, his parents create reasons for him, actually excuses, for these relative failures. Their own basic style is to project blame to others and, naturally, he uses this approach too. In his naive grasp of real academic competition he predicts that going to an elite high school for talented boys will be "fun." His parents secretly wonder if he is qualified, but they will be informed that he does not meet the school district's criteria for intelligence or for superior grades.

The C.'s are relatively open for suggestions on managing their son at home and wish to weigh their own impact on his lagging development in motivation and general self-responsibility.

## *Workbook Exercise: Prescriptions*

The specific intervention strategies used on this case are purposely omitted in this "typical" case of underachievement at the junior high level. The student reader may use this case material as a basis for creating individualized prescriptions for Charles and compare these possibilities with colleagues under the general supervision of a clinical instructor or supervisor. The case may be approached from a generally behavioral and/or psychodynamic vantage point, with strategies listed as a basis for further consultation and negotiation with parents and school professionals. It is apparent, in view of the complexities of style and the various needs in each of the family members, that many efforts, by both school personnel and parents, will be needed to redirect Charles's energy and help him mature.

### EXTINCTION OF SEVERE CRYING

An attractive, likeable couple sought to admit their profoundly retarded daughter Debbie, age four, to a residential home for fifty crippled children. The facility specialized in physical therapy and a general program of stimulation in speech, occupational therapy, music and recreation therapy, psychological services, education, and medicine. Red-haired, blue-eyed, and beautiful, Debbie unfortunately had epilepsy with grand mal seizures and was so paraplegic as to require a wheelchair. Her parents had previously enrolled her in an outpatient program for physical therapy, which required them to drive her a considerable distance three times weekly. After two years of this inconvenience and the recent birth of a younger daughter, the parents and a physician felt that a more intensive habilitation program was required to optimize Debbie's overall development.

After a review of medical information and an appraisal of Debbie by department heads in a residential school, she was accepted by the staff as a new patient, but her admission was postponed for six months by reason of temporary overcrowding in the facility.

The consulting psychologist had been involved in the admission screening and noted through parent interviews the additional reason behind their application: "She's driving us crazy with her crying and screaming," reported the mother.

Upon further inquiry on the day of the screening, the psychologist learned that this couple (1) had always wanted children, (2) were initially and normally distraught at the realization that Debbie was multiply handicapped, (3) had been quite unable to change her severe crying "no matter what we did," and (4) felt "like terrible parents." The mother analyzed, "My daughter must hate me. What else can I conclude? Every time I look at her face, she cries and screams. What have I done to make her so afraid of me?" Their only approach in stopping her crying was to pick her up immediately and soothe her. This stopped Debbie's crying.

The psychologist indicated that an alternative explanation was available and proceeded to outline various behavior considerations: Debbie's normal crying was reinforced early by being picked up, leading to more crying when wanting to be picked up, then reinforced further by parents becoming anxious and relieving themselves by picking Debbie up, etc. His explanation both puzzled and interested the parents, whereupon the psychologist summarized a few vivid examples of extinguishing unacceptable behavior in your children e.g. thumb sucking, enuresis, phobic conditions, etc.

The mother indicated eagerness "to try anything" at home during the ensuing six months to get Debbie to stop screaming every time she saw her mother's face, while the equally baffled father wanted relief for his wife and quiet for himself. Apparently the mother's face had become a conditioned stimulus to crying, which, in turn, made the mother put Debbie on her shoulder for soothing.

The psychologist suggested, as a first approach, that they simply place the girl alone in a room at home and allow her to cry until she stopped, then reward her with affection by picking her up when she ceased crying. The mother immediately had three objections: (1) "I can't be so cruel to leave my handicapped daughter alone," (2) "This will not get at the real reason my daughter hates me," and (3) "We've already tried this for a day or two and neither my husband nor I could stand it. We finally picked her up and she stopped crying." No amount of consultation, reflection, or explanation helped them to adopt the psychologist's plan.

After the parents' return to the residential facility a week later, the psychologist was ready with a second plan. This involved gradual desensitization in a series of successive approximations with the mother coming into the room where Debbie sat in her wheel chair. The mother was not to show her face except briefly and partially, even if she had to turn her face sideways while coming into the room. If the girl began to cry, the mother was to turn her back, begin house chores, or walk out again. The mother was also to present her face, partly averted, near faces of the grandparents, for whom the girl revealed no crying. The instructions to the father were identical. They were also to associate the pleasure of Debbie's eating and being touched with gradual full-face views of the parents. They now indicated that this was "the weirdest thing" they had ever heard and objected also that since Debbie had to be looked at to be fed, the face-view of the mother would evoke immediate crying.

With this last consideration in mind, the psychologist then advised them to peek over the top of a magazine while feeding the girl. Greater portions of the face were to be revealed over consecutive feedings and, of course, considerable attention and affection should be offered to Debbie during noncrying periods. The mother and father quickly rejected the plan as "silly." "Why can't you analyze her to get to the roots?" questioned the mother angrily.

A telephone call from the social worker of the residential school to the parents the next day found them disappointed and furious at the suggestions they heard from the consulting psychologist. "That psychologist is a quack," said one of the parents. "He suggested that we train her in the silliest ways. Our neighbors and my parents would think we have flipped if we did this. We've never heard anything so ridiculous. Please call us when Debbie can come to stay for the other therapies and we'll try to survive in the meantime." The social worker tactfully informed the psychologist of their reactions (and wondered privately if indeed the suggested plans were anything more than a whim).

Debbie, crying and screaming, was finally admitted six months later, the parents having struggled unsuccessfully and without relief from her severe crying and tantrumlike behavior. Guilt-ridden and convinced of their ineptitudes as parents, they reluctantly left their child while clinging to their only evidence of parental skill: the totally normal behavior of their other daughter.

After the staff listened to an additional five months of severe crying behavior in the residential home, which stopped only when Debbie was picked up, the head nurse finally requested help from the same consulting psychologist, who was there on a weekly basis. The request had a special urgency because various department heads in physical therapy, occupational therapy, speech, and education complained that Debbie was not profiting from the specific programs by virtue of incessant crying. Further, the administrator of the home wondered if Debbie's enrollment should actually be terminated to make room for other crippled children more likely to profit from the multi-therapy habilitation program.

In the past, the personnel had developed reasonable confidence in the consulting psychologist and his behavior modification programs in changing head-banging behavior, excessive dependency, lack of punctuality, etc. manifested by the crippled and often retarded children. Despite the contention of some therapists that behavioral techniques are easily learned and generalized by nonpsychological staff, the authors' clinical experience indicates that each new program had to be carefully explained, reexplained, and monitored frequently.

Generalization of the behavioral principles to the next child's problem rarely occurred in spite of in-service training and succession of successful cases. In addition, the values of this particular facility did not permit the gathering of quantitative base-line behaviors or frequency counts or the introduction of empirical approaches. Should such quantitative approaches be forced upon the staff, it was likely that all consulting might terminate, such was the extent of the suspicion.

In Debbie's case a special factor, the seizure condition, was discussed. Medical personnel believed that no change in medication was required, although it was hypothesized that the grand mall seizures might somehow "trigger" her crying episodes. In consideration of the complex values of the facility, the following program was designed for Debbie by the psychologist in consultation with key staff members:

1. Whenever Debbie starts to cry, in whatever therapy department or room she is in, she is to be *turned in her wheelchair toward a corner or a wall and totally ignored.* No one is to attend to Debbie's crying in any way until she stops: no picking her up, no talking to her, no criticizing or encouraging her while she is crying and, certainly, no one is to face her. Instead, personnel are asked to stay alert to react as soon as she stops crying whether this takes two minutes or two hours.

2. Only when Debbie stops crying should one go immediately to her. Reward her for stopping her crying by, first, turning her away from the wall and, second, picking her up, hugging her, and saying approving words (even though she does not comprehend). After a few moments of calm behavior, Debbie may be returned quietly to her wheelchair and pushed into her respective training program, the dining room, etc.

3. Please alert all other staff members, volunteers, and visitors about Debbie's program and encourage their total cooperation. Stop others who interfere and show them how the girl is to be handled by following this plan.

4. If while being held up or returned to her wheelchair Debbie starts to cry, she is to be placed in the wheelchair and turned again toward the wall until she stops crying. Any attention she gets while crying will be a signal for her to persist. She must be trained to learn that crying will not lead to being picked up, and that being quiet will result in attention and affection.

5. It is imperative that staff members attend to Debbie's er-

ratic seizure condition by offering the prescribed medical approaches and attention (see medical file in physician's office).

6. The parents have been requested not to visit Debbie for twelve weeks so that the behavior modification program can be carried out without their interruption. (With pronounced misgivings, the parents agreed to cooperate.)

7. Lastly, do not change this training program in any way without prior discussion with the consulting psychologist.

During the first two weeks of the program Debbie's crying became worse. The head nurse reported that her staff was getting demoralized, not so much by the crying, but by the fact that the child-care workers could not execute their typical maternal and protective behaviors toward Debbie when she was in distress. The psychologist urged them directly that the program should be continued without change and requested that they control themselves. Only then could it be determined if the behavioral strategy was effective. One child-care worker was admonished by the head nurse for picking up Debbie while she was crying. The worker, a twelve-year employee who exuded considerable affection for the children, was offering Debbie intermittent reinforcement.

At the end of the fourth week, the child-care staff and the speech therapist reported a slight decrease in the length of Debbie's crying when she was turned toward the wall. Several volunteers were overheard to say that the program was "inhuman" and that they would pick up Debbie anytime they wanted when the head nurse was absent. They were asked to cease their volunteer activities if they could not follow the program. It was explained to them for least the third or fourth time and all gave verbal agreement.

At the end of the sixth week, all therapy department heads, except one, reported a marked decrease in Debbie's crying behavior. The head nurse threatened the same child-care worker noted previously with instant dismissal if she was found to pick up Debbie once more, as. this had been observed three times within the past week. The worker was reassigned to another department to guarantee adherence to the program. The social worker kept the parents informed weekly of their daughter's marked improvement in "self-control." They were requested to stay home without seeing Debbie.

By the end of the eighth week the staff reported excellent cooperation by all volunteers, nurses, visitors, etc., and that Debbie's crying behavior was replaced by smiling behavior and attention to others. Suspicion among several nonpsychological personnel was still present that Debbie's crying was diminishing for perhaps "biological" rather than "training" reasons even though her medication stayed exactly the same. The psychologist complimented the staff members individually for their adherence to the behavioral guidelines and mentioned that the program was working as expected (although he wondered privately if the staff would still maintain their new practices).

At the end of the ten-week period only one department head complained that there was absolutely no decrease in crying behavior while Debbie was in her department. The psychologist suggested that he observe this therapist deal with the girl to see "what was reinforcing Debbie" but this idea was met with icy and stern disapproval. Prior conflicts in programming for certain children had occurred frequently between this department head and the consulting psychologist. She permitted no observations of her work and was sometimes contentious. The psychologist hypothesized to her that since she and the mother, both red haired and attractive, bore a rather striking facial resemblance (especially to this retarded girl), this similarity could be the evoking stimulus for her behavior. This interpretation was rejected instantly.

On the final day of the twelfth week, a conference had been scheduled for the anxious parents to meet with the psychologist, head nurse, and all the department heads. The parents insisted that they were going to take Debbie home for that weekend "whether the crying program works or not." With some genuine apprehensions, the psychologist arrived for the conference knowing that the crying was still severe in one department from the report of the last week and that the parents would be "objectively" informed of the "failure" of the program by this one particular therapist.

The department heads testified to Debbie's calmness, her newly discovered affectionate behavior and attentiveness to her surroundings, her comfort while eating, and the lack of sustained crying beyond a minute or so. The previously objecting therapist announced, "I know that the psychologist didn't expect to hear this, but Debbie has been a perfect angel for me all week and I wanted to give the good news to her parents. The program really works."

Debbie's mother began to smile and cry at the same time, and the father let out a large sigh of relief (so did the psychologist). The administrator then informed the delighted parents that since the disruptive behavior was almost extinguished (except during epileptic seizures), Debbie was to be allowed to stay at the rehabilitative facility for at least another year or two, since she could now benefit from the many therapies available.

Two final episodes of interest followed. After the staff meeting with the parents, the mother rushed to pick up Debbie, who beamed at her mother's face and did not cry after being put back in the wheelchair. But, as the parents pushed her down the long hall toward the front door, Debbie began, for no observable reason, to scream and cry. The parents, in panic, looked at the psychologist walking behind them and heard him say, "Just face Debbie toward a wall and walk into that side room until she stops. Leave her alone." They did this and waited with all their original apprehensions bubbling to the surface. After thirty seconds, Debbie stopped crying, and the parents continued uneventfully and gratefully to take her to their car for the trip home. Later they reportedly trained their three-year-old daughter to push Debbie in her wheelchair toward the wall whenever she cried.

Four months later the parents sent a note to the psychologist:

Miracles never cease. Debbie is doing so well with her crying, or lack of it, that we felt that we just had to drop a note and thank you for the program you designed. It seems to have been very successful. We think enough time has passed now that we can say with confidence that those bad crying sprees are a thing of the past. We're not saying that she doesn't cry at all, but the unnecessary, uncontrollable crying is gone. She's much happier and we're enjoying her so much more. We thank you for your concern, your time, and your patience.

## HYPNOTIC DESENSITIZATION FOR ANXIETY

Name:  Bill B.          Age:  15 Years          Grade:  Tenth

Bill was a white, Jewish youth who was referred because his school achievement had been deteriorating and he had earned failing grades. The family reported that they were also having a "discipline problem." Bill was the elder of two children. His sister, Marcia, was two years his junior and was an excellent student. The family claimed that the two children got along relatively well together. The father, forty-five years old, was an established dentist in an urban community. The mother, forty-three years of age, was his dental hygienist. They worked in an office in their home. They were American born and educated and had been married eighteen years. They described their own relationships as excellent, having worked and travelled together extensively.

Bill was a wanted child. Birth and delivery were uneventful. He was full term, and the mother reported that there were no complications. Developmental milestones were within the normal range, perhaps slightly accelerated. He walked at ten months, spoke individual words at approximately fourteen months, and was speaking two-word sentences at approximately twenty months. Bowel and bladder training occurred at approximately age three. The parents reported that there was no history of any unusual conditions of high fever or convulsions. He had the chicken pox when he was twelve years of age and had hay fever. Bill was still allergic during the ragweed season, but his reaction was controlled with antihistamine medication.

Up until the ninth grade he was an *A, B* student. When he entered high school his marks suddenly began to deteriorate, but he was still passing subjects. However, in the tenth grade he failed history and English on his first report card. The family reported some discipline problems with him relating to bedtime, finishing his homework, neatness in room and appearance, and not doing his chores around the home, which included helping to clean the father's office.

While an extensive battery of psychological tests was given, only the essential test results will be summarized below. The WISC IQ scores were Verbal IQ 116, Performance IQ 120, Full-Scale IQ 121. On the Kuder Preference Record he earned high percentile scores in artistic, musical, and scientific areas. On the Mooney Problem checklist, Bill listed the following problems:

> Wanting more time to myself. Nothing interesting to do on vacation. Not allowed to go around with people I like. So often not allowed to go out at night. Losing my temper. Getting excited too easily. Not taking something seriously enough. Sometimes wishing I'd never been born. Parents old-fashioned in their ideas. Parents expecting too much of me. Wishing I had a different family background. Not spending enough time in study. Not interested in some subjects. Can't keep my mind on my studies. Don't like to study. Poor memory. Worrying about examinations. Subjects not related to everyday life. Teachers too hard to understand. So often feel restless in class. Too little freedom in classes. School is too strict. Classes are too dull. Teachers lack in personality. Too many teachers. Grades unfair as measures of ability.

On the Descriptive part of the Mooney he summarized his chief problems: "I seem to be one who can't stand most of my teachers. Either they bug me, mark unfair, etc. Also, in talking about my friends, my parents would say, 'Why do you hang around with that person?' "

### Thematic Apperception Test

Bill's responses are noted below:

*Card 1:* This kid has just started playing the violin. He just started to move the bow and his fingers. He put the object down and he started to wonder how the music is made. He is . . . he hasn't learned anything about how the music is made. He feels confused. Eventually he'll ask the teacher or his parents and eventually he'll find out how the music comes about.

*Card 2:* She's in a small type town and a girl just said goodbye to her mother and is on her way to school. While the mother's husband is working in the fields with the horse the girl is wondering about what's going on in school. It's probably going to be a test or quiz. I guess when she comes home a couple of hours afterwards, they'll eat dinner. It'll probably be something the husband took out of the ground. Vegetables or something. I guess the father will probably have some pride in himself. (Why?) Because when you build something it is something you've done by yourself. You get accomplishment or something like that.

*7BM:* This is the father and the son. The son is asking him some kind of important question. It's a serious discussion. It seems like the son looks sad. Father is kind of happy that the son came and asked him. (Outcome?) The boy gets help.

*Card 10:* Seems like something tragic has happened. This I say looks like mother and father. Mother starts to cry and grabs hold of the husband for security. The husband is whispering, "It's all right, it's all right." (Tragic thing?) They just received a message that the son was killed in Vietnam.

*13MF:* The guy just came home from work. He went upstairs to get undressed and all. He found his wife in bed, dead. He has his arm over his eyes because he doesn't want to look. That's it. (Outcome?) They find the guy that killed her. He gets life in prison. (How about the husband?) He finds another wife.

*17BM:* This guy is in the school gym. He is getting marked for climbing the ropes. This guy looks like he's a pretty good rope climber mainly because he's going up without his feet. That's it.

*18BM:* This guy is ready to leave home for good. A wife is trying to hold him back because she loves him so much. (What led up to this?) He came home for dinner from a hard day's work. He expected dinner on the table and it wasn't there. (Outcome) He leaves her for good.

## Rorschach

*Card 1:* (6 seconds) It's a butterfly. (Inquiry): It's a butterfly with its wings spread out. It's the whole card. (Most people see more than one thing. Does it remind you of anything else?) Does it matter which way I hold it? Oh no, okay. Some kind of fly or insect. (Inquiry): It's a fly, some kind of fly. (Is that a different response than the butterfly?) Yes, some kind of fly and it's also the whole thing. (Card held to the right.) Possibly a map of some sort, that's about it. (Inquiry): I don't know the position but it's all the rest. It's the whole card held this way (to the right). It would be a couple of continents. I don't know where on earth it would be. It's no special continent, just looks like a map. (Total time, 68 seconds)

*Card 2:* (4 seconds) It looks like a mask. Some guy who hasn't shaven in a long time. (Inquiry): The red things were eyes. The white is where the nose would come out. It looks like it would be human, the mask of a human being. The guy has red eyes, and the heavy beard shows that he hasn't shaved it for a couple of days. (Heavy beard, what makes it look that way?) It's dark, it's a real dark beard. It kind of looks like some spaghetti was on the floor and someone stepped in it, that's about it. (Inquiry): [Area surrounding D3] That's what happened to me in school today. I dropped my spaghetti and someone stepped in it. The red is the sauce, the black is where the person hit it with his shoe. It's like dirt. (Total time, 62 seconds)

*Card 3:* (3 seconds) It looks like two people. That's about it. (Inquiry): [D1 area] It's two women with high heel shoes. (What makes it look that way?) It's the shape, that's all. It's shaped like it. (Total time, 55 seconds)

*Card 4:* (3 seconds) It looks like another insect. (Inquiry): [D1 upside down] It looks like an insect. Here are its fine parts and tentacles. (Any special kind of insect?) No, no special kind, just an insect. Looks like maybe one pair of shoes, that's about it. (Inquiry): [D6] It's a boot, there's the toe part and it's the shape of it. That's about it. (Total time, 35 seconds)

*Card 5:* (5 seconds) Looks like a bat. (Inquiry): It's the whole card, there's the two tentacles and two hind legs and big spread-out wings and it looks like it's flying. It could be a plane of some sort, that's about it. (Inquiry): Well, it's an airplane. It's kind of like looking from the top down at it, it looks like an airplane that's flying, it's kind of shaped that way, it's the whole card. (Total time, 49 seconds)

*Card 6:* (14 seconds) It looks like another insect. (Turns card in all directions) No, nothing else. (Inquiry): [W less the upper two thirds of D8] No insect in particular, it has a long straight body and wings, it just looks like some insect. (Total time, 52 seconds)

*Card 7:* (7 seconds) It looks like two little kids on a seesaw. I can't tell if it's male or female. (Inquiry): It looks like it's about to be put in motion, it's flat and on the ground and looks like one is about to start, it's the whole card. [The seesaw is D4 and the people are D2.] Possibly a map of the top of the world with a bottom. (Inquiry): [D9 less D5] White is water, like the Arctic Ocean. Russia [D10] and neighboring countries. [The card is upside down, D1 is the U.S. and Mexico, and Canada is D3.] (Total time, 50 seconds)

*Card 8:* (5 seconds) It could be a mask. It's the whole card, it's not a full mask, no special kind of mask and could be of a person but, no, more like a dog. (Inquiry): (What about it makes it look like a mask?) Well, it's the shape of a mask. It's not the colors, just the shape. It could also be a dirt stain. (Inquiry): I had a T-shirt that looked like that at one time. It was a big blotch shaped just like that. No, it's not the colors, just the shape. (Total time, 47 seconds)

*Card 9:* (8 seconds) (Upside down) A volcano erupted. (Inquiry): [D9 upside down] The red is the flame and the lava. Only the red reminded of lava burning. Maybe another map, (card turned to the right). (Inquiry): Just the orange part reminded me of half of Greenland with islands on the side [D3]. It's all surrounded by water. (Total time, 42 seconds)

*Card 10:* (4 seconds) Looks like a group of insects of all kinds. (Inquiry): [All except D9] Just a group of insects. Worms (D4). The worms are long, the spiders are here (the worm) and all kinds of insects. (Card upside down) Looks like another mask, that's about it. (Inquiry): It's the shape of a mask. It's just the shape, not the color. It's the mask like of a person (upside down). The nose is here [D3]. The eyes are here [D2]. [The mask includes D9 and D11.] (Total time, 40 seconds)

## *Rotter Incomplete Sentence Blank, High School Form*

1. I like: "cars."
2. The happiest time is: "at a basketball game."
3. I want to know: "more about the human body."
4. At home: "I get treated fairly good."
5. I regret: "not being able to get my license."
6. At bedtime: "I read a book."
7. Boys: "are boss."
8. The best: "car is a Corvette®."
9. What annoys me: "I can't go on a trip with my friend."
10. People: "are sometimes stupid."
11. A mother: "is a good companion."
12. I feel: "I am mature."
13. My greatest fear is: "flunking."
14. In the lowest grades: "I was a good little boy."
15. I can't: "understand why kids can't vote at eighteen."
16. Sports: "is a good hobby."
17. When I was younger: "I never went out with friends."
18. My nerves: "are sometimes on edge."
19. Other kids: "have more freedom."
20. I suffer: "from strict parents."
21. I failed: "because I don't do my homework."
22. Reading: "is very good."
23. My mind: "seems to wander."
24. The future: "seems unpredictable."
25. I need: "more freedom."
26. Dating: "is terrific."
27. I am best when: "with friends."
28. Sometimes: "I feel like running away."
29. What pains me: "is that I'm not allowed to drive."
30. I hate: "school."
31. At school: "I meet my friends."
32. I am very: "truthful."
33. The only trouble: "is I can't pass school."
34. I wish: "I would get *A*s."
35. My father: "is terrific."

36. I secretly: "wish I were not born."
37. I: "am for peace."
38. Dancing: "is a good way to have fun."
39. My greatest worry: "is not passing school."
40. Most girls: "seem to like me."

The authors have deliberately left the test data open for the readers' own interpretation and for classroom discussion. The Rorschach areas delineated are described by Beck (1950) and are reiterated by Small (1956). While the authors use the Piotrowski system (1976) of interpretation and find it effective, the readers may score the material in the system most familiar to them.

The treatment approach used with Bill consisted of a number of individual psychotherapeutic sessions as well as joint sessions with the parents. During the joint sessions, Bill was able to observe that the parents truly cared for each other and were quite happy together in spite of their struggles with him. It was equally evident that they also cared for him and loved him. They had some definite expectations in terms of chores involving the care of the house and the small lawn. The father also expected him to help in the office, having taught him how to develop and mount his dental X-rays, in order to speed the efficiency of the office. Bedtime, decided by the parents by fiat, was 10:00 PM. The therapist served partially as a facilitator for the parents to include the boy in negotiation and discussion on the above expectations. The following are some excerpts from the therapy sessions:

*Father:* I believe a boy his age should go to bed at 10:00 PM.
*Therapist:* Every night?
*Father:* Well, they start school early and he gets up about six-thirty in the morning.
*Mother:* Doctor, don't you believe he has to get enough sleep? I believe a parent has to make sure her children take care of themselves.
*Therapist:* I guess the key to your question is the word "enough." How do you determine how much sleep is enough?

*Bill:* Yeah, I'm never late for school. I don't wake up tired and I'm not always tired at exactly ten o'clock. How about weekends when I don't have to get up early?

*Therapist:* What's your proposal, Bill?

*Bill:* (Addressing his parents) See, at least he asked me what I think. You make up all these rules and you don't ask!

*Therapist:* And how do you feel about that?

*Bill:* Angry! Goddammit!

*Therapist:* Okay, we'll analyze your anger later on to discover how you make yourself angry, but for now (addressing the parents), how do you feel about what Bill is saying?

*Father:* Well, I guess what he says is right. I never really thought about it. I guess we do make all the decisions.

*Mother:* But our decisions are not made to hurt the boy. I believe they are right.

*Therapist:* I understand your motives are fine and you really want to be helpful and caring. If he were given the choice, do you think Bill would make poor decisions?

*Mother:* Gee, that's a hard question. I sort of do and I don't. That's an interesting question.

*Bill:* (Beginning to shout) See! She don't even ask me for my opinion and she's not sure I can make a good decision about weekends when I don't have to get up early.

*Father:* Okay, Bill, what do you think is reasonable?

*Bill:* Well, actually, ten o'clock isn't bad on weekdays but I think I should be able to stay up till eleven or at least until the nine o'clock movie finishes on TV when there's no school the next day.

*Mother:* And all this is so important to you?

*Bill:* Yes, dammit, I'd like some say on some things that affect me.

*Mother:* Well, I can go along with that but if you are going to stay up late I expect you to do all your homework.

*Father:* Okay, your request seems reasonable. Why didn't you ask before?

*Bill:* What for, would you have listened?

*Therapist:* Okay, so everyone gets uptight in your family based on what they think. Your parents say to themselves, "Bill doesn't usually make mature decisions so why ask him for his opinion and get into arguments." And you say to yourself, "Why ask them anything. They'll only turn me down." Then you probably make yourself angry by saying, "They should listen to me and hear what I say. They are unfair and that is terrible for me. It's awful to have parents who are unfair" and then you lose your temper and yell.

*Bill:* Well, I don't know whether I use those exact words but, yeah, I remember thinking things like that and you know I really believe it's awful when parents don't listen to teenaged children!

*Therapist:* Well, it may be inconvenient and annoying at times, but how awful and terrible is it? Are they threatening your life?

*Bill:* Well, no!

*Therapist:* Do they attack you, beat you with a whip?

*Bill:* No, nothing like that.

*Therapist:* Well, I guess those things would be awful.

*Bill:* Well, I agree but I think it's awful when they don't listen to me!

*Therapist:* So you would like your parents to listen to you and respect your point of view.

*Bill:* Yes.

*Therapist:* Well, let's see what you do to get what you want.

*Bill:* But I don't get what I want.

*Mother:* Never?

*Father:* That's not a fair statement.

*Therapist:* Before we go into that, let me pursue my point a little further. Bill wants you to listen to what he says. Now what does he do to accomplish this goal?

*Father:* I get your point. He wants us to listen to him but he doesn't communicate to us.

*Therapist:* Bill, what do you think?

*Bill:* I see what you're driving at. I decide I'm gonna be put down so I don't even tell them what's on my mind.

*Therapist:* Exactly, and then how do you feel?

*Bill:* I feel angry because they're not listening to me.

*Therapist:* Without even giving them the opportunity to listen and at worst turn you down.

*Bill:* I never thought about that.

*Therapist:* Right! Your anger was being created in your mind. You were angry because they were *theoretically* or *possibly* going to turn you down and you didn't even wait to see what they really would say.

*Bill:* I kind of thought they were bastards without giving them the chance to prove it.

*Therapist:* Right, and you probably also added that those bastards shouldn't think the way they do or act the way they do because I don't like it: Change your style, you bastard parents, because I, King Bill, demand it!

*Father:* (Laughing) Sounds dramatic, but I guess that's right. I guess we all get upset. . . .

*Therapist:* Make ourselves upset.

*Father:* Okay, make ourselves upset when people don't act exactly the way we want. I see your point, Doctor, I guess what you're saying isn't only directed at Bill.

*Mother:* You mean I make myself angry if people, or my children, are not exactly the way I want them to be. What should I be then?

*Bill:* Understanding! If I try something and do it wrong, don't scream. Help me instead of screaming at me or be patient or something.

*Father:* Okay, so we should be more tolerant of other people, even our children. I see the point you expressed in an earlier session. Something happens, we think or assess what happened, and then we make ourselves angry. So when we find ourselves getting angry, we should try to find out what that B step or middle step is.

*Mother:* B step?

*Bill:* Yeah, you know what we tell ourselves that makes us angry. Remember the Doctor said before that something happens and that's point A; then we think something about it and that's point B; and point C is how we feel or act.

*Mother:* Oh yeah, I remember, the B step is the important step.

The sessions proceed along these lines with the family members. The therapist in this circumstance attempts to serve as a catalyst to open communications between the child and the parents to get them to think more logically and to diminish anger and antagonism toward each other.

As these particular therapy sessions progress it becomes clearer that Bill is having a great deal of difficulty studying for his examinations and doing his school work. He reports tremendous anxiety at even opening his books and asks for some private sessions to discuss this difficulty. Bill states, "I just flunked another history test. I tried to pass it, but when I went to study I got real nervous and couldn't even look at the book. My hands began to shake. I'm so scared of failing that to look at the book makes me nervous. I know you'll say I'm overreacting to the fear of failure and that I think I'll be a no-good person if I fail and all that, but I really need help with this."

Behavior therapy techniques are essentially consistent with rational emotive therapy. The therapist in this case decided to use a desensitization approach similar to that described by Wolpe (1958). Since Bill was failing history, the therapist established an anxiety hierarchy with him, which involved history homework and his reactions. Bill noted what he would be least anxious about to what he would be most anxious about. The hierarchy consisted of (1) thinking the word *history*, (2) imagining the teacher giving the homework assignment, (3) approaching his desk at home with his history book in his hand, (4) opening the history book and reading it for five minutes, (5) reading the history book for ten minutes. For steps 6 to 15 the period of reading was increased to sixty minutes by five-minute intervals. For steps 16 to 19, the reading period was increased to two hours by fifteen-minute intervals.

An hypnotic relaxation technique was used. In the initial phase the client received a brief explanation of hypnosis, which would aid the muscular relaxation process:

*Therapist:* I mentioned that we would be using an hypnotic relaxation technique. Do you know anything about it?

*Bill:* Well, I once watched a show where some people were acting like dogs and doing funny things but I don't really know anything about it.

*Therapist:* Well, we're not going to get involved in a show or funny things.

*Bill:* Good.

*Therapist:* Basically, hypnosis is not a strange or mysterious thing. It's something normal for most people. What the hypnotist does is to teach the person to go into one of his normal states. That's called the hypnogogic state. That's the state we're in just before we fall asleep at night or just before we get up in the morning. Sometimes people will say that they had a conversation with someone and they might not even remember it.

Now, almost anyone can be hypnotized. Contrary to what most people believe, the brighter you are the easier it is to be hypnotized because you understand what the hypnotist is saying. People who have difficulty with being hypnotized are the severely mentally retarded, who may not know what you're talking about, or the psychotic individual who isn't communicating with you and is in a world of his own, and the stubborn person, who will do the opposite of what the hypnotist says. So that if I were to say "relax" to the stubborn person, he would say to himself, "No, I'll tense up and show that son-of-a-bitch he can't hypnotize me." Other than that, most people can be hypnotized. Hypnosis also has some good side effects. It increases the person's ability to relax and to concentrate. Do you have any questions, Bill? (Now the stage is set. The message is: Smart, normal people can be hypnotized and the effect is beneficial. Further discussion followed and issues were clarified.)

*Bill:* Okay, I trust you, let's try it.

*Therapist:* I'm going to start by asking you to look at the tip of my pen. As I count you'll find your eyes beginning to blink and you'll want to close them and relax. When that happens just let them close and begin to relax. (The therapist began to count and simultaneously suggested that Bill's eyes would close and he would relax.) One-two-three . . . your eyes are beginning to flicker and you'll want to close them. Let them close.

*Bill:* (Finding his eyes flickering, he laughs nervously.) This is really funny. It might actually happen.

*Therapist:* Good, just let it happen. Relax. It's not unusual the first time someone is being hypnotized to begin laughing. It's a combination of being nervous and also a little disbelief that it could really work. Don't worry about the laughing, I'll just resume my count . . . eighteen-nineteen-twenty. (On the count of forty his eyes close.) You are doing fine; remember, you're not to wake up or open your eyes until I tell you. Now I'm going to count to ten again, and as I count you'll begin to relax all the muscles of your body, your arms, your legs, thighs, shoulders, chest, neck muscles. Relax the muscles of your neck, forehead, all your facial muscles, even the tongue muscles. (Counting) One, two — ten. Now each breath you take will make you relax more and more. Now as you're relaxing you'll also be able to talk. How do you feel?

*Bill:* (Speaking softly) More relaxed than before but I'm not really fully relaxed.

*Therapist:* Okay, you're doing fine. Let's try the muscles of your arms. Just relax them so completely so that you give up control over them. Make it so I can move them and not you. (The therapist moves Bill's arms.) Your muscles are still a little tight, continue loosening them. (At this point his arms become limp.) Now you have it. You're doing fine. Now let's continue to relax. (Relaxation continues for about 5 more minutes.) Are you completely relaxed?

*Bill:* Everything is relaxed except my chest muscles.

*Therapist:* Show me where you feel tension. (Bill points to his chest.) The therapist touches the area and says. "This part will also relax. The relaxation is coming in and you will feel a pleasant, good, relaxed feeling in here. Let the relaxation come in." (Another 2 or 3 minutes pass.) How do you feel now?

*Bill:* Good, relaxed.

*Therapist:* Okay, now I'd like to see if you can visualize things. Picture yourself eating supper tonight. Have that picture?

*Bill:* (He nods his head.)

*Therapist:* Can you see it like something in a movie?

*Bill:* Yes.

*Therapist:* Okay, now let your mind wander to a pleasant relaxing experience at any time in your life. Signal me by raising your right thumb when you have this picture.

*Bill:* (Signaling)

*Therapist:* Okay, tell me what the scene is.

*Bill:* It's a beach scene when I was thirteen. The family was down the shore; I got on the beach by myself at about ten o'clock in the morning. The weather was nice and it was quiet. I just got on this beach chair and just lay down there in the sun. It was warm and relaxing; the beach was still quiet.

*Therapist:* Good, can you project yourself into that scene? Now relax and feel the sensation of the warm sun. Do you feel it?

*Bill:* Yes.

The first session was further devoted to the production of pleasant images and the ability to relax. Before ending the hypnotic session the following was said:

*Therapist:* Each time you try this you will find yourself able to relax more deeply, and eventually you will feel relaxed almost as soon as you sit down in the office. Eventually you will be able to think the word *relax* and turn off your tension quickly. One further suggestion. Remember each time you come here you will be able to relax more and more, but if someone suggests hypnosis at a party game, you will be resistant to it. You will not want to be hypnotized at a party or a show. You will be resistant to hypnosis under those circumstances. You will be able to cooperate here, or if a physician, surgeon, or dentist needs to use it for a therapeutic purpose, then you will be able to cooperate. Is that clear?

*Bill:* Yes.

(The above suggestion was given as a caution. Since a person's normal resistance to hypnosis may be reduced as a function of any type of hypnotherapy, this prudent warning helps the client resist nonscientific and amateur efforts in hypnosis, which might be destructive.)

The proceeding sessions continued through the hierarchy, in a manner similar to that described by Wolpe (1958), to establish a pattern of reciprocal inhibition regarding Bill's anxiety. The following excerpt came three sessions later:

*Therapist:* How have you been doing?

*Bill:* Well, I'm not as nervous as when I started. I don't get real nervous now when the history teacher gives assignments. I can open the book and look at it, but I can't study for more than fifteen minutes.

*Therapist:* Okay, we'll work on that shortly to see if we can stretch that out. How are you getting along with your parents?

*Bill:* Better, since they started to listen to me. I've tried that A-B-C stuff and it's interesting to see how often I will tell myself that they won't listen before I even ask them anything. Now that I'm talking they do listen, and sometimes I even get my way. (The therapist and Bill discuss this for awhile.)

*Therapist:* Now, Bill, get into a relaxed position. Just look at my pen; as I count aloud your eyes will close and you will relax. One, two, three, . . . ten (eyes are closed). Each breath you take helps you to relax more and more. Think of that relaxed beach scene. Do you have it?

*Bill:* Yes (appears quite relaxed and is breathing deeply).

*Therapist:* Are you completely relaxed?

*Bill:* Yes.

*Therapist:* Remember now, if you feel the least bit anxious, signal me by raising your right thumb, understand?

*Bill:* (Softly) Yes.

*Therapist:* Now, let's construct this scene. You are home and you know you have a history assignment. (Pause) Good, no anxiety signal. Look over your assignment and you see it will take about ten minutes (Pausing; no anxiety sign is indicated). Change that scene. You have the assignment that takes fifteen minutes of homework. (The patient signals anxiety by raising his thumb.) Turn that scene off, completely relax yourself. (The thumb comes down and the patient relaxes.) Now let's repeat the scene. The fifteen-minute homework assignment. (The patient is still completely relaxed.) Now let's picture a twenty-minute homework assignment. (The patient signals anxiety.) Turn that scene off, relax again. (The patient indicates that he is relaxed.) Okay, turn the scene on to a twenty-minute history assignment. (The patient signals anxiety again.) Relax again; okay now let's see if you can hold the relaxation. (Short pause) Fine, now picture yourself doing your history homework for twenty minutes and you are staying relaxed. (The patient stays relaxed.) Very good.

The therapy continues along this line for approximately ten more sessions. The patient becomes able to relax himself by thinking the word *relax* to himself. He finds that he can attend to an individual homework assignment for up to two hours without debilitating anxiety, sufficient time for completing most of his assignments. He becomes much more open to his parents, most likely a result of the prior psychotherapy and of his ability to complete some homework assignments. They, in turn, respond by allowing him to express his opinions more frequently and giving him more choices because they recognized that he is becoming more mature. As his grades in school improve, the parent-child relationships also improve. After a total of thirty desensitization sessions, plus the individual and family counseling combined, both parents and the boy felt that he was sufficiently improved to terminate treatment.

For several years thereafter the therapist had no contact with the family. Six years later, the parents telephoned the therapist to refer a friend with similar problems. Doctor and Mrs. B. indicated that their son was "fine," having received his B.B.A. degree recently. He was now working for an insurance firm and was "happy" at his job. Bill was also dating and had an active social life. The parents reported that the relationship with him was quite good and that he was also making enough money to move out of their house and into his own apartment. The parents recognized that many young adults his age have this legitimate desire. While they considered it unnecessary for him to move, they recognized his need for privacy. They added an expression of their gratitude for what they considered a truly successful outcome to their family problems.

# CHAPTER IV

# MENTAL RETARDATION

O NE of the most common varieties of referral for psychoeducational evaluation deals with suspected mental retardation of the school-age child. Although in earlier years identification of the retarded provided only educational intervention by reassignment to special classes, current assessments additionally prescribe the following: speech and physical therapy, some "mainstreaming" with regular classes, considerable medical attention to physical causes and correlates, music therapy, an adjusted curriculum, behavior modification, and counseling. Others suggest sex education, occupational therapy, psychiatric evaluation, parental education, vocational training, on-the-job placement, and supervision at work. Such services are triggered by a valid diagnosis from a psychologist, who also identifies related problems that detract from the child's learning and social adjustment.

The clinical and school psychologist seeks, then, not just a psychometric score and a diagnostic classification, but rather an opportunity to describe, cross-sectionally and longitudinally, (1) the strengths and weaknesses of the suspected retardate, (2) the possible causes of the retardation (often with the aid of medical specialists), and (3) an array of recommendations to eradicate or minimize the social, personal, and educational problems of the client in question (Wisland, 1974). Further, the psychologist will (4) counsel the parents about their grief reaction to the diagnosis and its implications, (5) stimulate professional action regarding the therapies deemed necessary to minimize weaknesses, (6) accept the legal responsibility of making a formal diagnosis of retardation so that the child can partake of special education services, (7) summarize the clinical impressions in consultation with other professionals, and (8) follow-up the case insuring that maximal services are rendered according to the child's needs (Ross, 1964).

The procedures and actions noted above are time-consuming, often difficult to initiate, and all too easy to disregard in view of the community's pressures for psychological services for other children who are handicapped or disabled in some other way. Yet, there are few other clinical syndromes that have such a profound effect upon the child's life and that of the parents. Often, it is emotionally devastating to siblings and even distant relatives who fear a vague "contamination" by association (Noland, 1970).

It behooves the professional psychologist to exert the utmost care in arriving at the initial diagnosis of mental retardation in view of the complexity of the problems and the severity of the consequences: special stigma ascribed by our achievement-oriented society, general rejection by "normal" peers, guilt on the part of the family members, greatly lessened potential for academic success, and termination of the American Dream of "Going To College And Getting A Good Job." Retardation itself, the sheer lack of mental ability to solve normal social and academic problems rapidly, will constitute a perplexing series of dilemmas for the child and his parents. Marriage potential is often questioned, especially if genetic and/or hereditary factors are suspect. Indeed, some parents are terrified at the thought of sexual drives in their retarded adolescent children (De La Cruz & LaVech, 1973; Grossman, 1972).

It is necessary that psychologists provide differential diagnoses between three categories of pathology: learning disabilities, emotional disturbance that makes a child *appear* to be mentally retarded (pseudo-retardation), and mental retardation. Each diagnostic concept is an "umbrella" term incorporating an almost infinite variety of subclassifications plus separate signs, symptoms, and/or criteria and relatively discrete treatment considerations. The effect of a misdiagnosis can be damaging, especially if one examines the educational goals of the three main categories.

For the learning disabled and the emotionally disturbed youngsters, the classroom aim will be to improve their academic and social skills, respectively, to achieve eventual competency with normal peers in regular classes. The retarded child will, to a certain extent, be given a developmentally slower program, depending upon the degree of retardation, wherein stress will likely be put upon academic, self-help, social, and vocational skills. Presumably these emphases will aid him in developing maximum capabilities. The program for the genuinely retarded will not aim at return to full-time, regular class, although part-time "mainstreaming" may eventuate. On a cautionary note about the reverberatory effects of mainstreaming, however, the data-oriented studies of Kehle and Guidubaldi (1976) of Kent State University should be seriously considered by educators, psychologists, and parents alike. In their stratified, random sample, they determined, by using the powerful assessment tool, the Barclay Classroom Climate Inventory (1975), that there were definite detrimental effects in the mainstreaming stages of educable retarded children.

The original diagnosis is crucial and must be completed with great care and rigor. In order to verify or refute these critical assessments, repeated team evaluations should be made at least every two years during a child's school career even if not legally mandated.

Some professional workers act as though retardation will somehow fade away once the typical adult retardate reaches the world of work. On the contrary, the limitations of the mentally retarded person may become even more pronounced once he or she leaves the protected environment of the school or training program and enters the competitive world of work. Then, the minor and understandable inabilities of the retardate in telling time and grasping work procedures, or being unreliable, childish, or egocentric will stand out in bold relief to the detriment of the retarded worker. These behaviors, even if found in many "normal" adults, often form the basis of rejection by co-workers and employers.

In our combined experiences covering forty-five years in schools, residential institutions, private practice, consultation and university clinics, the authors have examined over 1,000 retarded children and consulted on the educational and therapeutic programs of at least another 1,000. These experiences have led us to the impression that, although retarded children and adults can substantially profit from intensive and individualized intervention, we believe equally that there is an upper limit of development, perhaps set genetically or based in "tissue" adaptability, beyond which genuinely retarded people cannot achieve. No doubt that such limits have been underestimated in individual cases for a variety of reasons, but a limit is nonetheless present. The goal, as Sarason (1969) has so effectively noted, is to help each retarded person develop close to that vaguely known upper limit without excessive stress or anxiety.

It often falls to the psychologist, pediatrician, or child psychiatrist to be the first professional person to offer the parent the diagnosis of mental retardation. The term itself is abhorrent to parents anywhere at anytime (Wolfensberger & Kurtz, 1974). Merely changing the word will not necessarily change the implications of the pathology. For example, for those who learned very slowly nearly a century ago, they were labeled as "dumb," and regarded as hopelessly incapable. Later, these slow-learning people were classified into three rough categories: moron, idiot, imbecile. In the 1920s new terms evolved through general reaction against the previous categories to become "mental deficients" or "mental retardates." As educators contributed their pedagogical expertise, a presumed refinement in the language came into being with four, more educationally relevant classifications: educable retarded (approximately 75-55 IQ range), trainable retarded (55-35 IQ range), severely retarded (35-20 IQ range), and profoundly retarded (below 20 IQ), among the relevant criteria noted below.

Although the term *mental retardation* is sanctioned by professional groups working with this exceptional group (Heber, 1961), various parent and other professional groups have suggested another, presumable less stigmatized label: the developmentally disabled child. Whether or not new terms add anything significant to clinical thinking remains to be seen, but there is no doubt that retarded persons do tend to behave differently if treated differently by persons who regard them in a less derogatory fashion. It is also obvious that all retardates are not alike regardless of the label.

To evaluate the retarded school child via psychoeducational instruments, the psychologists should first be intimately familiar with not only seven basic criteria for the diagnosis of retardation, but also be capable of obtaining specific kinds of data through tests, interviewing, and observations to determine if the child has, in fact, met those criteria or not. The issue about what constitutes a comprehensive diagnosis of mental retardation is complicated but not unfathomable and is one that falls squarely in the camp of clinical and school psychologists. How does one know when a child is genuinely retarded or invalidly diagnosed and whether the apparent retardation is relatively permanent, e.g. Down Syndrome, or possibly transient, e.g. pseudoretardation due to psychosis? At what age is the diagnosis relatively certain and when, if ever, is it positively certain? Is a developmental history imperative? Must there be a school program available before one makes a diagnosis of retardation? Can a child be both learning disabled and mentally retarded? Such questions, although important, cannot be dealt with extensively in a case study book except by illustration and inference.

For the purposes of providing (1) special class placement, (2) parent consultation, and (3) prescriptive intervention for the additional problems of the child, the following criteria for mental retardation are recommended for clinical consideration (Doll, 1941; Heber, 1961; Kessler, 1966).

The mentally retarded child of school age, compared to children of normal development, is assessed, rated, and observed to be:

(1) socially incompetent or lagging significantly in social adaptability;
(2) intellectually deficient by more than one and one-half standard deviations below the mean on individual and appropriately normed intelligence tests, optimally administered;
(3) significantly delayed in most developmental areas, i.e. receptive and expressive speech, fine- and gross-motor coordination, visual and auditory perception, and other learning modalities;

(4) damaged (assumed) in the central nervous system by virtue of genetic, hereditary, toxic, and/or prenatal, natal, and postnatal circumstances;

(5) unable to comprehend abstract concepts;

(6) markedly deficient in comprehension of all academic areas of learning; and

(7) slow in learning not due to lack of opportunity, emotional problems, sensory impairment, learning disabilities, or social isolation.

To give life to the abbreviated criteria noted above, two relatively clear-cut cases are offered for illustration. Secondary to the retardation problems are the unique dramas behind each case, the rejection or acceptance of the retardation by the parents, the personality strengths and weaknesses of each child, the coping mechanisms, and finally the individualized prescriptions specific for implementation in the home and the school.

Both of the cases have a follow-up to indicate, to some extent, if the prescriptions were effective or not and how the child or parents reacted. The cases selected for inclusion in this chapter represent not only a variety of mentally retarded children of different races and socioeconomic levels, but also those typically occurring in the practice of clinical and school psychologists.

## MILD RETARDATION: PASSIVE-DEPENDENT

Name: Thomas T.   Age: 9 Years, 9 Months   Grade: Ungraded
School: Private School for the Learning Disabled

Mrs. T., a mother with two sons, was dissatisfied with Tom's current school placement and progress. She felt that (a local private school for learning disabled children) was not providing the educational program to foster his academic progress. She requested a psychoeducational evaluation to determine whether or not the present placement was appropriate for her son. She also wondered if Tom's progress was being "blocked" by an inability to concentrate on school matters caused by emotional problems revolving about the absence of his father in the home.

Mrs. T. had had Tom evaluated at several reputable clinics previously and received varying results, all of which were at the disposal of the present psychologist. Throughout this process of searching for a "satisfactory" diagnosis and class placement, Mrs. T. has worked very hard to change those placements, noted momentarily, with which she disagreed.

### School Information

After a full year of school, Tom's kindergarten teacher recommended that he repeat kindergarten because he had not shown sufficient development or readiness as required for entrance into first grade. However, Mrs. T. insisted that he enter the first grade, and school personnel acquiesced. He quickly dropped behind the other youngsters in academic learning and was evaluated by a school district psychologist. The diagnosis indicated that Tom was mildly retarded (Stanford-Binet L-M, IQ 63), with the recommendation that he be placed in a special class for retarded educables at a second school. This was done, although Mrs. T. disagreed with the diagnosis and then contacted the Child Guidance Clinic at Center Hospital to get a second evaluation for her son. The second evaluation found "borderline" intellectual functioning (WISC-R, 78 IQ), with evidence of a learning disability linked to minimal cerebral dysfunction and having an emotional overlay. Although Mrs. T. wanted Tom placed with learning disabled children in his present school, the hospital's psychologist was not supportive of this placement due to the relatively low level of Tom's intellectual functioning; nevertheless, the placement was effected through the pressure of both parents.

Tom has attended the learning disability school for the past three years. His current teachers believe that he is working "close to his limited capacity" and perceive him as a mentally retarded boy. They do see an improvement in his fine-motor coordination and socialization with others. Initially he was an isolated child, but now, feeling more self-confidence and showing the first signs of social acceptance, he plays with other children, often much younger than he.

Currently, Tom is seen as a "tease" who strikes out by kicking and spitting at others. When confronted he often tries to shift the blame to another child and does not accept responsibility for his actions, thereby showing generally immature characteristics more typical of a younger, insecure child. His social behavior suggests that he operates at a six- or seven-year-old level, well below his actual age of almost ten years. Academically, Tom is now achieving at first grade levels in both reading and math and cannot focus attention to tasks for more than a minute or two, although he cannot clearly be called hyperactive.

The school social worker related that Tom was working close to his mental capacity and that part of his problem was that his mother pressed him to perform at unrealistically high levels, or those appropriate for a normal child. For example, Mrs. T. has been to the school several times to complain of his lack of difficult homework and has belittled his instructional program as "inadequate" because she felt that the school merely repeated what he had previously learned. She also complained about the disciplinary treatment her son received there. School officials felt that Tom manipulates his mother through the use of "horror tales," exaggerating the reactions of the class to his annoying behaviors. Mrs. T. explained that Tom has been emotionally upset over events that happen at school, which the teachers claimed are "farfetched."

### Family Background

The father, separated from the mother but living nearby, promised to come for one interview but failed to appear.

Mrs. T., a dynamic, forceful woman, acknowledged that she is now tired of her efforts to aid her son and that this present evaluation is her last "go round." She feels that Tom's main problem is an "emotional" one caused by the absence of his father and the resultant lack of male guidance. To fill this void, Mrs. T. has contacted the Big Brothers Association to provide him adult male contacts but determined that they were unable to send a volunteer since the father is still available. She is also convinced that Tom suffers a secondary problem, mild brain damage of an unknown cause, which limits his motor coordination.

The father, as she reported, was a former retail clothing salesman who characterized his son as lazy and shiftless.

Migrating from the South to Philadelphia after graduating from high school, they met and eventually married after an eight-year dating period and after the birth of Tom. Mr. T. refused to acknowledge that he was the father and waited two years after the boy's birth to marry her, perhaps a sign of his reluctance to enter a marriage relationship and accept family responsibilities, a pattern that proved to be true. The marriage was a "rocky" one in which he failed to provide a strong, dependable male image. Taking little interest in the home and none in Tom, he preferred instead to "dress up" and "hang out" with his male friends. Later he stayed out all night with his male friends, and Mrs. T. suspected that her husband was bisexual.

Although she has previously worked at several jobs, usually as a clerk, Mrs. T. now supports herself, Tom, and her other son, Billy, age four, with money from the Department of Public Welfare. She first tended to "baby" and overprotect Tom and still spends considerable energy on him about school problems. Now, however, she is trying to "force" Tom to grow up by teaching "manners" and age-appropriate behavior. She seemed confused in regard to child-rearing practices and needful of guidelines and a professional person to trust.

Tom believes that she likes Billy better, for the latter must sleep in his mother's bed, due to room size and budget limitations, while Tom sleeps alone in his room. Eventually, Mrs. T. plans to have both boys sleep in the same room when she can afford a folding bed. She will not use bunk beds for fear one of the boys might fall from the upper level, another symptom of overprotection and anxiety.

Mrs. T. feels that Tom is quite unhappy, for he has no friends, in contrast to Billy. Tom stays constantly by her side and complains that he is lonely, expecting her to produce friends for him. This childish behavior causes her to feel quite depressed and frustrated in combination with her own problems: separation, loneliness, and several unsatisfactory dates with men "selected by a computer." Both she and Tom currently receive psychotherapy at a mental health clinic.

Mr. T., although refusing to disclose his address to his wife or pay any support, still visits his family about three times a month. He attends little to either of the boys except to criticize and punish, usually for what he calls "back talk." He also promises to take Tom to exciting places but fails to keep his promises, greatly disappointing the boy.

Mrs. T. feels that out of constant disappointment she "yells" at the children too much. When she is aware of this she will take a sedative prescribed by the mental health clinic. The attention and energy required to raise her boys seem to leave her with little time for a life of her own, and being in her early thirties, she is starting to feel cheated.

Mrs. T. would like to see Tom complete high school and grow into a strong, dependable, stable man who is not easily influenced by his friends. She has forcefully resisted the earlier diagnosis of mild retardation and does not accept his many limitations, feeling that they can be overcome by training and hard work.

### Developmental History

The mother revealed that she had a long, difficult labor after having been hospitalized during her ninth month because of toxemia and elevated blood pressure brought on by improper diet. At birth, Tom weighted 5 pounds, 4 ounces. At eleven months Tom had to be hospitalized for pneumonia with an unspecified high fever. Tom was "normal" in his development except for a delay in his speech and language, so often indicative of intellectual deficiencies, and in his not using sentences until long after his third birthday.

Tom has sustained minor head injuries in two falls and injured his head in an automobile accident, but this was apparently of no medical consequence. In the past, Tom has suffered headaches, allergies, and an asthmatic condition, for which he has been treated.

Frequently, Tom has been the target of verbal teasing and physical abuse from other youngsters. He is afraid of other youngsters and has difficulty in making friends. Mrs. T. sees him as a sensitive little boy whose feelings are easily injured. When he becomes extremely upset and anxious he is subject to chronic bodily complaints, nausea, and diarrhea. At times he has become physically ill from anticipating events before they happen, a common symptom of high anxiety. She also says that, at times, he lacks strength and energy, especially when called upon to clean up his room or help at home. She often wishes he were energetic, for she feels that his sedentary activities, such as watching television, have been part of the cause for his recent weight gain.

### Physician's Information

A telephone interview with Tom's doctor revealed that, aside from a noticeable "slowness" in his intellectual functioning, the boy was in good health and mentioned only mild respiratory illnesses and an allergy. He noted confidentially that the mother has been bitterly critical of professionals who diagnosed her son as retarded, a topic that he has avoided with the mother to concentrate instead on minor health concerns.

A previous neurological report determined the presence of minimal cerebral dysfunction, for which medication was not advised.

### Test Results

| WISC-R: | | Binet L-M: |
|---|---|---|
| Verbal | 58 IQ | CA  9 Years, 9 Months |
| Performance | 71 IQ | MA 6 years, 5 Months |
| Full-Scale | 62 IQ | IQ  66 |

*Key Math:*                          *Informal Reading Inventory:*

  Grade 1.4                                Instructional Level: 1st Gr. Pl.

                                          Frustration Level:    2nd Gr. Pl.

*Bender-Visual-Motor-Gestalt:*      *Wide Range Achieve. Test:*

  Perceptual Level: 5 Years,             Word Recog. 1.8 Gr. Pl.
                 4 Months

                                       Arithmetic      1.5 Gr. Pl.

*Vineland Scale of Social Maturity:*   *ITPA:*

  Social Age: 7 Years, 3 Months         Psycholinguistic Age:

                                       5 Years, 10 Months

### Behavioral Observations and Clinical Information

Tom is a neatly dressed, passive youngster who is over-weight, giving the impression of being soft and almost effeminate. He is a quiet child who enjoys solitary activities rather than those in which he would have to relate with other youngsters. He has a good deal of difficulty with peers, reporting that they tease him, often by calling him names, indicating they think he is dumb or sick. His reaction to this abuse is to strike out by spitting, teasing, or kicking at his tormentors. However, his usual method for dealing with aggression is to withdraw from contact.

During the testing situation Tom was initially apathetic and listless. He slouched in his chair and generally seemed to lack interest and energy for the tasks presented. He failed easy items and then passed more difficult ones. His early demeanor seemed to indicate initial resistance to the testing situation as did his tendency to give rapid responses simply to supply an answer as required. Once Tom became more familiar with the testing surroundings he became more comfortable and began to work much harder and function at his estimated potential. Once at ease he slipped from one-word answers to much more responsive sentences, again indicating that he now felt comfortable with the examiner and the material presented. He seemed to be fairly easily distracted both by sight and by sound, causing him to misinterpret directions. His walk and general motor coordination gave the appearance of awkwardness. In addition, he revealed inability to tell time, confusion in telling direction, and mislabeling of colors.

### Test Interpretation

The results of testing indicate that Tom is a mildly mentally retarded child, educable level. Throughout the test his vocabulary reflected concrete rather than abstract thinking ability. In none of the subtests did the youngster show evidence of any mental functioning in the average or low average range of mental abilities.

Perceptually, although Tom shows more strength in auditory channels than in visual channels, he is quite low in both, functioning near the five and one-half-year level.

In general academic achievement Tom is currently working at the first grade level in both arithmetic and reading, which is consistent with his mental age expectations. His reading skills are limited to simple word recognition, and he possesses no word-attack skills. Arithmetic skills include single-digit addition and subtraction; he requires the use of his fingers for all computation.

Projective testing (C.A.T.-Animal Figures; Sentence Completion) revealed a great deal of pressure in trying to meet his mother's standards for academic growth (while being handicapped by insufficient intellectual ability to do so). He views his mother as demanding and restrictive, not allowing him the freedom given his younger brother. Tom is faced with a threatening and hostile environment and does not feel confident in his ability to meet personal and academic problems. He has feelings of inadequacy caused by constant failure. Aggressive tendencies are handled through withdrawal or teasing behavior.

### Psychological Diagnosis

Tom is a mildly retarded youngster who is working very close to his academic capacity in school. He has weaknesses in his visual-motor functioning as well as in his ability to memorize and recall information provided him either through sight or sound. His anxiety stems not so much from the absence of a guiding male but rather from the pressure he feels to meet his mother's expectations and his inability to do so. He further suffers from a failure to match his peers in his current classroom setting, since they are learning disabled and not additionally handicapped by being mentally retarded like Tom. His mother has tried desperately to develop normal traits in him beyond his limits, and he has become withdrawn and defeated from constant failures and a sense of rejection.

### Psychoeducational Recommendations for the School Personnel:

1. Tom is recommended for placement in an intermediate class for the educable mentally retarded, such as those presently housed within a nearby public school, but only after Mrs. T. has had the opportunity to visit and examine the classroom setting and compare her goals for her son and the goals of the school. This visit is to be made only after Mrs. T. has had an explanation for the need of such a placement for Tom by the present psychologist and understands the necessity for it. Until such a placement can be realized, it is recommended that Tom remain in his present school setting.

2. The best educational setting for Tom is a well-structured one in which visual and auditory distractions are kept to a minimum.

3. Intermittent feedback should be given to Mrs. T. in the

form of regularly scheduled conferences between her and the classroom teacher. It is further recommended that Tom's teacher be a male if possible so as to help provide a masculine figure with whom to identify.

4. Use concrete teaching techniques such as the Fernald VAKT system or the ITPA curriculum. To increase tactile and kinesthetic sensations, sandpaper letters or finger paints can be used for tracing activities.

5. All verbal directions must be clearly and simply stated in language appropriate to his intellectual functioning so that Tom can readily understand.

6. Have Tom listen to, identify, and repeat specific sounds. With his eyes closed, have him discriminate sounds to judge whether they are near or far, loud or soft, high or low.

7. To improve Tom's short-term memory, have him look at pictures and try to recall as many objects, letters, or numbers as possible.

8. Initially, assign a youngster to be Tom's "pal" while he becomes acclimated to his new classroom setting and to introduce him to the other members of his class.

9. Provisions should be made to give Tom a program of gross- and fine-motor instruction. Throwing a ball back and forth or simple games such as "Simon Says" can be used to foster balance, body movement, and coordination. This may also help introduce Tom into more social games.

10. Continuation of speech therapy is recommended.

11. Levels of expectations for academic success should be consistent with Tom's capacity for learning. Expect relatively slow progress and do not express disappointment, thereby increasing feelings of worthlessness.

## Recommendations for the Parent

1. It is recommended that Mrs. T. transfer Tom to a public school class for the mildly retarded after discussion with the private school personnel (the latter have already

agreed to the plan).

2. Give all instructions and directions to Tom appropriate to his mental age of six and one-half years rather than at his actual age of late nine years.

3. Enroll Tom in YMCA intermediate-age sports activities, starting with swimming, which he particularly enjoys.

4. Give him a list of small chores he can do at home, e.g. picking up toys and clothing, making the place settings for dinner, and going to the store for small, inexpensive items. He could watch his favorite television programs contingent upon doing these tasks. Reward him with verbal and tangible approval.

5. Make a visit to the special class teacher to discuss the nature and structure of the retarded class as well as their common goals for Tom. The mother must have hope for the boy's future and her own as well.

6. Move the sons into the same bedroom as soon as it is economically feasible, and reduce Tom's feeling of rivalry or jealousy.

7. Discover and verbally recognize what Tom does right rather than focus on what he does wrong. Avoid much criticism on what Tom cannot do, and emphasize through praise, hugs, and other displays of affection those things he does right. He must realize that he does not have to be perfect to be loved.

8. When it becomes necessary to discipline Tom, try to do it in a calm, consistent manner. Make sure that he understands exactly what the punishment (deprivation of a privilege) is for.

9. Keep in contact with the classroom teacher through regularly scheduled conferences to keep abreast of Tom's progress.

10. Listen to Tom when he comes home from school, but do not react immediately to negative complaints of maltreatment by the teachers or classmates. Instead, calmly discuss the incident later with the teacher when conferences are scheduled.

11. Encourage him to practice his homework at a regularly

scheduled location and time. Only give assistance when he actively seeks it and demonstrates difficulties in doing the assignment. Staying up to watch a favorite television program or a movie can be used as an incentive. Avoid teaching him new school material, but instead practice well-learned material with him at the first grade level.

12. Encourage him to select his clothing, dress himself, and perform his personal grooming. Praise him for those things he can do successfully.

13. Allow Tom to make small purchases for personal items when he accompanies his mother to the store. He should be allowed to make his selection, pay for the the item, and accept his change.

14. Mrs. T. should reserve the correction of Tom to herself and not allow her visiting husband to discipline Tom, as this confuses the boy.

15. Encourage him to ride his bicycle and to play with younger children as an alternative to his constant television watching.

16. Encourage him to have his friends come to his home to play and occasionally stay overnight.

17. Continue to work with the family physician to control Tom's weight.

18. The mother should continue with personal therapy. This report will be mailed, with the mother's permission, to her agency so that the boy's therapist may incorporate the current information in his counseling with the boy. She should also continue to discuss during therapy the father's relationship with her and their sons.

## Additional Information from Mrs. T.
## (5 Months Later)

September: Tom was placed with her permission in the recommended class for the retarded by the Chief School Psychologist of the city. Mrs. T. reported that she was "pleased" by the placement but complained about disruptive children in the class she observed. She said that the "thoroughness" of the evaluation convinced her of Tom's retardation, and her confidence in the psychologist left her no reasonable alternative explanation.

The following May: Mrs. T. called to indicate that Tom had a "successful" school year, was more comfortable with other retarded children, and would stay in this class for another year or more. She complained obliquely that the principal and special education teacher had "strained relationships" but that the class, although somewhat noisy, was well-run and active. She said that although she knows that her son is retarded, she finds him much more interested in learning and "more relaxed" at school and at home.

## MILD RETARDATION: AGGRESSIVE

Name: Henry H. Age: 8 Years, 8 Months Grade: Educable Retarded
Siblings: Willa, 6 Years; Alfred, 4 Years; Tina, 2 1/2 Years; Freida, 18
      Months

Mrs. H. requested a psychological study at the suggestion of Henry's teacher, Mr. R., who instructs retarded children. Since kindergarten Henry has frequently fought at school and in the neighborhood, last year almost daily. His parents also expressed concern about his inability to control his temper, his lack of coordination, hostility toward siblings, aloof and sometimes hostile attitude toward his stepfather, enuresis, lying behavior, and fascination with violence. Apparently his parents accept his intellectual limitations and speak well of the school program.

### *Family Background*

Henry, a small, black retarded boy, lives with his mother, stepfather, brother, and three sisters in a five-room house located in an overcrowded ghetto neighborhood. Upon visiting the home, it was seen that the home is amply supplied with story books, which Mr. H. reads to his children three or four times a week. The family also goes out together on frequent excursions to the zoo, drive-in movies, short trips, and summer picnics.

Mrs. H., age twenty-five, a pleasant, overweight housewife, was born the fourth of eight children and grew up in ghetto poverty. She described her mother as a strong, dominating, nervous little woman and the sole disciplinarian in the family. Her father, a hard drinking but gentle and compassionate bricklayer, was "ousted" by her mother when Mrs. H. was fourteen. Unhappy at home from that time, Henry's mother left home at age sixteen after having completed tenth grade.

Mr. H., Henry's stepfather, twenty-nine, is tall and soft-spoken. The younger of two children, he was raised by his mother in an urban ghetto, quit school one semester before graduation from high school, served in the army in Vietnam, and has worked at several jobs. Trained as an auto mechanic, a trade that he loves, he was unemployed nearly a year before gaining employment in his field. Referring to his own child-hood, Mr. H. stated that not having had a father distressed him greatly. A church choir member, Mr. H. regards cursing and immoderate drinking as wrong; he believes strongly in the importance of a father's role in his children's lives. The parents generally use spanking with a belt and/or confining Henry to his room with denial of television privileges as disciplinary methods. Henry is much less inclined to try anything wrong when Mr. H. is around the house. They reported that Henry presently shows considerable enthusiasm for school work, vol-untarily beginning his own homework after supper every night and eagerly talking about learning to read and write. He is also quite fond of his teacher.

## Developmental History

Henry was born two months premature and weighed 4 pounds 1 ounce. The delivery was described as easy, and no drugs or instruments were used. Born cross-eyed, he was taken to an eye clinic at nine months and has been treated there regularly. He wears strong glasses and has 20/25 corrected vi-sion in both eyes. Henry contracted mumps at thirteen months and for four or five days ran a temperature of 104 degrees, his only serious illness.

As an infant Henry learned to sit and stand alone, walk, and to speak words and sentences later than the children of friends and neighbors. The boy returned to soiling after beginning first grade, but this stopped after he was placed in a Retarded-Educable class. Enuresis continues to be a problem, occurring about three times a week. Language development was extremely slow except that he has "mastered" all curse words, to the parents' dismay.

### Educational History

Henry began schooling with first grade at age five. He "hated it" and became a problem child, frequently soiling his clothes and fighting with peers. He passed first grade but after psychological evaluation was recommended for placement in a Retarded-Educable classroom, a move that did not occur because of crowded conditions. The family moved to a new neighborhood and Henry was placed in a Retarded-Educable class. Continuing in R.E. classes since then, he has shown much less anxiety about attending school. However, his behavior has continued to grow more aggressive; his parents were called to the school several times yearly.

Mr. R., Henry's teacher, described him as one who tries "too hard to please," responds very favorably to behavior-modification techniques, tends to shy away from his peers, stay at the teacher's side, and daydream excessively. According to Mr. R., Henry is achieving satisfactorily in the classroom. At recess he is impulsive, provocative, and very aggressive.

Henry presently is unable to read sentences, but he works hard, without much prodding, at learning to spell and count. His parents reported that only recently has Henry begun to appear to take satisfaction from learning itself, rather than striving solely to please his parents or teacher.

### Behavioral Observations

Henry, who appears to be about a year younger than his

chronological age, came to each testing session dressed in clean but faded shirt and trousers. He wore strong but scratched eyeglasses to correct esotropia. Reflecting his low socioeconomic background and language background, he sometimes slurred words but generally was able to be understood. Always pleasant, cooperative, and eager to please, he smiled freely and apparently enjoyed the testing situation, although he grew tired before each session ended, manifesting shorter attention span, less persistence at completing a task, and more physical movement (squirming, standing, and stretching).

Henry exhibited impulsivity in testing by acting without plan or forethought. He also displayed inability to conceptualize abstractly, responding in very concrete terms and actions. Gross and fine coordination were poor for his age.

## Psychological Test Results

| WISC-R: | | Stanford-Binet | |
|---|---|---|---|
| Verbal | 74 IQ | CA | 8 Years, 8 Months |
| Performance | 48 IQ | MA | 6 Years, 6 Months |
| Full-Scale | 58 IQ | IQ | 73 |

| Beery-Buktenica Visual-Motor Integration Test: | Bender-Gestalt: |
|---|---|
| VMI Age Equivalence: | Perceptual Age Level: |
| 5 Years | 6 Years, 0 Months |

| Wide Range Achieve. Test: | | Wepman Auditory Discrim. Test: |
|---|---|---|
| Reading: | Grade 1.3 | Approx. 5 Year Level |
| Spelling: | Grade 1.3 | |
| Arithmetic: | Grade 1.8 | |

*Illinois Test of Psycholinguistic Abilities:*

Psycholinguistic Age: Approx. 5 1/2 Years

Strengths: Auditory Sequential Memory   8 Years, 3 Months

Limitations: Visual Association          4 Years, 2 Months

                Visual Sequential Memory   3 Years, 4 Months

*Projectives:* (Children's Apperception, Blacky, House-Tree-Person).

### Discussion of Test Results

INTELLIGENCE TESTING: Henry's scores on the WISC-R and Stanford-Binet tests place him in the mildly retarded (educable) range of intelligence. During testing Henry operated at a concrete level in quantitative and qualitative areas; he was unable to handle concepts of similarity and differences between things at his age level. His fund of information and experience is limited. On WISC-R performance items (Picture Arrangement, Block Design, Object Assembly) the boy showed gross visual perception deficiencies, being unable to reproduce even the simplest block pattern or to (correctly) juxtapose more than two pieces of a puzzle. The Stanford-Binet (Basal Age 4 Years, 6 Months, Ceiling 9 Years) also showed his greatest difficulty with items involving geometric designs.

WRAT scores indicate that Henry is achieving academically at a low first grade level in spelling and word recognition, which is commensurate with his six and one-half-year mental age; he has no word-attack skills. His arithmetic reasoning ability is only slightly better, being limited to simple concrete addition and subtraction involving use of fingers and counting aloud. The appropriate instructional level appears to be not much above the kindergarten-readiness stage.

Bender-Gestalt and Beery VMI results indicated that Henry's visual-motor perceptual level is one-half to one and one-half years below his mental age, indicative of possible neurological impairment. ITPA results indicated both auditory- and visual-perceptual development of five and one-half years, with auditory-perceptual skills being the stronger of the two. The most severe areas of deficiency involved the ability to relate and organize visually presented concepts (Visual Association) and the ability to reproduce visual sequences of geometric designs. The Auditory Memory score, on the other hand, was 8 Years, 3 Months, indicating that this is probably Henry's best channel for learning.

EMOTIONAL FUNCTIONING: Results of the projective tests of personality indicated that Henry has strong feelings of aggression, which he expresses through fighting with siblings and peers. He also feels deprived of love and attention yet considers himself undeserving because of his own "bad" behavior. Thus he understandably feels defeated, helpless, and lonely in a world in which he cannot cope. He does not believe in his own value or worth as a human being, as evidenced by his immediate destruction of what he has created in drawings and games. He views his siblings as rivals for parental attention.

### Diagnostic Summary

Henry is an educable retarded child whose perceptual handicaps, poor coordination, impulsivity, and concrete thinking suggest minimal cerebral dysfunction, which may have been caused by premature birth and/or by a high fever or trauma suffered in infancy. Mild to moderate behavior problems are also present: Henry attempts to compensate for his learning deficiencies, short stature, and lack of physical skills with highly impulsive, aggressive behavior directed toward siblings and other children.

### Workbook Exercise

Previous to noting the authors' treatment plans for Henry as listed in the Appendix, p. 217, it is recommended that the student construct a series of strategies predicted to be successful in minimizing the many problems in the case. One must focus not only on the primary diagnosis, but also seek to alleviate, for the teacher and parents, the many other problems of the child in learning, self-control, sibling rivalry, inappropriate language, etc. Essentially, if there are many problems, there will likely be required many solutions.

### Psychologist's Follow-up (5 Months Later)

I just called Henry's home. Mr. H., his stepfather, answered the phone, recognized my voice instantly, and was pleased to be contacted.

He informed me that Henry no longer fights or displays such aggressiveness toward his siblings or peers; on the contrary, he is now quite proud of the fact that he's the "oldest child" and displays rather protective behavior toward his brother and sisters, e.g. making sure their jackets are buttoned properly, etc. He no longer vents his frustration by destroying his sisters' dolls. He still occasionally tells a "whopper" of a lie, but this is not nearly as frequent as it once was.

Mr. H. mentioned that it took a while to adjust to Henry's retardation by lowering his expectations, etc., but he thought that he and his wife had done so successfully. He is still determined to be the "best possible father" to his children.

He mentioned that Henry had a new teacher since January and that Henry had had some trouble grasping the English accent of Mr. W., of Caribbean origin. After about five weeks, however, things seem to be going well for Henry at school now. According to Mr. H., Henry no longer is getting into so much trouble at school with his fighting.

I then called his previous teacher at home, who said that to the best of his recollection Henry's fighting had indeed decreased. He recalled Henry as acting "somewhat more quiet."

# CHAPTER V

# LEARNING DISABILITIES

CHILDREN with specific learning disabilities, not due primarily to mental retardation, emotional stress, environmental deprivation, or sensory handicaps, have become better understood through research in recent years (Hammill, 1972; Locher & Worms, 1977; Neurological and Sensory Disease Control Program, 1969; O'Grady, 1974; Seiderman, 1976; Wender, 1971). Although the phenomena within this general category of pathologies are often quite baffling to parents of such a child (Brutten et al., 1973; Freeman, 1974), writers in a variety of professional disciplines (Clements, 1966; Cruickshank, 1971; Vance, Gaynor, & Coleman, 1976) have suggested understandable etiologic patterns, while others (Blanco, 1972; Myers & Hammill, 1969; Valett, 1968) have offered remedial prescriptions and strategies. Still, a few varieties of learning disabilities, with apparently irreversible aphasic or dyslexic conditions, do exhibit minimal progress even after substantial educational and therapeutic efforts.

Although protean and often puzzling at first glance, the learning disabilities have signs and symptoms that cluster in sufficiently observable patterns to render them identifiable and treatable. Such groups of causes or descriptors are labeled for simplification purposes as follows: minimal cerebral dysfunction, hyperkinetic, mild motor impairment, mild brain damage, the awkward child, perceptually handicapped, neurologically impaired, etc., with full recognition that no two learning disabled children are alike, a fact leading to the federal mandate of Individual Educational Programs for exceptional children.

Some of the most frequently observed symptoms include impairments in the visual and auditory perceptual areas, problems in receptive, associative, and expressive language, often in combination with motor and neurological functioning and, of course, serious underachievement in school for the child's estimated abilities. The symptomatology of the learning disabled is extensive and has been listed in several sources (Birch, 1964; Clements & Peters, 1962; Clements, 1966; Wender, 1971). Psychologists and related specialists need to familiarize themselves with test performance indicators, dysfunctions in perceptual functioning, neurological "soft" signs, disorders of communication, diagnostic achievement tests, variants in motor functioning and attention span, as well as the correlates in behavioral traits, personality, and development — no simple assignment even with interdisciplinary assistance.

Since the symptoms are multi-dimensional and individual for any case in question, so must be the remedial strategies to circumvent, adjust to, or compensate for the special limitations discovered. Nor should these prescriptive interventions be merely educational, pharmacological, or physical in nature, as it becomes obvious to the diagnostician that parents (Brutten et al., 1973) and peers (Ledebur, 1977) can also play a role in exacerbating or reducing the child's reactions toward his or her limitations. The attitudes held and the behavior executed toward the affected child by family members, siblings, and teachers must often be changed as radically as the educational program if the child is to develop a greater sense of competence and self-worth. Remediation of educational problems is assuredly a fundamental step in this direction, but such academic efforts alone are often insufficient for the morale problems of the child by the time the difficulties are identified. If the child's motivation to learn and to develop is seriously impaired, as is so frequently the case, then much of the educational thrust is diminished or ineffective. The learning disabled child must be changed, through perhaps psychotherapeutic or behavioral strategies, to be a motivated learner who will respond positively to the assistance offered.

In the cases presented in this chapter, an effort has been made to illustrate not only "typical" cases of learning disabilities but also to highlight the dynamic and behavioral styles of the affected families. This is done to document the need for a comprehensive psychosocial appraisal of such relationships, which have frequently contributed to the child's demise: severe over-protection, rejection, broken family ties, anxiety states that further disable the child, environmental conditions that overwhelm the parents' normal ability to guide, nurture, and stimulate their offspring. Sometimes relatively massive intervention has been required: attendance at private schools for the learning disabled with a special "academic" curriculum including physical therapy, motor training, perceptual training, occupational and speech therapy, group psychotherapy, behavior modification, etc. Other cases, which could have been included but for space limitations, require private tutoring, attendance at resource rooms in local schools, and even family therapy to reduce scapegoating and hostility toward the disabled child for his failure to execute the parental aspirations and roles demanded of him.

The following cases illustrate not how to solve each and every problem presented in the referrals of present and future clinicians, but instead offer models of interesting yet common problems that the practitioner will likely experience. Such materials provide examples of good psychoeducational practices, the comprehensive integration of clinical data, and the creation of appropriate strategies to suit the many problems of the clients.

## A LEARNING DISABILITY

Name:  Alice A.      Age:  6 years, 5 months  Grade:  First (Nov.)

Mr. and Mrs. A sought a psychoeducational evaluation because Alice was having difficulty with school work. They felt that she was unable to concentrate on her work and was having difficulty in learning to read.

### Background Information

Alice is the only child of Mr. and Mrs. A. Mr. A. is a thirty-two-year-old X-ray technician who works in partnership with two physicians. Concerning his educational background, he had great difficulty learning to read and was considered learning disabled, although he later attended college for two years. The mother, Mrs. A., twenty-nine years old, is a high school teacher. She holds a bachelor's degree with thirty additional graduate credits. Born in Holland, she moved to the United States with her family at eleven years of age. The couple has been married for approximately nine years, and they reported that their marriage relationship is genuinely stable.

During her pregnancy Mrs. A. had headaches, and she received Darvon® medication. She also had some problem with water retention. The birth of Alice was approximately two weeks premature. From all reports, developmental milestones appeared normal. Alice walked and spoke single words at twelve months. Two-word sentences appeared somewhere between eighteen and twenty-four months. Control for bowel and bladder was achieved at approximately thirty months. Regarded as well coordinated, Alice rode a two-wheel bicycle at five years and likes bicycling. She was sent to ballet school and likes to dance.

The only serious illness that the parents could recall was a virus and ear infection at age three. She ran a temperature of 104 degrees, and tubes had to be inserted in her ears for them to drain. She was also reported to be a poor eater when younger, regurgitating at will. Hearing and vision were normal.

At about age two and one-half Alice began nursery school, where she reportedly enjoyed most of the activities and had friends. She memorized songs and melodies taught at the school, socialized well, and revealed no learning problems. Currently Alice attends first grade in a large suburban school district in a middle-class neighborhood. Many of the children in her class have bright normal to superior intelligence, and a number can easily read in primary level books. Alice appears quite inattentive, struggles with the academic program, and reverses many letters and numbers. These problems have led to other children calling her "dummy," making it difficult for her to relate well to them. She has also been the recipient of some antireligious comments by a few students, and understandably this has caused her marked discomfort. While initially enthusiastic about school, she no longer looks forward to it and prefers to stay home.

**Test Results**

*WISC-R:*

| Verbal Subtests | S. Sc. | Performance Subtests | S. Sc. |
|---|---|---|---|
| Information | 6 | Picture Completion | 5 |
| Similarities | 10 | Picture Arrangement | 11 |
| Arithmetic | 8 | Block Design | 10 |
| Vocabulary | 13 | Object Assembly | 6 |
| Comprehension | 11 | Coding | 8 |
| (Digit Span) | (2) | | |
| Verbal S. Sc. | 48 | Performance S. Sc. | 40 |
| Verbal IQ | 97 | | |
| Performance IQ | 86 | | |
| Full Scale IQ | 91 | | |

*McCarthy Scales of Children's Abilities:*

| Scale | Scale Index | Percentiles |
|---|---|---|
| Verbal | 60 | 85 |
| Perceptual Performance | 39 | 14 |
| Quantitative | 40 | 15 |
| (General Cognitive Index) | (96) | (40) |
| Memory | 29 | 2 |

Motor                                    42                    20

*Wepman Auditory Discrim.*        *Beery-Buktenica Visual*
*Test:*                           *Motor Integration:*

   Two errors: (Normal)          V.M.I. Age: 5 Years, 3 Months

*Peabody Individual Achievement Test:*

|                      | Grade Level | Percentile |
|----------------------|-------------|------------|
| Mathematics          | 0.6         | 32         |
| Reading Recognition  | 1.1         | 43         |
| Spelling             | 0.8         | 33         |
| General Information  | 1.4         | 54         |
| TOTAL TEST           | 0.8         | 39         |

*Woodcock Reading Mastery Test:*

|                       | Grade Level | Percentile     |
|-----------------------|-------------|----------------|
| Letter Identification | 1.4         | 58             |
| Word Identification   | 1.0         | 9              |
| Word Attack           | 1.2         | 43             |
| Word Comprehension    | 1.5         | 25             |
| Passage Comprehension | 1.1         | 29             |
| TOTAL                 | 1.0         | 29 percentile  |

*Vineland Social Maturity Scale:*

*Social Age: 8 Years, 0 Months*

*Sentence Completion Test Responses:*

1. All my life I: "love you."
2. If I were bigger: "I were you."
3. If I were smaller: "you were bigger."
4. Sometimes I'm afraid: "of you." (Tell me more about it.) "About a boy, a scary boy who goes 'Boo.' He lives near me."
5. When I'm afraid I: "am mad and frightened and sick and tired. That's what I am now."
6. If I were a boy: "I would be a girl."
7. My mother thinks I: "am mad, frightened, and sick and tired."
8. I get mad when: "the days are happy. Sometimes when I'm happy all the people around me are mad." (Tell me more about that. Do you like when people are mad?) (Speaking to the examiner.) "No, I don't."
9. My father thinks: "I'm happy."
10. My mother thinks: "I am happy."
11. I often wish: "you are sad."
12. My friends think I am: "sad and frightened."
13. I like to: "play out in the summer swimming in the pool."
14. I want to be like: "a grown-up down at the street who shouts at the school. That's the funniest part."
15. I feel best when: "I am happy when I got out and be happy on the way and that's all."
16. When I'm alone: "you are so mad and happy and singing a song."
17. When I am sick: "I am in bed having a temperature."
18. My father expects me to: "go shopping at Wawa's."
19. I feel terrible when: "I'm happy."

20. My mother wants me to: "go into the store and get a toppy in the tippy. Like a top in the ceiling and a tip down from the ceiling" (laughing).
21. I feel ashamed when: "I am mad and a munster." (What's that?) "Like a boogie man."
22. School is: "in school."
23. I worry when: "I'm a busser" (meaning a student who takes a school bus to school). "And I fall in the ground in the ice" (laughing).
24. I feel disappointed when: "I am mad." (What makes you mad?) "I don't know, when someone gets angry at you."
25. When something is hard for me I: "am going to sit down and play with your pan." (Tell me about that.) "It's a pan that you bag. Once there was a man who came to me who said my mother was going to sneeze and to get me to the druggist."
26. When I break something I: "am in trouble."
27. When I am punished I: "am mad."
28. When someone fights with me: "I am mad."
29. My teacher thinks I: "is bad."
30. I don't like to: "be in bed."

Her frustration is quite evident, as is her desire to be loved and accepted. While some of the responses seemed quite atypical for her age and inappropriate in character, she laughed frequently and seemed to offer her responses facetiously. Alice revealed language impairments, word substitutions and word confusions not only in the Sentence Completion Test but also in general conversation. She required rather frequent repetition of instructions and gave inappropriate verbal responses arising mainly from her misinterpretation of words rather than from any bizarre ideation or emotional disturbance. When Alice responded in vocabulary, she approximated an eight-year-old level, using such words as "disappointed, frightened, and druggist." She showed some learning disability in her receptive language areas, which may contribute to her problems with the phonic-visual associations so crucial in the learning of words. However, one would have to carefully follow her progress to be certain that continued stress does not lead to decompensation in the direction of a psychosis. One would hesitate to keep Alice under the stress and anxiety she currently feels.

### Blacky Pictures

The interrogation questions come from Appendix C of the manual.

*Card 1:* (Oral Eroticism) They're digging. Is the Mama hurt? Maybe she's resting.

*Inquiry:*
1. How does Blacky feel here: Unhappy.
2. How does Mama feel here: Sad.
3. How much longer will Blacky want to stay there: Long enough, a long time.
4. When Blacky grows up will she rather eat than do other things: No.

*Card 2:* (Oral Sadism) She has her own collar on. She wants to take Mama's because Mama is grown-up and she wants to be like Mama. When it says Mama she feels mad and then she feels happy when she puts the collar on her neck. She wants to take the collar because she wants to have a new brand collar (reversal of brand new collar) that's Mama's.

*Inquiry:*
1. Why is Blacky doing that to the Mama's collar: Because she wants to take it because she likes her collar.
2. How often does Blacky feel like doing this: One time, two times, three times, four times, five times.
3. What will Blacky do next with Mama's collar: Dig it someplace. (What do you mean?) Like hide it.
4. What will Mama do when she comes: She'll dig and find it.

*Card 3:* (Anal Sadism) Blacky's going to the toilet next to Mama and Papa. Mama will be mad and Papa will say who did it? Then she runs back to her house. In the morning she climbs up the tree to see her Mama. Tippy is the brother and he comes out and he climbs up to the tree with Blacky.

*Inquiry:*

1. Why is Blacky doing it over there: She doesn't want to mess up her ground. She wants to mess up Mama and Papa's.
2. Why is Blacky covering it up: She doesn't want Mama to see it because she would be mad at her.
3. What will Mama say to Blacky: Bad girl, go back to the house, go to sleep until morning. Don't sneak in the nighttime because I'll find out. One day she sneaked up the tree without Mama knowing.
4. What will Papa say to Blacky: Nice Blacky. You are a good girl.

*Card 4:* (Oedipal Intensity) Mama and Papa kissed because they loved each other. She liked to get married and couldn't. One day she grew older and got married and is so happy that she made the Mama and Papa jealous. She was so mad at them now that she bit them.

*Inquiry:*

1. How does Blacky feel about seeing Mama and Papa make love: Jealous. (Why?) She's unhappy because they kissed each other.
2. How often does Blacky feel this way: Whenever they kiss.
3. What will Papa do if he sees Blacky peeking: He'll say bad girl. This time you're going to get a different punishment. You can go out but you can't see us kissing anymore.
4. What will Mama do if she sees Blacky peeking: She'll say the same thing because the father made the rule. Don't cry because I'm so angry at you. You better believe it.
5. Which would be better, Mama with Blacky or Papa with Blacky: Mama with Blacky.

*Card 5:* (Masturbation Guilt) She has fleas and wants to take them off.

*Inquiry:*

1. How does Blacky feel here: Happy, sometimes sad,

sometimes mad, sometimes she feels frightened.
2. Who is Blacky thinking about here: I don't know.
3. Is Blacky afraid here: He just wants to be happy, not afraid.
4. What will Mama say if she comes over and finds Blacky: Nice girl, you're a very good girl. Sometimes you're bad but sometimes you're good.
5. What will Papa say if he comes over and finds Blacky: The same thing.

*Card 6:* (Penis Envy) What's the knife for? To cut off Tippy's tail? He'll get a cut if the knife gets on the tail. If he gets a cut, he'll cry.

*Inquiry:*
1. How does Blacky feel about her own tail: Her tail is more interesting, it's a nice and pointed one and can do more things.
2. Which one of Blacky's family planned for Tippy's tail to be cut off: Blacky.
3. What will Tippy think about losing the tail: Sad, she'll be sad.
4. How will the other dogs in the neighborhood feel when they see Tippy's short tail: They'll cry.
5. Would Blacky like to trade her tail for a pretty bow: Yep.

*Card 7:* (Positive Identification) Once upon a time this toy dog just moves his tail and he gets the string and he gets mad and he got lost with the toy dog.

*Inquiry:*
1. Who talks like that to Blacky: Papa.
2. Who is Blacky most likely to obey: Mama.
3. Who is Blacky acting like here: Papa, no Tippy.
4. Which one would Blacky rather be like: Mama, Mama is so pretty.
5. What would Blacky feel like doing if she were the toy dog: Nothing, she would just be unhappy.

*Card 8:* (Sibling Rivalry) Once upon a time, Blacky came and saw all the people, all her family, so she was growling.

172 Clinical and School Psychology

*Inquiry:*
1. What does Blacky feel like doing now: She feels like walking away.
2. Does Blacky think Tippy deserves the praise: She wants to join everybody but she's not allowed to.
3. Who does Blacky think is paying more attention to Tippy: Mama and Papa are both paying the same amount.
4. How often does Blacky see this: A long, long time.
5. Blacky is angry, at whom is she most angry: Mama, no I mean Papa. Mama and Papa and Tippy because Tippy is having more attention than Blacky.

*Card 9:* (Guilt feelings) Once upon a time Blacky was crying. She ran all the way home and never came home again. (Can you explain that?) She ran away from her house and ran north. She built herself something. Are there any parents, I mean human beings to take care of her? (It s your story, you decide.) Okay, so she found a lady to take care of her and told her she didn't like her parents. (Why did she run away?) Because she didn't like them, because they were paying more attention to Tippy.

*Inquiry:*
1. What might have happened between the last picture and this one: They were paying more attention to Tippy.
2. Whom does this remind Blacky of (the pointing figure): Of herself.
3. Who is really to blame for Blacky feeling this way: Papa and Mama and Tippy.
4. What might Blacky do now: Cry.
5. How long will Blacky feel this way: One minute, two minutes, three minutes, four minutes, five minutes, six minutes.

*Card 11:* (Positive Ego Ideal) That's Mama. She is so sad for her because the kid is going away and that's all and that's the end of the story to me.

*Inquiry:*

1. Of whom does this remind Blacky: Mama.
2. How good is Mama compared to this dream: I don't know.
3. Will Blacky want to be like this dream: Yes.
4. Will Blacky grow up to be like this dream: Yes.

*Card 10:* (Love Object) Blacky is dreaming and it's about Papa. He's a boy and he's strong and wealthy and he picks everything up and that's all.

*Inquiry:*

1. Who is this that Blacky is dreaming about: Papa.
2. Whom does this remind Blacky of: Papa.
3. How good is Papa compared to this dream: Good.
4. Would Blacky want to grow up like this dream: No, Blacky is a girl.

### Further Inquiry

Her favorite card on the Blacky was Number 1: "Because Mama is begging. She's lying down and that's what dogs do when they beg for things." She disliked Card Number 5 but did not know why.

From the Blacky it is evident that her desire for attention and affection is quite strong. Her feelings toward the parents are ambivalent. She resents anyone who infringes on her desire for attention and affection. She is likely to resort with hostility toward the failure to gain recognition and may use passive-aggressive measures to retaliate. Blacky would like the mother to spend more time with her. She is feminine identified and would like to emulate her mother. Some Oedipal feelings are present. She is jealous of the affection the parents show to each other. However, she does see the resolution of this conflict, getting married and having her own husband. While Father likes to give the appearance of being stern, it is Mother whom she is more likely to obey, although she does want the attention and affection of both parents.

The following interpretations were excerpted from the psychological report:

At this time Alice functions in the average intelligence range (WISC-R, Verbal IQ 97, Performance IQ 86, Full Scale IQ 91). In accounting for the variability of her performance, her potential ability is at least in the 100 to 110 IQ range.

On the developmental test of visual-motor integration, she achieved a V.M.I. age equivalent of 5 Years, 3 Months, indicating at least one year developmental delay in this area. Auditory Discrimination as measured by the Wepman Scale was within normal limits for her age.

The McCarthy Scales of Children's Abilities approximate her WISC-R IQ with a GCI of 96. The Memory score is the lowest, indicating difficulty in focusing her attention on a task at hand and retaining information presented auditorally. These limitations would create a handicap in her learning to read unless there was much repetition to the point of overlearning. As with the Beery, her Perceptual Performance score was below age level.

The achievement scores are noted previously and attest to her variability in achievement with some delay clearly evident. Her social age of eight on the Vineland indicate the presence of considerable social maturity and self-sufficiency.

In terms of personality she was perceived to be an energetic little girl who wants lots of love and affection and likes to be the center of attention. She does want to succeed in what she undertakes. Alice wants the positive attention that success brings and therefore has the necessary motivation through social approval to do her work. Although she would like to be a dependent child she recognizes, especially from the mother, the parental encouragement toward independence. Thus, if not successful at a task, she is more likely to express hostility toward her mother. In spite of her desire to be dependent she is jealous of adult privileges and occasionally is envious of the affection the parents show to each other. At times she enjoys behavior that irritates adults as a way of making herself feel more important and gaining attention. Making adults feel uncomfortable gives her some recognition in light of her inability to gain this legitimately by successful achievement. In situations that she perceives to be extremely difficult or tension ridden, she is more likely to retreat rather than aggressively attempt to overcome them. In the absence of sympathetic support, this retreat goes into fantasy and day-dreaming.

She is feminine identified, interested in making friends and getting along with them. She shows signs of anxiety and emotional immaturity. The signs are not serious at this time as long as she is not placed in a highly stressful situation; otherwise she might decompensate.

### Conclusions and Recommendations

Currently Alice is functioning in the average intelligence range. While she has adequate vocabulary development, there appears to be unevenness in both visual and auditory perceptual development coupled with a short attention span. Difficulty in writing on lines and letter reversals are also found more frequently than normal for first graders. In light of the fact that she seems unable to develop an adequate sight vocabulary and learn the basic phonic skills despite classroom instruction, the conclusion is reached that she is a learning disabled child.

Since at the time of testing she has only been in first grade for three months, she is not significantly behind her peers to warrant a grade retention. Further, since she is already behind in her class work in both reading and arithmetic, moving her for intervals during the day to attend a resource room will not help her to keep up with her peers academically, though she would benefit from such instruction. The effect would be to increase her feelings of inadequacy and would likely put her under further stress. The following recommendations are made to alleviate her problems:

*For School Personnel*
1. Alice should be placed in a transitional first grade with children at her ability and achievement level who have academic and language problems and where the pace of instruction will be slower, the curriculum will stress readiness materials, and individualized attention will be available.

2. The initial emphasis should be on developing a sight vocabulary and then on phonics.

3. The teacher should indicate an attitude of acceptance of the fact that Alice will make errors and will need much repetition of instructions in reading and arithmetic.

4. In order to foster Alice's sense of self-esteem, the teacher should call on Alice when she knows the answer so that she develops a greater feeling of success in relation to school work.

5. When Alice attends to a task for a longer period of time than usual, she should be noticed and praised by the teacher in front of her peers. To help her focus attention on academic tasks, distractions should be limited by not seating her near a window, open door, or a colorful bulletin board. A study carrel or "office" or corner of the room may be quite helpful in this regard.

6. If the slower and more repetitive instruction of a transitional first grade is not successful in improving her reading, then she should be reevaluated diagnostically and considered for a learning disability class that utilizes the kinesthetic and tactile approaches to reading in addition to the visual and auditory approach in the regular class.

7. A conference between the psychologist and teachers of Alice's regular class and resource room is being arranged to discuss curricular materials and a reinforcement program to aid her motivation.

*For the Parents*

1. The parents should continue to provide home chores for Alice to do and, when she does them correctly, to notice and praise her for it in order to foster her sense of self-esteem and confidence.

2. They should encourage her to watch various educational television programs involved with counting and reading e.g. "Sesame Street" and "The Electric Company."

3. Have games at home that involve drawing and tracing. Follow-the-dot games and puzzles would be helpful to her as well as those involving counting and solving simple

arithmetic problems.

4. Cut out some pictures from a magazine or catalog. Put the name of the object under the picture and show it to her in flash card fashion. After she is able to pair the picture with the words, separate the two and let her match the words to the picture. Eventually let her read the words in isolation.

5. Increase attention span, notice and praise her each time she is able to complete a task or chore without becoming sidetracked. Speak to her slowly with simple language, asking her to repeat instructions.

6. Obtain a pediatric neurological examination and evaluations for possible sensory impairments that might interfere with learning.

7. The psychologist will reassess Alice in one year to determine her progress and make necessary academic adjustments in her program in consultation with her teachers.

8. If stress continues or Alice continues to feel unhappy, consider family psychotherapy or counseling to alleviate anxiety and to aid the parents in dealing with Alice.

9. A parent-psychologist-teacher conference has been arranged to explain Alice's particular problems to the parents.

## Follow-up Information

A pediatric neurological examination was performed, and a second independent psychological examination later confirmed the diagnosis of learning disability. For budgetary considerations the school personnel had discontinued its transitional first grade classes and placed Alice instead in the learning disability first grade level program. The follow-up assessment the following June indicated that Alice was beginning to make academic progress but required a good deal of practice and repetition in the language areas. She appeared much less tense and anxious than before, gave more typical responses in a second Sentence Completion Test, and reported to her teachers and parents about her many friendships in class.

## A LEARNING DISABILITY

Name: Barry B.   Age: 9 Years, 3 Months   Grade: Second Parochial
Siblings: Lenny, 13; Sara, 10; Agnes, 6; Charles, 4

Barry was brought for psychological evaluation by his mother because of her concern regarding his inability to learn to read and identify the names and sounds of letters. Difficulty following verbal directions and poor school performance in all subject areas except math were also indicated. At home he frequently engaged in temper tantrums, fought with siblings, and had difficulty sleeping.

### Previous Examinations

Barry was referred to a local hospital a year earlier for a psychological, neurological, and medical evaluation because of poor school performance. He was diagnosed as having minimal cerebral dysfunction with an adjustment reaction to childhood, and no recommendations were offered except psychotherapy, a treatment neither understood nor accepted by the mother.

### Family Background

Mrs. B., a white, heavy-set woman, age thirty-four, was born in an urban area, the first girl and the second oldest of four children. The economic circumstances of her home life were described as lower middle class. Her father was employed as a laborer, while her mother was a housewife who generally had the final authority. Home life was characterized by much hardship.

After dropping out of the eleventh grade, Mrs. B. worked as a sales clerk at concession stands for two years until she married her husband, a gas station attendant. She described her husband as a gentle person.

The couple moved to rural Georgia where her husband worked as a construction laborer while she handled child discipline and financial matters. Following a tragic auto accident that killed her husband and daughter, Mrs. B. lived with her parents-in-law, a period marked by great stress. When Barry was nine months old Mrs. B. moved to another city to live with her mother and a sister. She is presently supported by a monthly allotment from welfare. Confident of her authority, Mrs. B. prefers a slow pace of life with minimal aggravation. Her affection fluctuates toward Barry. The younger children were born out of wedlock.

## Developmental History

Prenatal history was marked by Mrs. B. losing 60 pounds as well as suffering from the shock of her husband's death. After a lengthy labor (17 hours), Barry was delivered at full term weighing 6 pounds, 7 ounces and was a healthy baby. He was described as an active infant who constantly cried until age two and one-half, an irritant to a mother under stress without a husband.

All developmental stages were within normal limits except for language development and toilet training, which were delayed. Daytime wetting occurred until age five and one-half while nighttime wetting continued up to eight and one-half.

Because Mrs. B. gave Barry little extra attention as an infant, she feels guilty. She indicated that her guilt may be related to her present tendency to shower him with attention, i.e. hugging, kissing, and indulgence.

When he was seven, Barry broke his toe and finger on separate occasions but refused to tell his mother both times. Social immaturity is indicated by a two and one-half year gap between chronological age (9.3 Years) and social age (6.8 Years) on a test of social maturity and suggests indulgence and infantalization of the boy rather than sheer social incompetence.

## Educational History

After attending an enjoyable public school first grade, Barry was, for obscure reasons, placed in a parochial first grade, where a sharp decline was noted in his school performance. Despite remedial reading, he continued to do poorly and had to repeat the second grade. In general, he dislikes school and refuses to talk to his mother about his school activities.

Sister Rita, the second grade teacher, indicated that Barry is doing poorly in all school subjects except math, which he enjoys. His greatest area of weakness is reading in that he does not know the letters of the alphabet and cannot recognize or spell simple first grade words. A phonics approach is used to teach reading, most likely a handicap to children deficient in the auditory perceptual channels. Poor handwriting, letter reversals, and difficulty following verbal directions were also indicated. His teacher has lowered her expectations for him since the beginning of his school year.

In terms of classroom behavior Barry reportedly is easily distracted, has a short attention span, is frequently out of his seat, talks without raising his hand, and takes things from his classmates. He is described as being afraid of making mistakes and when pressured, withdraws. On the playground he prefers playing with younger children. He is accepted by his peers but is not popular.

### Family Dynamics

Mrs. B. described Barry as a tense, immature child who is dependent upon her but confides in his grandmother. He regards his aunt, age twenty-eight, as a playmate. Sibling rivalry is indicated, as Barry hits all his siblings except his oldest brother, Lenny.

When disciplined or when demands are placed upon him he regularly pouts, whines, and engages in temper tantrums. Because he dawdles while doing chores, Mrs. B. expects less from him than the other children. Barry also has a history of sleep disturbances and on occasion has been cruel to animals. Frequently teased by his peers, he lacks close friends and gets along best with younger children.

Mrs. B. views her family role as being "the head of the house." She feels responsible for everything within her home and receives little help from the sickly mother but gets some assistance with child care from her sister, who is employed as a cleaning lady. Although Mrs. B. enjoys her responsibilities, she becomes overburdened at times and is easily irritated by her children. Mrs. B. spends little time alone with Barry.

Mrs. B. believes that Barry is generally helpless and incompetent. Rather than allow him to try a task and perhaps fail, his mother does things for him, thus keeping him at a dependent, infantile level. For example, because she does not want him to be "punished" for not doing homework that he is incapable of doing, she does it for him.

Mrs. B. also strictly supervises Barry's behavior. His independent play activities are limited to a one-block radius of home; he cannot cross intersections by himself; he is not allowed to spend the night at a friend's house, etc., even though he is nine years old. Mrs. B. frequently comes to his defense when he encounters difficulty with his peers.

### Behavioral Observations

Barry is a handsome boy who spoke in a whisper, appeared tense yet cooperative and eager to please. Offering few spontaneous remarks, he was generally unable to relax later and engage in casual conversation with the examiner. Barry appeared to be more comfortable with structured tasks. When presented with open-ended questions or asked about his feelings, he became rigid in posture and silent, withdrawing from eye contact and hanging his head. He was also reluctant to talk about his family; however, he did state that he would like his mother to pay more attention to him.

Significantly, the examiner had to repeat test instructions, as it was apparent that Barry did not understand what was expected of him, perhaps an indication of auditory difficulties. For example, when asked to identify the missing part in pictures, Barry responded by naming the picture. Easily frustrated with difficult tasks, he frequently required the encouragement of the examiner. Barry exhibited an overreaction to both success and failure. On several occasions after responding correctly he smiled and exclaimed, "I did it!" He also became noticeably upset after an obviously incorrect response.

### Test Results

*WISC-R:*

| Verbal | 84 IQ |
|---|---|
| Performance | 98 IQ |
| Full-Scale | 89 IQ |

*Stanford-Binet:*

CA 9 Yrs., 3 Mos.

MA 7 Yrs., 11 Mos.

IQ 86

*Bender-Gestalt:*

Below-normal visual-motor

perception skills (7½ yrs.)

*WRAT:*

| Reading | Grade Kg. 5 |
|---|---|
| Spelling | Grade 1.1 |
| Arithmetic | Grade 2.4 |

*Gray Paragraphs:*

Reading: Primer Level

*Vineland Social Maturity Scale:*

| Chronological Age | 9.3 |
|---|---|
| Social Age | 6.8 years |

*ITPA:*

| Auditory Reception | 8-7 Yrs. | Visual Reception | 9-3 Yrs. |
|---|---|---|---|
| Auditory Association | 6-6 Yrs. | Visual Association | 6-6 Yrs. |
| Grammatic Closure | 7-7 Yrs. | Visual Closure | 10-5 Yrs. |
| Auditory Memory | 4-10 Yrs. | Visual Memory | 10-5 Yrs. |
| Verbal Expression | 5-0 Yrs. | Manual Expression | 10-4 Yrs. |

| *Wepman Auditory Discrim. Test:* | *Projective Tests:* |
|---|---|
| Impairment in auditory | T.E.D., C.A.T. and |
| discrimination | Sentence Completion |

### Test Interpretations

Barry scored in the upper limits of the low average range of intelligence on the WISC-R and the Binet. The discrepancy between the verbal and performance scores is indicative of his perceptual problems in the auditory and language areas. Considering this and the fact that his Performance IQ score is in the average range, it is believed that he possesses average scholastic aptitude. Barry is generally better at manipulating objects than dealing with verbal concepts.

Evaluation of visual-motor perception revealed a performance a bit below normal limits for a child his age. In general, Barry demonstrated low average ability in understanding and interpreting what he sees. However, greater difficulty was revealed in the ability to discriminate words presented verbally and, in general, to understand and comprehend what he hears. Difficulty in verbal expression was also indicated. The above is suggestive of perceptual impairment in the auditory channels associated with mild cerebral dysfunction.

An informal assessment of the child's gross- and fine-motor coordination indicated poor balance, sloppy handwriting, difficulty skipping, inability to tell time, and difficulty lifting his fingers one at a time when his hand is placed on a table. His poor coordination is also indicative of mild cerebral dysfunction.

Considering his mental ability, Barry has the potential to achieve at the mid-third grade level. Barry is currently achieving from one to three years below his intellectual capacity in the three areas assessed: Reading (Grade Kg. 5 to Primer), Spelling (Grade 1.1), and Arithmetic (Grade 2.4). Chronic underachievement is indicated in reading and spelling, factors that most likely negatively affect his self-concept and behavior.

In terms of personality, Barry perceives himself as inadequate and inferior on an array of projective techniques. He feels rejected by his family, especially his mother. Although he likes being dependent and indulged, he is also angry at his mother because she is reluctant to allow him to try things on his own. He expresses at least some of this anger by displacing it onto siblings and animals. Anxiety and mild depression are evident in that Barry is tense, unhappy, and has little hope for the future.

### Diagnostic Impressions

Barry, a learning disabled child of low average to average intelligence, is presently underachieving for his intellectual capacity to a severe degree in reading and spelling. Poor coordination and defective auditory perceptual functioning suggest minimal cerebral dysfunction. Visual perception was found to be below normal. Mild emotional disturbance is indicated by anxiety, mild depression, poor self-concept, and displaced aggression.

### Workbook Exercise

Prescriptive strategies may be created by the interested student or clinician in relation to the above case of a learning disabled child. Separate listings will likely be required, as changes are needed in both the school and the home setting. The recommendations of the authors are listed for comparison purposes in the Appendix, p. 225.

### Follow-up 16 Months Later

Barry attended the recommended private day school for the learning disabled through local school and state funding. Within the multi-disciplinary setting, he received an intensive auditory perceptual training program, classroom instruction with nine other similar pupils, and an adaptive physical education program to help integrate his perceptual- and gross-motor functioning. The boy was reportedly especially delighted with the latter program. He earned extra "points" in a behavior modification arrangement for extra time in the gym, his special interest being street hockey where he was, several times, "Athlete of the Week, Younger Boys' Section." Barry, now ten, made reading and spelling gains to the early third grade level, showed significantly greater ability to concentrate, and almost extinguished his fighting. At home, the mother said that he was still a "complainer" but learned that temper tantrums led to the isolation room. Mrs. B. was frankly surprised that school reports had been so encouraging, and she has attempted ("I forget alot") to reward him for improvement. She still "criticizes" and then "forgives" him and is ambivalent about him as a person. His school has informed her that although Barry has made definite progress academically, motorically, and socially, he needs their special programs for another year or two before being "mainstreamed" to his local school.

CHAPTER VI

# GIFTEDNESS

T HE possession of high intelligence is almost always considered a virtue in our society, especially by educators and related specialists, who identify and cultivate such unique talent. Not all parents, however, feel elation or pride at the news that their son or daughter is a gifted individual, even if the parents are well informed about the possible origins and potential uses of this high ability.

## The Objecting Parent

One parent of a twelve-year-old, gifted (148 IQ) junior high girl was most disturbed when school personnel and the psychologist recommended part-time placement for her in an "accelerated class" with other gifted students. The girl was thrilled at the idea of such a placement. Although the mother was nearly euphoric at this development, the father, a truck driver of modest education, forbade his daughter's enrollment in the forthcoming gifted class.

The school psychologist talked intensively with the man about his daughter's unusual potential and the need to cultivate her rapidly developing intellect and interests. The father understood all that was said but had a distinctly different value system with which all had to contend. He believed that women were not only inferior on all dimensions but should be relegated to housework and raising babies — hardly an original set of beliefs. Further, if women were kept "in their place," i.e. subdued, they would make better wives, cause less trouble, and recognize their dependency as "part of natural law." The professionals in the case were frustrated in their attempt to dissuade his deep beliefs; likely these were defenses against his own sense of inferiority: he was impervious to reason. Furthermore, he really wanted "peace and quiet," since his wife had

186

learned long ago that he could not tolerate "nagging."

Thus informed, the school psychologist met with the brilliant girl in June and explained all that had happened in not receiving her father's permission to enroll her in the gifted program.

She was extremely disappointed and angry. How dare her father deny her a privilege that she had earned, she retorted. She would not be in the advanced classes with most of her friends, and she would miss out on the learning of her favorite subjects, such as space exploration and astronomy, including visits to a local astronomy club for telescopic views of planets, etc. Wasn't there any way she could get into the advanced group?, she questioned.

The school psychologist devised a plan to which this most talented girl gleefully agreed. She was to "nag" her father all summer long about permission to enroll in the gifted classes, feign depression, complain loudly, ask many difficult questions, yet not provoke him into an angry rage. The particular strategies for accomplishing this were left to her imagination, as she knew her father extremely well, loved him for his kindnesses, and felt sorry that he could not "see the big picture" of female rights and the uniqueness of her individual abilities. No contact was made with the girl during the summer.

However, three days before school began, the administrator in charge of the gifted program received an urgent telephone call from the father. He said, "I've had to listen to my girl bellyache all summer about this gifted program that you folks feel is so wonderful. I can't take it no more; she wore me out with a hundred questions about space shots. And you know, I think that she really is different. Put her in the gifted classes so I can have some peace and quiet."

### The Responsive Parent

One case will be presented here that reveals the constructive reaction of parents, although dynamic elements are always involved in their individual dispositions.

The selection criteria of the gifted vary between states, counties, and school districts depending on federal and state laws operative at the moment, the vision of local school boards, the funding available, and often the leadership within administrative ranks. In general, since about 1 or 2 percent of the population could be expected to score in a gifted range, a frequent cut point to make the group truly "elite" and special is a minimum of 130 IQ on an individual intelligence test. Occasionally to allow for a Standard Error of Measurement, some school districts will accept a 125 IQ as an absolute minimum. Supplemental criteria often involve teacher rating, high percentile scores in group achievement tests, high GPA, etc.

Other programs have considered two levels of gifted children, the higher level being those over a 150 IQ, unique for the incredibly bright children who seem to exist almost everywhere. One of the authors has examined at least six children over 160 IQ on the Binet.

It is the contention of the present authors that early identification and special training of the gifted are essential and, in fact, undeniable once the children make themselves known with or without testing. They almost force adults to teach them. The culture should adapt to the talents as well as the handicaps of its youth in an even-handed way. Too many gifted youth (Goertzel & Goertzel, 1962) have not been recognized as unique at a young age and were rejected or penalized in various ways by parents, teachers, and society generally. Of course, others were recognized early and stimulated profitably. Indeed, repression of intelligence is frequently one of the defense mechanisms of many brilliant children with the presumption on our part that this created, if not maladjustment per se, at least temporary discomfort during the school years of the child.

A clear acceptance of the child's intelligence is revealed in some detail in the case reported below. It is equally as important to recognize how the child and parents adapt to or use the intelligence as it is to recognize the fact of intelligence itself. The initial identification of the gifted is one of the more pleasant tasks of a school psychologist, since it involves in most cases the giving of "good news." However, the one exception occurs when a parent fervently expects a "gifted" score on the IQ test and the child does not earn it. The parent may become quite irate at the psychologist and blame him or her personally for the child's inability to solve very complicated test items. Fortunately, most parents are quite reasonable.

The following case with the gifted deals with Jeff J., who was followed up for two years after his initial evaluation by a school psychologist. The verification of brilliance produced a major educational and social change and perhaps effected a special life-style of one child with accepting parents.

Name: Jeff J.    Age:   10 Years, 6 Months    Grade:   Sixth

## Tests Used

Stanford-Binet, L-M, Gray Oral Reading Paragraphs, Thematic Apperception Test, Sentence Completion Test, Clinical Interviews, and Parent Conferences.

## Test Results

*Binet*                          *Gray Reading Paragraphs*

166 IQ                           Reading Level:   College (13)

The parents of Jeff requested that the psychologist evaluate him, as problems had arisen recently involving a declining interest in academic work, as well as a concern whether he was a "well-adjusted" youngster and one of such high intelligence as to require special education planning. Jeff had also been involved in minor pranks around the public school recently in conjunction with other boys, i.e. changing the order of library books, staying away from school after recess was over, making believe that he comprehended nothing in class, etc.

The mother was seen prior to psychological evaluation of the boy and offered information regarding his background. She was concerned whether Jeff was sufficiently "extraverted" to be "normal" and wondered whether his three or four hours of reading per day were excessive to the exclusion of social and athletic activities. The obtained developmental history was positively remarkable in the sense that it revealed rapid development of vocabulary, i.e. sentences at twelve months, reading at three years, and very advanced conceptual abilities. Jeff was perceived by her as a boy who was "very amenable to reason." In addition, his motor development was considered somewhat above average, and he was physically healthy.

### Educational History

On previous group intelligence tests, Jeff had always scored in the upper 1 percent of the norm group and was considered to be an extremely intelligent child. Even before he entered school the parents found him reading quite fluently. During the first grade he would frequently glance through the newspaper headlines and magazines and discuss his interest in events. The mother indicated that the boy had "forced" them to teach him to read because he constantly came to them asking for interpretations of words and letter combinations and the meanings behind the words themselves. He excelled at Scrabble® and difficult crossword puzzles by the fourth grade. His work was so outstanding in the first grade that a perceptive teacher recommended his acceleration to the third grade the following year. The parents and administrator agreed to this recommendation. This is, of course, the reason why he is about a year younger than his current classmates.

Jeff had always done exceptionally well on achievement tests by scoring in the 98th or 99th percentiles in all areas. For the first few years of school most of his work had been at the *A* level, but in recent months some homework and class assignments had not been handed in punctually, and he has developed a careless attitude toward his sixth grade studies. Apparently, mischievous behavior was replacing conscientious attitudes toward learning. The investigating psychologist began to wonder if the boy was learning anything new in school at all.

### Family Background

The father, Mr. J., appeared for a conference and seemed to

be a competent, managerial-level computer specialist. He currently works for (a major company), having been a graduate student majoring in mathematics and computer sciences. About six years ago he was stationed with his family in India as a company consultant to that government.

The mother is also a college graduate having majored in the social sciences at (an Ivy League university) but never really pursued her own career. Part of this reason is that they have four sons of whom Jeff is the oldest. This family has lived in an upper-middle-class suburban community for the past six years, generally encompassing Jeff's educational career.

The parents' general reputation is one of wholesomeness, genuine concern for their children, and excellence in participation in community affairs. The younger brothers do not present special academic or social problems in school. According to the parents, these younger boys, although above average students, are "different" from Jeff in that they appear to have "more normal interests" in sports and a great variety of friends.

Jeff has been somewhat of a "loner" and preoccupied with reading matter at very high levels. Presently Jeff has been seen at home to be a procrastinator in his chores and school responsibilities. He has been known, according to the mother, to read books pulled out of various hiding places during his assigned time for work. The mother has wondered if she is competent enough to raise such a child. Her call for guidance and support was undeniable. The father, in contrast, suggested that his wife has become overanxious about "small problems," and she admitted this tendency. Neither parent would elaborate on this point in spite of several general inquiries by the psychologist. They kept their attention instead on Jeff's educational future.

At the end of the interview Mr. J. informed the psychologist that Jeff had received special attention from a private psychologist when Jeff was in kindergarten. For our records, a copy of the psychological report was obtained, which indicated a resulting 157 IQ on the Stanford-Binet. At that time a recommendation was made that the boy should enter a class for gifted children. For various reasons the plan did not seem feasible for the parents at that time, i.e. no local schools had such facilities then, the parents did not wish special recognition to come too early for the boy, and a relative had suggested that they not "exploit" Jeff.

### Tests and Clinical Interpretations

Initial contact was held with Jeff, age ten and one-half, to establish rapport. He seemed somewhat tense and uncomfortable when asked personal questions. He volunteered information, however, rather freely regarding his activities at home, which included three or four hours reading per day, approximately two to three books completed per week, and the absorption of most of the newspapers and two or three periodical magazines, including *National Geographic* and *Time*.

Jeff spoke in a quiet voice but indicated immediately his exceptional intelligence and his ability to quickly see verbal relationships. He recognized fully that his homework was not adequate and felt, "I'm in trouble with both my teacher and my Mother" because of this tendency. He admitted freely that he was negligent about his chores but merely waits "until my Mother forgets her threats; she usually does." This and similar comments spotted throughout the interview indicated a low level of follow-through on and control of Jeff by the mother. This permissiveness has left him with no particular obligations to live up to. Much of this was verified by discussion with his parents. Jeff smiled tolerantly at the psychologist and assured him that, "I knew the free ride would be over some day and I see you're the one to terminate my frivolities. It was childish and I'm about to get to work anyway." His perceptions were very accurate.

This boy is extremely enthusiastic about the written word. Upon request he read, in addition to the formal testing, a psychology textbook with fluency and then demonstrated his comprehension of the material through inquiry. In terms of his recreation, he prefers to read by himself but occasionally gets tired of this and joins his playmates for outdoor sports such as "playing cowboys" and riding bikes but admitted getting "a little disappointed" at the level of thinking of his comrades, whom he finds somewhat immature. He suggested the games were too simple and not sufficiently imaginative to keep him captivated. He also seemed disappointed at the *World Book Encyclopedia* at home and hoped that a more adult level reference would be purchased by his parents. He very much enjoyed the cultural opportunities offered by his parents when visiting the city to attend its science and natural history museums. In this semirural community, Jeff has not had a great deal of opportunity to receive intellectual stimulation.

In terms of his parental relationships, Jeff seems to have a balanced view. He feels keen affection for his parents and his younger brothers but is not overtly demonstrative. He felt that disciplinary procedures when used were "quite fair" even though he believed that he was not affected by them very much. In listening to his perception of his parents they seemed like very normal, adequate, and sensible people who may need to take a bit more control of the boy and help redirect his educational program. In all major respects he is quite a normal boy with no unusual problems worthy of clinical attention. Although capable of independent judgment, he does have minor difficulty handling face-to-face relationships with adults. His reasoning is lucid, and he gave many indications of being a truly remarkable boy who is capable of outstanding academic and perhaps professional work. Although somewhat withdrawn, he has strong interests that compensate for social deficiencies. He has not found any children with similar intellectual abilities even in this upper-middle-class community.

### Discussion of Results

The most significant observation through formal intelligence testing relates to the IQ score of 166. Apparently this is a reaffirmation of the previous testing, although higher. A simple descriptive statement of his performance on the present intelligence test is that it was brilliant. Although the boy is only ten and one-half years old, he successfully passed all the items typical of a fourteen-year-old child, missed one item at the average adult level, missed only two items at the superior one adult level, and made successful passings at the last two levels. He mentioned casually after we were done, "I've spent more time thinking during this test than I've done the whole past semester in school." Jeff was delighted with the difficulties encountered in the test.

On the surface the inquiries revealed that Jeff had no genuine difficulties in school, stated that he felt everything was "going along well," and that the curriculum was "adequate." However, in the projective materials contradictions were revealed where he referred to boys who were "bored," who found school material "dull and uninteresting" and not a "real challenge." Conceivably the "pranks" around the school have arisen out of his desire for excitement to relieve monotony. His aspirations at the present time include going to college and eventually becoming an aeronautical engineer.

### Diagnostic Summary

Jeff appears to have a normal personality structure, although he is somewhat withdrawn socially but is compensated well by strong interests in reading, play activities, science interests, and a desire to seek intellectually challenging tasks (chess, mathematical puzzles). The lenient parents have not exerted controls necessary for any ten-year-old boy to meet his obligations. It seems that they have been somewhat fearful about "inhibiting" his intelligence and potentially creative talents. The case was reviewed with the superintendent and the boy's present teachers. The recommendations noted below were found to be acceptable to all concerned in the school.

Both parents were given a lengthy feedback interview. They were quite fascinated with the findings and willing to give serious considerations to the recommendations proposed. The mother seemed to grasp with more certainty the role that she might play with the boy, and the father was requested to offer more involvement in occupational and mathematical activities with his son.

## Recommendations

1. It is recommended that Jeff be placed in a preparatory school or a public school program catering to gifted children. A book about such private facilities, and the expenses of these schools, is being obtained and will be reviewed carefully with the parents. They are most willing to consider this information and will review their finances and the other personal variables in this decision. We feel that the mother was enthusiastic about this recommendation; although Mr. J. showed initial reservations, he became more interested as we developed the full implications of the boy's need for a strenuous educational program so that he might be in full flight intellectually for his adult life. We suggested further that beyond the boy's intellectual needs he also required social experiences to learn leadership skills, self-confidence, and a sense of responsibility. We recommended that Jeff not be placed in a military school, the latter being vehemently ruled out by the boy himself, although the psychologist never considered this as any possibility. The boy's own reaction to a private preparatory school for accelerated students was very positive. The psychologist and boy discussed it in considerable detail after the parents were found to be responsive.

2. In the meantime, as the parents planned for the fall term elsewhere, the teachers, superintendent, and psychologist planned to meet to devise a special curriculum in major academic areas for Jeff. This may take the form of high level reading, summarizing, reporting on current events, space projects, art, drama, history, and perhaps creative projects of his own construction. There are endless variations to such a curriculum, which may meet this boy's needs and the needs of similar students in local schools.

3. If the boy does not attend a special class or preparatory school elsewhere, then the school personnel must continue to revise his public school curriculum frequently and must give special attention to his enrollment in the "honors program" in the local high school. The administra-

tors of three adjacent school districts are already discussing the need to develop a tridistrict "gifted program" for such exceptional pupils.

4. Highly specific home recommendations were made to the parents in regard to Jeff's discipline and the stimulation that he needs culturally. They were to deal with Jeff at an intellectual level of at least a middle-teenager although to recognize that his emotional maturity is that of about a typical eleven-year-old.

### Additional Information (5 Months Later)

After considerable investigation by the parents, they enrolled Jeff the following September into a prestigious preparatory school, an excellent facility catering to talented boys and preparing them for college and professional life. The demands for intellectual excellence were very high, yet the social and athletic programs were also emphasized.

### Follow-up Information (2 Years Later)

The Headmaster of the school sent a letter to the psychologist thanking him for originally recommending his school to the parents of Jeff J. He reported factually that Jeff had achieved "in the most outstanding manner in practically all academic areas, having highest honors in science and foreign language." He noted further that the faculty had nothing but praise for Jeff's conscientious efforts and performance. The Headmaster also said, "Jeff is the best organized child I have ever seen in my long tenure at ——— School as a teacher and Headmaster. I'm also happy to tell you that Jeff and another equally talented boy soon became good friends, selected each other as roommates, and succeeded in capturing most of the academic prizes for their levels. Both are now vigorously athletic and are potentially first-rate young scholars."

CHAPTER VII

# SENSORY IMPAIRMENT AND MULTIPLE HANDICAP

## HEARING IMPAIRMENT

Name: Sandra S.  Age: Six Years, One Month  Grade: Kindergarten

$S$ANDRA has a moderately severe, sensori-neural hearing loss; her speech and language production and verbal comprehension are below expectancy levels. She was fitted with a hearing aid three months after an audiological evaluation was conducted at a local university audiology department. Currently, a psychological evaluation was requested by the school principal and speech therapist to assess Sandy's intellectual and perceptual levels so as to provide the regular classroom teacher with recommendations for enhancing Sandy's communication skills and learning.

### Family Background

Sandy lives with her mother, father, a sister who is nine, and a brother who is eight. Both of her siblings attend a local parochial school, while she is enrolled in a public school.

Both parents are high school graduates. Mr. S. is a sales representative of a shirt company, whereas Mrs. S. has never been employed, having been married right after her graduation.

### Developmental History

When Sandy was born Mrs. S. was twenty-three and her husband was twenty-eight years old. The mother reported no difficulties during pregnancy or birth. Sandy was described as a "quiet" baby, since there were no sleeping or eating problems.

Sandy sat up by herself at four months; she crawled at six months and walked at fourteen months. Toilet training was initiated when she was twenty-four months, and it was completed in one week, all of which are indications of normal development.

During Sandy's first year, she spoke single words such as *mama* and *dada*. Although the number of objects she could name increased somewhat, she still spoke single words at age three. Because of her lack of progress with language, the parents took Sandy to their family doctor for an examination. He reportedly said that there were no auditory defects and that she was in excellent health.

However, her language development since the age of one had not progressed further than the use of single words. The parents, upon being interviewed by the psychologist, revealed that they were "not alarmed" because their family doctor had remarked that Sandy was probably a "late starter" and gave "no evidence" of a hearing deficit, although a hearing test was not performed.

Mrs. S. recalled that Sandy did not respond to the doorbell or to the telephone ringing. At times she would sit and watch movement on television with the volume off. This behavior finally alerted the parents enough to consult a hearing specialist just before Sandy began to attend kindergarten.

The mother described Sandy as a "happy child," for even now she rarely cries or whines. She is generally quiet, sometimes passive, and very patient; she will sit quietly and wait for a desired item. She smiles or claps her hands when she is happy and if something is amusing, she laughs out loud normally. Sandy attends to loud noises, especially since the fitting of the hearing aid two months ago.

### Health History

Mrs. S. described her younger daughter as being unusually healthy. With the exception of having the common cold approximately once or twice per year, Sandy has never been ill. She has had none of the common childhood diseases and nothing to account for her auditory problems via heredity or infection.

In October, the school's hearing therapist confirmed the results of the original audiological examination. Sandy's hearing loss for both ears was again reported to be between 50 and 80 db (while the normal range for hearing is between 0 and 20 db). The delay on the part of the parents in getting her a hearing aid resulted because of their "shock and disbelief" over the fact that their physician had made an error in judgment, and perhaps also because they wished to believe that she was truly normal. They now feel that the hearing loss was obvious from the start and are still angry with the physician for his misdiagnosis.

### *Hearing Information*

The audiometric report indicated that Sandra's hearing loss varied with the frequency, in that she has a severe loss of 80 db in the high frequencies and perhaps only a 40 to 50 db loss in the lower (speech) frequencies, essentially a sloping loss. The losses as measured by testing through air conduction and bone conduction were similar. With the hearing aid on, she now hears most speech sounds but likely with distortion in the high frequency sounds: *s, z, sh, ch.* Sandra's voice quality is quite hyponasal, typical of children manifesting this type of hearing loss. (The speech pathologist's report describing her articulation and language skills was in her cumulative folder.)

### *Educational History*

Because of Sandy's apparent deficiency in language development, Mrs. S. did not send her to kindergarten until one year later than usual. Thus Sandy was six years old in December though most of her classmates were still five.

Sandy's kindergarten teacher reported that her readiness and academic functioning are quite low. She has not yet learned the names of the letters, numbers, or colors. Her ability to copy letters and numbers is also below average. She has difficulty following verbal directions or comprehending a story read to her, all very understandable in view of her diagnosed hearing loss and lack of opportunity to learn language.

Sandy functions in the kindergarten by imitating her classmates after observing their actions carefully. She is very much aware of the activities and immediately copies the group's behavior, but she is able to comprehend key words such as *yes, no, book, paper,* and so on. When spoken to, Sandy intently watches the face of the speaker for visual cues; she is able to lipread most efficiently to the surprise of all who work with her, since she has just begun formal training in lipreading on a weekly basis.

During the first month in kindergarten, Sandy did not speak unless it was absolutely necessary. After that, her spontaneous speech increased greatly. Yet at times it is difficult to understand her; however, when her articulation is corrected, she is able to repeat correctly. Sandy has been receiving speech therapy since September, and her therapist confirms the tremendous improvement in the quality of her articulations.

Mrs. S. reported that she believes Sandy is "very bright" because she is able to "catch on" to things very quickly. She can imitate activities and verbalizations quite accurately during the first or second attempt.

### Social History

Mrs. S. described the relationships between Sandy and her brother and sister as very close. Both siblings enjoy her company, and they spend an appreciable amount of time with her. Her sister enjoys "playing school" with her, while her brother is constantly showing her how to play simple games. Quite often Sandy plays with the neighborhood children and seems to be accepted by them. The mother reported that Sandy shares candy and toys with her friends. Sandy grew up with a neighborhood girl, Adele, a five-year-old. The two girls are inseparable both in the community and in the same kindergarten class. During the school day, Adele takes care of Sandy by helping her with activities and school tasks. During recess, Sandy always follows Adele and imitates her activities. In fact, Sandy is unnecessarily dependent upon her best friend, but this has generally worked for her advantage in school.

### Family Dynamics

Sandy's role in the family is "the baby," and consequently, she receives a great deal of attention. Her brother and sister "watch over her," and both parents tend to spend a great deal of time with her as well as overprotect her. Because she is the youngest, as well as being hearing impaired, her mother has been reluctant to encourage independent behavior, such as completely dressing herself or taking a bath unassisted, although the mother reported that Sandy is quite able to perform these activities by herself when a baby-sitter stays at home.

Every day after supper, Mrs. S. helps her two older children with their homework. During this time, Mr. S. plays with Sandy. The family often engages in activities together such as visiting friends, going to the park or a picnic, or to the zoo; apparently they are closely knit people who care for one another. The parents hope that all three of their children will attend college. However, this expectation is "mandatory" only for their son, who reportedly is an honor student in school although only eight years old.

### Previous Psychological Examination

In September, a psychologist at the local university evaluated Sandy by administering the Hiskey-Nebraska Test of Learning Aptitude, a test designed for the hearing-impaired child. She scored an IQ of 87, which places her within the low average range of intelligence. However, he believed this IQ to be misleading, since her visual retention and recognition were normal to superior, and the poorer scores centered around the culturally oriented areas. He noted further that she required frequent repetition of instructions when he gave some verbal subtests of the Binet to check her comprehension.

Sandy's strongest skills were visual attention span and the

ability to remember visual stimuli; her scores were on the eight-year-old level. Her visual-motor skills and her ability to discriminate the differences between visual stimuli were on the five- to six-year level. Motor coordination and the utilization of spatial relationships were on the five-year level. Sandy's poorest scores were on those tasks that required her to relate to concepts presented visually. In summary, Sandy could utilize her visual memory, concentration, and attention quite well, but only in a rote manner. Her comprehension of what was seen was quite poor and at the early four-year-old level.

### Observation and Behavior

Sandy is a very attractive, brown-haired, thin girl who seemed to be happy and content. She was quiet, but not passive, and actively participated in class. Her interaction with her classmates was by using single words such as *wait, gimmie, yes,* and *no.* She functioned in the classroom by imitating the other children; however, during a "free play" period, she went by herself to get a puzzle.

Sandy went willingly with the examiner to the testing room. The extra attention of the one-to-one situation seemed to please her; her level of cooperation and effort were excellent. She tried very hard on all the tasks no matter what the level of difficulty.

Her perception of visual cues was quite good. While attempting a certain task, she watched the examiner's face for any cues as to whether or not her performance was correct.

During the first two brief testing sessions, Sandy did not speak spontaneously; however, during the last two sessions, she attempted to talk a great deal. For example, after seeing a picture of an object, she tried to relate that they had one at home by saying "Me . . . at home" while pointing to the picture.

### Test Results

*Wechsler Preschool and Primary Scale of Intelligence* (WPPSI):

Performance IQ:  86

*Bender-Gestalt:*

Visual-Motor Functioning:   7-year Level

*Illinois Test of Psycholinguistic Abilities* (ITPA):

| | | |
|---|---|---|
| Visual Reception: | 7 Years | 1 Month |
| Visual Association: | 5 " | 9 " |
| Visual Sequential Memory: | 3 " | 7 " |
| Auditory Sequential Memory: | 2 " | 7 " |
| Visual Closure: | 4 " | 6 " |

*Vineland Social Maturity Scale:*

Social Quotient:   98 (not an IQ)

Age Equivalency: 6 Years, 0 Months

On the performance subtests of the WPPSI, Sandy scored within the low average category. It is impossible at this time to determine if this is a valid and stable indication of Sandy's ability because her comprehension of verbal instructions is presently comparable to a four and one-half-year-old child. However, this is an indication of her present level of functioning and confirms the 87 IQ obtained on the Hiskey-Nebraska Test, clearly indicating no mental retardation.

Similar to a two-year-old, Sandy knows many nouns but few verbs. She does not yet have word concepts such as *same, opposite, smaller, biggest, absent, present, slow,* or *fast*. She can identify objects by name, but she does not know their functional value; for example, she can identify a "stove," but she cannot respond to "tell me what we cook on." Sandy comprehends a great deal more from visual symbols than she can demonstrate by the use of language. Her visual comprehension is on the early seven-year level, one year above her chronological age. She is able to relate concepts from visual information on a level comparable to her age as long as she is not required to verbalize the concepts. For example, she is able to associate an object such as a bat with an appropriate object, a ball.

Her ability to utilize her memory of visual stimuli is low. She has a good visual attention span; however, her ability to recall what she has seen is on the 3 Year, 7 Month level. If incomplete visual stimuli are presented, she has difficulty identifying the objects (4 1/2-year level). Her ability to reproduce sequences of verbal stimuli is her poorest skill. Here she scored on the two and one-half-year level.

The Vineland Social Maturity Scale, a measure of social competence, was administered to Mrs. S. Sandy earned a social quotient of 98, the age equivalency of 6 Years, 0 Months. This indicates that her ability to socialize with others and to do things independently, such as eating and dressing, are up to her age level, in spite of overprotection.

### Diagnostic Summary

Sandy is a six-year-old, hearing-impaired child whose academic functioning is categorized as below average for her age, intelligence, and grade level. However, she has very recently received a hearing aid and has since revealed a marked improvement in the amount and quality of her speech productions. Her low average intellectual functioning may be a low estimate of her eventual learning potential. Sandy relies much too heavily on visual cues in attaining information, to the significant exclusion of auditory cues so necessary for survival in school. Her comprehension of verbal stimuli and her ability to articulate correctly for communication are her poorest skills, as noted by the teacher, psychologist, and therapist.

She is a friendly, cheerful girl who is highly cooperative and whose level of effort to perform well is excellent. Sandy is dependent on visual cues from others; she is overly dependent upon Adele, a classmate and best friend.

### Recommendations

OVERVIEW: It is first recommended that she remain in a regular kindergarten class rather than be placed in a hearing-impaired class; speech and language services should be continued indefinitely.

The primary goal in helping Sandy to function better at home and at school is to increase her ability to learn through the sense of hearing and to decrease her dependence on visual cues. All speech behavior should be rewarded, and nonverbal communications should be totally ignored except for emergencies. At every possible moment, Sandy should be given the opportunity to verbalize. Attempts to communicate to her by gestures should be avoided. The focus should be on making Sandy rely more on the auditory modality. This is absolutely imperative.

*School Recommendations for Teachers and/or Speech and Hearing Therapists*

1. Capitalize upon her assets. Notice what she does well and praise her verbally. Avoid using gestures as substitutes for words.
2. Encourage classroom participation. Do not allow Sandy to "hang back" from the group. Continue to provide her with classroom responsibilities such as "teacher's helper" or wiping tables; however, give her assistance in getting her to perform adequately rather than have another child perform the job after she first attempts it.
3. Avoid exaggerated mouth movements when speaking to her and avoid raising voice volume. Face her while speaking.
4. Whenever possible, separate Adele and Sandy. Encourage Sandy to function independently and also with an array of children. Encourage them not to anticipate or interpret her needs; ask them not to "baby" her by doing her work.

5. Have her listen to music, help her keep time, encourage her to sing and hum to the music as a way of increasing her interest in the world of sound.

6. Have her memorize a song or poem and, after private practice, ask her to sing or recite in class. Such experiences may desensitize her eventually to speaking before groups of children and speaking up in the classroom.

7. To aid her in developing more auditory comprehension, have her respond to verbal directions. Keep the directions simple and brief. The "Simon Says" game is excellent for this, provided that no physical movements are used and only verbal instructions are used.

8. Repeat sounds in isolation or attach sounds to meaningful situations such as imitation of a fire engine after showing a picture of a fire engine to enhance vocal imitation.

9. Furnish sound effects for a story of various objects and animals to enrich her auditory associations when using visual cues.

10. Encourage her to use her voice in any manner of which she is capable. Provide her with as much language experience as possible.

11. Have her communicate with other children. During play period, have her talk to another child by the use of a toy telephone or puppets.

12. Provide her with opportunities to offer word labels (nouns and descriptive adjectives) to objects in the classroom. Since she is deficient in a rich vocabulary, Sandy must be taught the different qualities and characteristics of objects and pictures, which most kindergarten children already know. In this respect she is a child who needs to learn the English language, as she is uninformed about many vocabulary words.

13. Sandy also needs practice in classifying objects and qualities: colors, fruit, clothing, alike and different, large and small, soft and loud, etc. Trays containing small objects, toys, or perhaps pictures from commercial language kits could be offered to Sandy. She could be required to call

out names and several qualities of each item, a few added weekly.

14. Even with the hearing aid, she will have to be trained to improve her auditory perceptual and discrimination skills, her comprehension of language, and her verbal production in terms of quantity and quality. In the classroom she will have to be trained to understand and utilize words, since the new sounds per se are relatively meaningless.

15. Call on Sandy to recite when it is certain she knows and is able to articulate the answer. This may give her greater confidence in recitation.

16. When she verbalizes and simultanteously uses hand movements, hold her hands and tell her to repeat what she said. Help her with both correct word usage and with articulation of phonemes.

17. Teach her to complete sentences. "This is ———." Point to an object and have her name and describe it so that she will actively be involved with retrieving newly learned vocabulary.

18. Play games such as "I'm packing my trunk and I put in a ———." Add more items one by one. Have her repeat the sequence to enhance auditory memory.

19. Do not accept nonverbal communication. Make her ask for what she wants.

Many of the above activities can be done in the regular classroom involving the entire group. The same activities can be used by the speech therapist in a one-to-one situation. The individual help that Sandy has been receiving should be, naturally, continued.

Because Sandy needs extra training and more stimulation in the auditory realm, it is highly recommended for her to attend, if possible, the additional afternoon kindergarten session with another teacher in the same school. Sandy is six years old and physically strong enough to attend school for a complete day. By attending the afternoon session, she will not only receive more experiences, verbal and otherwise, but it will also create more independence from Adele, her best friend.

Perhaps under these conditions, Sandy will be ready to enter the first grade next September. A year in kindergarten, perhaps in double session, should help improve her language skills; however, this decision may best be made in June or September by her teachers, the assisting speech therapist, and her parents. If she is not ready, placing her in the first grade where more emphasis is on verbal stimuli will only increase her frustration of not understanding what is expected of her and perhaps provide her with an opportunity of experiencing constant failure. This certainly would injure her good cooperation and effort levels. If such lack of readiness prevails, our alternative will be to place her in a special class for the hearing impaired on a daily, part-time basis with "mainstreaming" in nonacademic subjects, e.g. gym, art, recess.

*Recommendations to Parents*

1. All the recommendations (noted above) for the teacher will be duplicated for and explained to the parents so that they will learn of the school's contributions.
2. Encourage Sandy to verbalize at any time. Reward her attempts to speak. Help her use correct vocabulary and pronunciation.
3. Ignore nonverbal communications. Avoid anticipating her needs; make her ask for what she wants.
4. Speak to her in normal tones without exaggerated lip movements or without raising voice volume.
5. Avoid communicating to Sandy by hand gestures.
6. Help her label objects around the house.
7. Encourage her to answer the doorbell, answer the telephone, and retell the stories or actions she views on television.
8. Read bedtime stories to her.
9. Help train the two older children to communicate to Sandy by words and not by gestures.
10. The primary principle is to encourage Sandy to verbalize and to understand the verbalizations of others and to avoid communication that is nonverbal.

## Follow-Up Information (11 Months Later)

Sandy progressed considerably in the double kindergarten program during the following months in both verbal expressive and receptive skills through the intensive program offered by school personnel. To help guarantee that she would not regress in communication skills during the following summer, Sandy was continued in speech and language training privately. Her parents and older siblings tried very hard to foster her verbal communication as well as her independence, and although Sandy initially resented her loss of support of having others solve her problems or anticipate her needs, she soon found success in using words to gain her ends. By mutual agreement of the professionals and parents, Sandy was permitted to attend a regular first grade the next September. By the middle of that term she was becoming even more sociable and talkative and learning "at an average rate" according to her teacher. No special education class was planned for Sandy unless further problems develop.

### BLIND, DEAF, CRIPPLED, AND RETARDED

Hunched over in his mother's lap, squinting, retarded, and speechless, feeble and extremely spastic, Freddie F. was a black, multiply-handicapped child with a devastating medical background. The intervention amounted to near zero, as no kind of habilitation, medical or educational, had ever begun. Freddie, age eight, smiled at his mother as she stroked his face while the psychologist interviewed her at a residential rehabilitation home during a screening interview.

"No, he ain't ever been to school 'cause he can't see or hear. A tutor came out once but left in ten minutes." This was the response of Freddie's mother when asked about how the local schools had met their legal obligations to teach him and place him in a class with similar handicapped children.

> A school psychologist saw him once at home, asked me lotsa questions and said he be back, but he neva come back. No, I

been in the same house fo' fifteen years and they knew where we was. Yes, I called the psychologist and the school four or five time, but nobody ever helps me wid Freddie. Once some doctor said to "put him away," but the boy is so easy to take care of and so sweet that I just feel he oughta stay wid me. Now, maybe he oughta come to folks like you for de help that he needs.

Crying, she kissed his cheek, and he smiled feebly again.

The psychologist, in conjunction with other professional staff, had virtually no medical or social records to review; however, Freddie was immediately accepted for early admission. The boy was to receive an intensive multi-therapy program in every department available to him. Funding, estimated to be $14,000 per year, was arranged by the Department of Public Welfare and the local city schools.

Within three weeks of the parent interview, Freddie arrived at the residential home to begin the training program of physical therapy, speech and hearing therapy, occupational therapy, medical treatment, and psychological evaluation plus education. The psychologist's work was relatively minor compared to the efforts in the medical and physical therapy departments. However, as coordinator of the departmental team meetings, the psychologist was instrumental in holding the focus of the child's total rehabilitation. By democratic processes, the team members during the first meeting on Freddie assessed his needs and developed appropriate programs.

For example, after several opthalmological evaluations, it was determined that he was partially sighted, much to his mother's surprise, but with the proper refraction he was then corrected to 20/40 vision, enabling him to see for practically the first time in his life. Simultaneously, an audiology department at a nearby university discovered that Freddie had an 80 decibel sensorineural loss in both ears and recommended that he be equipped with a powerful hearing aid to permit the reception of sounds. It was evident, however, that at age eight he would undoubtedly have great difficulty in perceiving and utilizing the sounds that he heard. Yet even loud noises are useful information to a hearing-impaired person. On this basis, the local school district sent a dedicated hearing specialist three times weekly to the residential home to teach Freddie during the school day about his new hearing device and how to use sound constructively. Now that he had glasses it was thought that he might be taught some sign language, but since he was so incredibly stiff because of the spastic condition in all limbs, he was unable to communicate more than a few signs with his hands and fingers. Furthermore, finger spelling was out of the question because the boy was totally uneducated and had not the faintest concept of the alphabet.

Upon subsequent visits, the mother seemed more and more delighted with the progress the boy had made, especially after six months of physical therapy when he began his first shuffling gait with crutches. The special educational program, operated in the residential school by the local school district, was mainly a visual experience for him because he had not yet learned how to use sound effectively, although he did seem to follow the teachers' and children's activities. He apparently needed no special training to use his eyes constructively. He began to imitate the children's drawings of geometric designs, numbers, and letters even though these were conceptually meaningless to him at first.

Throughout all of this activity, Freddie maintained an unbelievably pleasant disposition and was affectionate to all who cared for him. He was indefatigable in physical therapy, working very hard at the parallel bars, swimming gently in a heated pool, and adapting to the many muscle-relaxing techniques prescribed for him in physical therapy. The orthopedic surgeon operated twice on Freddie to minimize muscular problems.

After two years of the multi-therapy efforts, Freddie was able to walk with Canadian canes slowly but steadily. He also became so accustomed to his powerful eyeglasses that he could recognize people at a distance of 50 feet. Hearing, however, remained a special problem, although he was able to produce about four or five sounds, his own name, his age when requested, etc. Other crippled children sought to help this popular and smiling boy by encouraging him when he walked and tried to play their games.

Another six months later, through the combined efforts of the staff, application was made for Freddie to attend, on a daily basis, a "total communication" program about 8 miles away in a well-known residential facility catering to retarded children. Previous to this request, the psychologist had administered a series of intelligence tests with the following results: Leiter International Performance Scale — 47 IQ; Columbia Mental Maturity Test — 52 IQ; the Vineland Social Maturity Scale resulted in a social quotient of 45, in view of his many handicaps, with a social age approximately five years.

The administrators and teachers of the total communication school evaluated written reports sent by the psychologist and various department heads testifying to the boy's ability to profit from all varieties of training. The residential staff still believed him to be a moderately retarded child and so informed the school personnel. Further otological evaluations convinced everyone that Freddie was now capable of hearing more words but that he still needed a total communication program involving finger spelling, signing, possible lipreading, and verbal expression as well as the more adept use of receptive language. As hoped, the total communication program personnel accepted the boy and have trained him on a daily basis for the past year.

Psychological counseling, of course, has never been available to Freddie because he cannot comprehend beyond the most simple words and, frankly, because he also presents no emotional problems in terms of social adjustment, motivation, or behavior.

This case is considered to be most successful by the staff of the residential home. The psychologist played only a small part as a team member by aiding in diagnostic testing and helping to direct the boy's educational experiences at certain critical points. Currently Freddie remains a happy child who can now see, hear, speak slightly, and walk beyond those capabilities ever believed possible by his mother.

# APPENDIX

APPENDIX

# WORKBOOK EXERCISES

### Section 1: Prescriptive Interventions

### *I. School phobia: The Case of Kathy K. (from page 76)*

A. Recommendations for School Personnel
  1. With parental and administrative permission already granted:
     a. Permit the girl to telephone home when she is anxious and when she needs to be reassured of the mother's welfare.
     b. Allow her to eat lunches at home four days a week, gradually increasing number of lunches per week in school. She will be transported by the mother by car during this desensitization period.
  2. The psychologist will speak to the counselor and teachers to explain this program and request their cooperation. The tentative plans have already been discussed with Kathy and met with her understanding and approval. It will be explained to school personnel that Kathy's depression and anxiety stem partly from separation from the mother and certainly not from poor curriculum or deficiency in teachers or peers. The teachers will be asked to reassure the girl often that school personnel are aware of her needs.
  3. To make the school a more positive experience, teachers may:
     a. Ask Kathy what she really enjoys most in school and reward her with this for attendance if at all possible. She may be rewarded also with recognition, special commendations, and "helper" tasks in class.
     b. Involve her in small group tasks where she can experience social contacts and peer group approval (her special interests are in animal behavior and art). As-

sign her a "Big Sister" for support in school.

   c. Provide extra help for make-up work after her absence and find opportunities to give her personal approval.

   d. Reinforce the girl's attendance by enthusiastically greeting her when she attends and when she completes her assignments.

   e. Allow her to sit with students whom she selects and inform them privately that she needs friendship and their support.

  4. The psychologist, who has had training in behavior therapy, will become actively involved as Kathy's therapist by beginning desensitization procedures (to be explained to the staff) to alleviate and reduce the fear of separation.

B. Recommendations to Parents

  1. The mother should make arrangements to drive Kathy to and from school each day, meeting the girl at increasing distances from the school building. The mother's presence and praise upon meeting her should serve to reinforce "walking home" behavior. The mother must be absolutely reliable in punctuality so that Kathy does not become anxious at not seeing her mother as expected.

  2. The parents will be asked to give permission for the school psychologist to begin therapeutic sessions for desensitization of anxiety. This behavioral approach will be explained at length to both the K's and Kathy. Essentially, physical relaxation will be paired with pleasant imagery and, in hierarchical order, with anxiety provoking imagery.

  3. It will be explained to the parents that school teachers, the curriculum, and peers have little or nothing to do with creating her problems, but that Kathy's anxieties stem from stressful expectations of parents coming from their very high expectations for her academic future. Further contacts will determine if specific parental adjustments can be made in harmonizing the home rela-

tionships.

4. To reduce anxiety related to the school situation, the parents should lower expectations for school and social achievement. The parents will be asked to find places to praise her at home, reassure her of their continued interest, and to be patient during this period of therapy.

5. Parents must wholeheartedly support the expectancy that Kathy will attend school. Demonstrations of parental involvement in buying new clothes especially for school, creation of hobby areas in the home, and driving the child to school, are helpful in establishing this support.

6. To enhance her self-confidence and independence the parents should:
   a. Give Kathy a weekly allowance for carrying out specific responsibilities in the home and allow her to spend it as she chooses.
   b. Unless the girl asks for assistance, refrain from directing and criticizing her during home assignments and reports.
   c. Afford much praise for any positive efforts in the home. Point out her good qualities and not where she falls short or achieves inadequately.

7. As problems of school phobia and underachievement are related to dynamics within the K. family, the parents will be referred to (a local mental health clinic) for further counseling. The school psychologist will speak to the K.'s and Kathy in this regard.

## II. *Mental Retardation: The Case of Henry H.* *(from page 159)*

A. Recommendations for School Personnel
   1. Placement in Retarded-Educable classes should be continued; reevaluation in two or three years is recommended. In the future, Henry should also be assessed on cognitive measures, which may be developed for minority children.

2. To minimize aggressive behavior:
    a. Encourage and openly praise Henry every time he begins to cooperate with other children. Reinforce social behavior. Maintain close supervision at recess to help prevent his fighting, and deny recess for continued aggression.
    b. Henry should be taught to displace his hostile feelings into available neutral objects such as punching bags, heavy inflated balls, football dummies, during wrestling, etc.
    c. A behavior modification program to substitute cooperative behavior for Henry's peer-directed aggressiveness should be initiated. After the teacher establishes a baseline record for fighting behavior, Henry should be rewarded for acceptable, nonaggressive, yet social behavior for a gradually increasing period of time, utilizing snacks, sodas, and plenty of praise as reinforcers. Be sure Henry understands what is expected of him, and express confidence in his ability to improve even when he fails.
    d. Keep in close contact with Henry's parents, calling them weekly to report progress or incidents of fighting. Mr. and Mrs. H. are interested in Henry's progress, academic and social, and will cooperate fully with the school. They will also appreciate hearing "good news" about him.
    e. Avoid harsh verbal reprimands. Consistency, firmness, and repetition of expectations will more readily lead to less impulsive behavior on Henry's part. Likewise, physical restraint is to be avoided except when there is danger of injury to Henry or to another child.
3. Check Henry's glasses daily to see if they have been cleaned; if badly scratched or cracked, contact the parents and ask that Henry be given new glasses.
4. Individualize instruction insofar as possible. Allow Henry to overlearn material at his own ability level in the academic, perceptual, and motor areas. This may

reinforce his feeling of competency and reduce feelings of inferiority.

5. Henry requires a rather rigid schedule, with only a minimal amount of tasks requiring creativity, originality, or self-initiation.

6. Use a multi-sensory approach to aid in development of all areas of learning. Have Henry identify objects by sight, feel, sound, taste, and smell. Provide learning exercises that use vision and hearing in combination with the other senses. Because Henry's greatest perceptual difficulties lie in the visual channel, learning experiences should not be restricted to this channel alone. At best, he is an auditory learner.

7. To aid reading, the Fernald Visual-Auditory-Kinesthetic-Tactile System for presenting letters, sounds, and words might be employed. The teacher writes a word on paper with a felt pen; the child says the word as he traces it, first with his finger, then with a pencil. This is repeated until the child can write the word without looking at it. He writes the word, then checks it himself; upon learning it, he places it in a word file box.

8. Special perceptual training is needed in the visual perceptual area:

   a. To improve visual perception —
      (1) Draw forms on the blackboard; have Henry identify those alike.
      (2) Place cardboard cutouts over corresponding shapes.
      (3) Match pictures and concrete objects.
      (4) Cut out various geometric shapes outlined with heavy black lines.
      (5) Point out parts of figures — lines, angles, relationships.
      (6) Reproduce designs on pegboard, ceiling tiles with golf tees, etc.
      (7) Find missing parts in pictures.
      (8) Finish incomplete geometric forms.
      (9) Find hidden objects in pictures.

  b. To improve visual discrimination —
    (1) Practice matching colors, forms, noting differences between objects.
    (2) Observe and match objects of size and shape in the room.
    (3) Sort small objects by size and color — marbles, buttons,. etc.
    (4) Look at pictures of objects — describe how alike and how different.
    (5) Arrange pictures in (left-to-right) story sequence: beginning, middle, end.
  c. To improve visual memory —
    (1) Look at a picture, then try to recall as many objects seen as possible.
    (2) Reproduce sequences — beads, blocks, designs.
  d. To improve auditory discrimination, develop activities such as these —
    (1) Look at two pictures; choose one named turkey, one named turtle; then one named ax, one named eggs.
    (2) Ask Henry questions such as —
      "Which grow on chickens — feathers or sweaters?" "Which is an animal — a puppy or a puddle?"
    (3) Have Henry distinguish and identify sounds, e.g. scissors, a striking hammer, sweeping, a saw cutting, a bell ringing.
9. To aid in development of concepts and abstract thinking:
  a. Play games of how things are alike and how they are different.
  b. Have Henry place objects, then words, into different categories, e.g. fruit, school supplies, tools, toys — according to color, shape, function, etc. To gather a supply of ideas for a picture scrapbook of word concepts, he can cut pictures from magazines as part of a group or individual class project.
10. Provide activities for laterality and directionality

training: have Henry identify body parts, using himself and also pictures; have him imitate movements, play a game of "I touch my right ear, . . ." etc., marching; use left-right orientation in giving directions to Henry.

11. Provide activities for improvement of coordination:
   a. Jump from one foot to the other: forward, back, to the sides.
   b. Hop, keeping time to a drumbeat; first one foot, then the other.
   c. Walk on tiptoes; stop and begin on command.
   d. Walk a low balance beam.
   e. Walk a line, heel to toe.
   f. Throw a ball and/or beanbag at a target, aiming for improvement of both accuracy and distance.
   g. Imitate body movements and bodily position.
   h. Encourage Henry to join in competitive games at recess and on the playground. Simple straight-line activities such as foot races and relays require considerable exertion and obedience to rules but not much fine-motor coordination. This may improve both his gross coordination and his social behavior.
   i. For fine coordination, folding, cutting, collating, and tying activities are suggested, along with hand puppets and finger puppets.

12. Since Henry is particularly sensitive about his short stature, perhaps his teacher could occasionally point out to the entire class at appropriate times that "biggest" is not necessarily synonymous with "best." For example, the best modern televisions and radios are those that take up the least space for wiring, tubes, etc.; astronauts must be small enough to fit into space-vehicle compartments; very small U.S. soldiers have been called upon to play an especially difficult and dangerous role (underground missions); small cars are better for driving and parking on city streets.

13. The token economy successfully implemented last spring should be reinstated as soon as funds are made available. The behavior modification system utilized in

the classroom by the teacher has gained impressive results in motivating Henry to achieve academically. The system should be continued, utilizing both tangible (food, use of toys and games, token "money") and social (praise, recognition, favored classroom tasks) reinforcements.

14. Extinguish lying behavior by showing obvious displeasure and withholding reinforcers. Conversely, truthfulness, especially regarding his own behavior, is to be reinforced.

15. Assignment of Henry to male teachers is strongly recommended.

B. Recommendations to Parents

1. To extinguish enuresis, a chart on Henry's bedroom wall should be used to record his nights with no wetting. He can be taught to keep his own record with checks or stars. All progress should be praised and otherwise reinforced with tangible items and with affection and pride. If and when it becomes economically feasible, the Wee-Alert® (a behavior modification system) should be obtained as an aid for Henry, since the bell and light combination for bedwetters has been quite effective in training.

2. Make sure Henry is wearing clean glasses with the correct prescription and without cracks or scratches. Break-resistant, double-thickness, tempered glass is suggested as an alternative to easily scratched plastic lenses.

3. Do not express, by word or gesture, disappointment over Henry's poor coordination, slow academic progress, and occasional forgetfulness. Any sign of rejection or disappointment over manifestations of his retardation will only substantiate his feelings of rejection and worthlessness, possibly stimulating still more aggressive and violent behavior. Levels of expectation should be kept consistent with Henry's ability. In view of his limitations in attention span and verbal skills, he is not recommended for psychotherapy. It is predicted that if the above prescriptions are put into effect, a decrease in

his aggressive behavior will result, and there should also be reductions in other problems.

4. The meaning of "mental retardation" will be explained in depth to Henry's parents during the feedback session, so that they understand more fully his handicap. He is not like other children his age; he will always lag behind others his age in accumulated knowledge, learning skills, and learning rate; his condition is neither their fault nor his; it is relatively permanent; he is presently highly motivated and is learning to the best of his ability. With their firm expectation that he can and will achieve realistic goals, and with their support, sympathy, and understanding, there is reason to believe that Henry might be able to finish high school (in special classes), read, write, and hold a steady job. Mr. H.'s dream of having his two sons work with him, helping him in the auto mechanic business, might well be a possibility.

5. Mr. H. should continue taking an interest in Henry's progress, teaching him games, exercises, manual skills, and taking part in father-son activities. Henry desperately needs his stepfather's patient, caring, firm guidance and reasonable expectations for achievement.

6. Personal interest in Henry's homework and progress should continue as before, but with the new understanding that Henry will likely never match other children his own age.

7. The causes and possible results of Mrs. H.'s tendency to be overprotective of Henry will be discussed at length during the feedback session. She may realize that she must join her husband in making rules of behavior and realistic expectations for achievement and in enforcing them consistently and fairly. Such limits will be specified during feedback.

8. With regard to Henry's highly impulsive, aggressive behavior and his lying, parents were reminded that the boy will learn self-control only to the extent that they expect and require him to do so. They must jointly

undertake a consistent plan of action, refusing to reinforce or indulge (by attention, especially) any unacceptable behavior by Henry toward his peers and siblings. On the other hand, every positive social act, beginning with simple gestures such as greeting them with a "Good morning" at breakfast and gradually working up to going whole days without a quarrel, should be reinforced via praise, attention, extra privileges.

9. Mrs. H.'s attention, affection, and love presently constitute the single most powerful reinforcement device for achieving desired behaviors. She should therefore make such reinforcements contingent upon the behaviors Henry needs to increase, including affection toward siblings, truthfulness, responsiveness to Mr. H., satisfactory performance of chores.

10. Mr. H. should demonstrate more open affection and attention toward Henry, even though the boy may not be responsive to him for several weeks or months. He must try to win Henry's friendship by encouraging him for effort or interest even if Henry cannot yet perform successfully. He must not wait for Henry to accomplish something dramatic or unusual but rather watch for small accomplishments, small gestures of friendship, and so on.

11. Both parents should make it clear that they disapprove of cruelty; all such acts should result in deprivation of privileges. Special reinforcement systems will be detailed to the parents involving television privileges, money for food and clothes, the right to select his own clothes, the chance to act responsibly as the oldest boy, and signs of approval by adults. Further, he likes opportunities to swim, ride his bike, color and trace, and "play school."

12. In addition to improving his behavior at home, Henry's parents should also reward him for every day that he attends school without getting involved in a skirmish. In this case, the teacher should be contacted regularly by telephone so as not to reinforce lying behavior on

Henry's part.

### III. Learning Disabilities: The Case of Barry B. (from page 184)

A. Recommendations to the Parents

1. Special school placement is recommended for Barry to develop his overall academic skills. Contact has been made with the counselor at (a learning disability school), who has indicated that Barry would likely be accepted into their program in September once state funds are appropriated.

2. To reduce temper tantrums, Barry should be immediately placed in a room by himself every time he engages in a tantrum. This room should not contain any toys, games, or other enjoyable playthings. Before putting him in the room, Mrs. B. should inform him that if he becomes quiet within, say, twenty minutes, he will be rewarded by being allowed to leave the room and engage in a desired activity. If he is not, then he must remain in the room until he is quiet. When Barry becomes quiet following a tantrum, he should also be praised. Once he is able to calm down more quickly Mrs. B. may gradually reduce the amount of time in which he is allowed to become quiet.

   It is very important that Barry be rewarded as soon as he has settled down. For this reason, either Mrs. B. or the grandmother must remain nearby until Barry becomes quiet. After he comes out, they should be sure to discuss what made him upset in the first place.

3. Mrs. B. should not do Barry's homework, supervise, or prompt him. She should be available to help Barry should he request it; however, this assistance should only be enough to get him started on a task or to answer a specific question.

   To help Barry learn to assume the responsibility for his own homework, at his low level, set up a star chart in his room. Inform him that every weekday, if he does his homework with a minimum of supervision and help, he will get a star on his chart and will be allowed to stay up thirty minutes later than his usual bedtime, or some such privilege. Barry should be praised at these times when he assumes responsibility for his homework. On Saturday, if Barry has accumulated, say, three stars out of a possible five, then he can be rewarded by being allowed to engage in some special activity such as going to the zoo or a movie, etc. When Barry is regularly able to attain three out of five stars, increase the criterion for success to four out of five stars and finally to five out of five stars.

4. Barry should be consistently praised for good efforts, not just acceptable performances. Rather than informing him of his mistakes, say, "That was a good try." Praise him for doing part of a task well rather than criticizing him for not doing the entire thing. For school reports, praise him for average achievements and slight improvements from one grading period to another in particular subject areas. He should not be punished for poor school performances.

   Barry should also be praised for human acts and the many positive personal qualities he possesses, such as his handsome appearance, politeness, desire to please, etc. His mother should recognize and discuss with him the positive academic strengths revealed by this testing: average mental ability, good math achievement, etc. It is important for Barry to realize that he is loved at home just for being himself.

5. He should be given a greater amount of freedom to do things on his own. Allow him to cut his own meat and tend to his own needs at the table as do the other children. Supervision of his play activities should be gradually relaxed. Allow him to play within a two-block radius of the house on Saturdays, and gradually increase the amount of time and the distance he can play from home as he gets older. Perhaps Barry could be allowed to go to the nearby park by himself. Allow him

to spend the night at a friend's house when the situation arises. Mrs. B. should not intervene in Barry's behalf when he encounters difficulty with his peers. Let him meet all situations with his own resources even if it is evident that he is not performing well.

Communicate to him that he is allowed more freedom because he is a "big boy" and no longer a baby. Barry should be praised for his attempts to be independent and given encouragement when he fails. As he becomes more independent, his self-confidence should improve. Furthermore, by allowing him greater freedom, Mrs. B. will be giving herself more free time with her other children.

6. His mother should use as much of her free time as possible to do things alone with Barry, such as playing picture bingo and cards, putting together puzzles, and having a catch. Intensive efforts should be made to establish a closer relationship between mother and son, but not one of dependency and infantalization.

   Mrs. B. must learn to become a good listener to her children. She should encourage Barry to talk to her about whatever he desires. Furthermore, she should decrease the amount of talk and the speed and complexity of her speech when talking to Barry, in view of his limitations. Because of Barry's auditory handicap, he is frequently overwhelmed by these aspects of his mother's verbal expression. Weekend activities such as visits to zoos, museums, etc. can be used to provide the stimulation necessary for him to practice expressing himself.

7. Mrs. B. should not give Barry more than one thing to remember at once. Ask him to get only one item at the store or one canned vegetable or fruit from the basement.

8. Mrs. B. may want to contact the nearest district office of Family Services for counseling in family management and in adjusting to her problems with Barry when she feels she needs it. Barry should see an audiologist.

B. Recommendations for the School:

1. Because of his need for specialized instruction, he should be placed in a special education class for learning disabled children. He should never be placed in a class for the mentally retarded.

   If he is accepted into a program for learning disabled children he should be tested diagnostically by the reading and arithmetic specialists in order to determine his specific strengths and weaknesses beyond those assessed here. Specific instructional recommendations for remediation should also be made at this time.

2. To increase attending and in-seat behavior, his teacher should inform him that he will be given a rating, say, four times during class. The points that he can receive on each of these four occasions range from one to ten. These ratings should reflect the amount of time that he remained in his seat and attended to his school work during each quarter and are based on the subjective estimate of the teacher. At the end of each class quarter the teacher should inform the child how many points he has earned and write the number in a small notebook to be kept at his desk. After class the total number of points may be exchanged for anywhere from one to fifteen minutes of free time with which he can engage in some desired activity such as playing cards, going to the gym, etc. The amount of free time earned should reflect the number of points earned, i.e. five points should only buy one-half as much free time as ten points. Barry should be praised for the points he earns and encouraged to try to earn as many points as he can.

3. To improve Barry's knowledge of the letters of the alphabet, cut out posterboard letters of all twenty-six letters. Encourage Barry to study his letters in the following manner:

   a. Present one letter at a time telling him the name of each letter. Have him first look at each letter attending to the general visual configuration, straight or curved lines, etc.

   b. Have him close his eyes and visualize each letter in

his head.

c. Next, have him pick up the letter and feel its contours.

d. With the letter placed flat against his desk, have him trace over the letter with the index finger of his writing hand.

e. Have him write the letter from memory and say its name as he is writing it.

f. Next, tell him how each letter sounds, again one letter at a time starting first with the consonants, and then the short vowel sounds, etc. Have him repeat the sound. If he has difficulty with the sound, give him a word family of three words that all have that sound.

g. Repeat the above steps until he is able to associate the name of each letter of the alphabet with its sounds and visual image.

4. In order to improve Barry's spelling have him learn spelling words in the following manner:

a. The teacher writes each word on a separate card in marker large enough for him to trace.

b. He then traces each word with his finger as many times as necessary to learn the word.

c. When he thinks he knows the word it is removed from sight and he then writes it from memory.

d. Have him check his own words and repeat the above steps until he correctly spells each word.

e. He should then write a sentence using each word.

5. Reading may best be taught by the Fernald VAKT approach — stimulating all sensory channels.

6. To improve auditory perceptual skills:

a. Have Barry close his eyes and become auditorily sensitive to environmental sounds about him. Sounds such as cars, airplanes, outside noises, etc., can be attended to and identified. He can also be asked to distinguish and identify noises the teacher makes such as dropping a pencil, tearing a piece of paper, using a stapler, bouncing a ball, sharpening a pencil, opening a window, turning on the lights, leafing through the pages of a book, cutting with scissors, etc.

b. Present word families in which only the initial consonants differ. Then present families in which only the final consonants differ. Finally, change only the medial vowels. Encourage him to become used to listening to slight variations in sound.

c. Play "Simon Says" and other games requiring him to listen carefully and understand verbal instructions.

d. Read him a story or a sentence with a nonsense element in it, sometimes at the beginning, middle or end, and ask him to explain what is funny about the story or sentence.

7. It is believed that Barry would most benefit from a patient, reinforcing teacher who will consistently praise him for correct answers, slight improvements in his academic work, and good efforts. He needs contact with a male model with whom he could identify. Initially, call on him only when it is apparent that he knows the correct answer. Make a habit of praising Barry for human acts and his positive personal qualities. It is important for him to feel liked at school. Hopefully, with a special curriculum to develop his academic competence and consistent praise from a warm, accepting teacher, Barry will no longer view school as a frustrating experience.

8. To encourage the development of independence, give Barry special classroom responsibilities such as watering the flowers, taking attendance, and delivering messages.

## Section 2: Page References for Scoring and Interpretation of Test Responses

*See the following:*                                                      *page*

A. Ned Steer (Mixed Diagnosis)                                               8

# REFERENCES

American Psychiatric Association. *Diagnostic and Statistical Manual of Mental Disorders.* Washington: American Psychiatric Association, 1968.

Barclay, J. R. *Consultant's Handbook of the Barclay Classroom Climate Inventory.* Lexington: Educational Skills Development, 1975.

Bateman, B. B. Educational implications of minimal brain dysfunction. *The Reading Teacher,* 1974, *27,* 662-665.

Beck, S. J. *Rorschach's Test.* New York: Grune, 1950.

Bettelheim, B. *Love Is Not Enough.* New York: Free Press of Glencoe, 1950.

Bettelheim, B. *Truants from Life.* New York: Free Press of Glencoe, 1955.

Birch, H. G. (Ed.). *Brain Damage in Children.* Baltimore: Williams and Wilkins, 1964.

Blanco, R. F. *Prescriptions for Children with Learning and Adjustment Problems.* Springfield: Thomas, 1972.

Blanco, R. F. *Underachievers: Family Types I, II, and III.* Unpublished lectures, Department of School Psychology, Temple University, 1977.

Bricklin, B. & Bricklin, P. *Bright Child — Poor Grades: The Psychology of Underachievement.* New York: Delacorte, 1967.

Brutten, M., Richardson, S. O., & Mangel, C. *Something's Wrong With My Child.* New York: Har Brace J, 1973.

Clements, S. D. *Minimal Brain Dysfunction in Children: Terminology and Identification.* Public Health Service Publication No. 1415. Washington: U.S. National Institute of Neurological Diseases and Stroke, 1966.

Clements, S. D. & Peters, J. E. Minimal brain dysfunction in the school-age child. *Arch Gen Psychiatry, 6,* 1962, 185-197.

Cooper, J. A. Application of the consultant role to parent-teacher management of school avoidance behavior. *Psychology in the Schools,* 1973, *10*(2), 258-262.

Cruickshank, W. M. (Ed.). *Psychology of Exceptional Children and Youth* (3rd ed.). Englewood Cliffs, P-H, 1971.

De La Cruz, F. F. & La Vech, G. D. (Eds.). *Human Sexuality and the Mentally Retarded.* New York: Brunner-Mazel, 1973.

Des Lauriers, A. & Carlson, C. F. *Your Child Is Asleep: Early Infantile Autism.* Homewood: Dorsey, 1969.

Doll, E. A. The essentials of an inclusive concept of mental deficiency. *J Ment Defic,* 1941, *46,* 214-219.

233

Ellis, A. *Reason and Emotion in Psychotherapy.* New York: Lyle Stuart, 1962.

Ellis, A. *Humanistic Psychotherapy: The Rational-Emotive Approach.* New York: McGraw, 1974.

Freeman, S. F. *Does Your Child Have a Learning Disability?* Springfield: Thomas, 1974.

Goertzel, V. & Goertzel, M. *Cradles of Eminence.* Boston: Little, 1962.

Group for the Advancement of Psychiatry. *Psychopathological Disorders in Childhood: Theoretical Considerations and a Proposed Classification.* New York: Group for the Advancement of Psychiatry, 6, Report No. 62, June, 1966.

Grossman, F. K. *Brothers and Sisters of Retarded Children.* Syracuse: Syracuse U Pr, 1972.

Hammill, D. Training visual perceptual processes. *Journal of Learning Disabilities,* 1972, *5,* 552-559.

Hammill, D. D. & Bartel, N. R. *Teaching Children With Learning and Behavior Problems* (2nd ed.). Boston: Allyn, 1978.

Heber, R. (Ed.). A manual on terminology and classification in mental retardation. *Am J Ment Defic,* Monograph Supplement (Rev.), 1961.

Kehle, T. J. & Guidubaldi, J. *Effects of EMR Placement Models on Affective and Social Development.* Paper presented at NASP Convention, Cincinnati, Ohio, March 26, 1976.

Kelly, E. W. School phobia: A review of theory and treatment. *Psychology in the Schools,* 1973, *10*(1), 33-42.

Kessler, J. *Psychopathology of Childhood.* Englewood Cliffs: P-H, 1966.

Kirk, S. A. *Educating Exceptional Children* (2nd ed.). Boston: H M, 1972.

Kornrich, M. (Ed.). *Underachievement.* Springfield: Thomas, 1965.

Ledebur, G. W. The elementary learning disability process group and the school psychologist. *Psychology in the Schools,* 1977, *14*(1), 62-66.

Locher, P. J. & Worms, P. F. Visual scanning strategies in neurologically impaired, perceptually impaired, and normal children viewing the Bender-Gestalt designs. *Psychology in the Schools,* 1977, *14*(2), 147-157.

McDonald, J. E. & Sheperd, G. School phobia: An overview. *Journal of School Psychology,* 1976 *14*(4), 291-306.

Manchester, F. S. *Special Education Standards.* Pennsylvania Department of Education, Harrisburg, Penn., September 30, 1977, pp. 3-4.

Marine, E. School refusal — Who should intervene (diagnostic and treatment categories). *Journal of School Psychology,* 1968-69, *7,* 63-70.

Meyers, J., Martin, R., & Hyman, I. (Eds.). *School Consultation.* Springfield: Thomas, 1977.

Morrow, W. R. Academic underachievement. In C. G. Costello (Ed.), *Symptoms of Psychopathology: A handbook.* New York: Wiley, 1970.

Myers, P. I. & Hammill D. D. *Methods for Learning Disorders.* New York: Wiley, 1969.

National Advisory Committee of the Bureau of Education for the Handicapped. U.S. Office of Education, 1967.

Neurological and Sensory Disease Control Program: *Minimal Brain Dysfunction. Phase Two: Educational, Medical, and Health-related Services.* Washington: U.S. Public Health Service, 1969.

Noland, R. L. (Ed.). *Counseling Parents of the Mentally Retarded.* Springfield: Thomas, 1970.

O'Grady, D. O. Psycholinguistic abilities in learning-disabled, emotionally disturbed, and normal children. *Journal of Special Education* (Vol. 8), 2, 1974.

Palmer, J. O. *The Psychological Assessment of Children.* New York: Wiley, 1970.

Patterson, G. R. A learning theory approach to the treatment of the school phobic child. In L. P. Ullmann & L. Krasner (Eds.), *Case Studies in Behavior Modification.* New York: HR&W, 1965.

Piotrowski, Z. *Perceptanalysis.* Philadelphia: Ex Libris, 1976.

Quinn, J. A. & Wilson, B. J. Programming effects on learning disabled children: Performance and affect. *Psychology in the Schools,* 1977, *14*(2), 196-199.

Rosenfeld, J. G. & Blanco, R. F. Incompetency in school psychology: The case of "Dr. Gestalt." *Psychology in the Schools,* 1974, *11*(3), 263-269.

Ross, A. O. *The Exceptional Child in the Family.* New York: Grune, 1964.

Safirstein, S. Passive-aggressive personality disorder: A search for a syndrome. *A J Psychiatry,* 1970, *125*(7), 973-983.

Sarason, S. *Psychological Problems in Mental Deficiency.* New York: Har-Row, 1969.

Schulterbrandt, J. G. & Raskin, A. (Eds.). *Depression in Childhood: Diagnosis, Treatment, and Conceptual Models.* New York: Raven, 1977.

Seiderman, A. S. An optometric approach to the diagnosis of visually-based problems in learning, pp. 330-343. In G. Leisman (Ed.), *Basic Visual Processes and Learning Disabilities.* Springfield: Thomas, 1976.

Small, L. *Rorschach Location and Scoring Manual.* New York: Grune, 1956.

Tahmisian, J. A. & McReynolds, W. I. Use of parents as behavioral engineers in the treatment of a school phobic girl. *Journal of Counseling Psychology,* 1971, *18*, 225-228.

Ullmann, L. P. & Krasner, L. *Case Studies in Behavior Modification.* New York: HR&W, 1965.

Valett, R. E. *The Remediation of Learning Disabilities.* Palo Alto, California: Fearon, 1968.

Vance, H., Gaynor, P., & Coleman, M. Analysis of cognitive abilities for learning disabled children. *Psychology in the Schools,* 1976, *13*(4), 477-483.

Weiner, I. B. Psychodynamic aspects of learning disability: The passive-aggressive underachiever. *Journal of School Psychology,* 1971, *60*(3), 246-251.

Wender, P. H. *Minimal Brain Dysfunction in Children.* New York: Wiley

Interscience, 1971.

Wisland, M. V. (Ed.). *Psychoeducational Diagnosis of Exceptional Children.* Springfield: Thomas, 1974.

Wolfensberger, V. & Kurtz, R. A. Usage of retardation-related diagnostic and descriptive labels by parents of retarded children. *Journal of Special Education* (Vol. 8), 2, 1974.

Wolpe, J. *Psychotherapy by Reciprocal Inhibition.* Stanford U Pr, 1958.

# AUTHOR INDEX

237

**O**

O'Grady, D. O., 161, 235

**P**

Palmer, J. O., 5, 235
Patterson, G. R., 68, 235
Peters, J. E., 162, 233
Piotrowski, Z., 127, 235

**Q**

Quinn, J. A., 235

**R**

Raskin, A., 6, 235
Richardson, S. O., 233
Rosenfeld, J. G., 5, 235
Ross, A. O., 137, 235

**S**

Safirstein, S., 235
Sarason, S., 140, 235
Schulterbrandt, J., 6, 235

Seiderman, A. S., 161, 235
Sheperd, G., 68, 234
Small, L., 127, 235

**T**

Tahmisian, J. A., 235

**U**

Ullmann, L. P., 5, 235

**V**

Valett, R. E., 161, 235
Vance, H., 161, 235

**W**

Weiner, I. B., 235
Wender, P. H., 161, 162, 236
Wilfensberger, V., 140, 236
Wilson, B. J., 235
Wisland, M. V., 137, 236
Wolpe, J., 131, 236
Worms, P. F., 161, 234

# SUBJECT INDEX

## A

Abandonment, fear of, 86
Abstract thinking, 220
Achievement, 10
  tests, 17, 162
Acting-out
  acute transient situational, 53
  sexual, 100
Adaptive responses, 69
Affection, 173
Aggressiveness, 36, 42, 58, 74, 150, 230
  minimizing, 218
  verbal, 45
Alcohol abuse, 93
Ambidexterity, 41
American Psychiatric Association, 233
Anal sadism, 169
Anger, 74
Ankle jerk, 41
Anxiety, 15, 55, 68, 69, 131, 163, 184, 231
  desensitization, hypnotic, 121-136
  separation, 75
Apraxia, tongue, 41
Association
  free, 85
  phonic-visual, 168
Asymmetric reflexes, 52
Attention span, 162, 173, 175
Auditory
  discrimination, 220
  impairment, 197-209
  perception, 161
Autism, 6
Awkwardness, 52, 161

## B

Balance, 183
Barclay Classroom Climate Inventory
  (1975), 139

Beery-Buktenica Visual-Motor Integration Test, 157, 166
Behavior
  modification, 56, 116, 163
  problems, 4
  emotional disturbances, 55-136
  therapy, 131
Bender-Visual-Motor-Gestalt Test, 31, 32, 38, 82, 111, 148, 157, 182, 203
Big Brothers Association, 144
Blacky Pictures, 169, 231
Blindness, 209
Brain damage, 40, 41, 42
  minimal, 54, 145, 161, 183
  organic dysfunction, 52

## C

California Achievement Tests, 17, 111
Cerebral dysfunction, 40, 41, 42
  minimal, 54, 145, 161, 183
Change, accepting, 27-28
Columbia Mental Maturity Test, 212
Communication disorders, 162
Competition, 10
Competitiveness, 28
Concentration, 18
Concept development, 220
Conflict, psychological, 37
Coordination, 28
  improvement, 221
Crippled, 209
Cruelty, 224
Crying, severe, 113-121

## D

Deafness, 209
Death orientation, 34
Deconditioning, 69
Depression, 6

mild, 184
Desensitization, 15, 69, 76, 115, 131
 hypnotic, 121-136
Developmentally disabled, 140 (*see also* Retardation)
Diagnosis, 5
Dilantin-phenobarb, 52
Directionality, 220
Down Syndrome, 141
Draw-a-man-test, 32, 33, 88, 231
Drive, high, 10

**E**

Ego, positive ideal, 172
Educational perspectives, 4
Electroencephalogram (EEG), 52
Emotional
 disturbance, 4, 39, 42, 51, 55-136, 138
 stamina, 10
Encopresis, 55
Enuresis, 55, 80, 156, 222
Epilepsy, 52, 113

**F**

Family
 broken ties, 163
 therapy, 15, 56, 68, 163
 type I, 9-15
 type II, 103-113
Fantasies, death, 34
Father
 absent, 142
 passive, 104
Fernald Visual-Auditory-Kinesthetic-Tactile System, 151, 219, 229
Finger
 order, poor sense of, 41
 spelling, 211
Follow-up
Free Association, 85

**G**

Gait, tandem, 43
Giftedness, 4, 186-196
 parents
  objecting, 186-187

responsive, 187-189
Gray Oral Reading Paragraphs, 182, 189
Grief reactions, 137
Grimacing, 41
Group for the Advancement of Psychiatry, 234
Growth, maladaptive, 52
Guidance
 eclectic orientation, 4
 multi-theoretical orientation, 4
Guilt, 36, 55, 172

**H**

Hamstring tightness, 41
Handicap, multiple, 4, 209-212
Handwriting, 183
Hearing (*see* Auditory)
Hiskey-Nebraska Test of Learning Aptitude, 201
Hostility, 58, 163
Hyperhidrosis, 41
Hyperkinetic, 161
Hypnogogic state, 132

**I**

Id, 34
Ideation, prepsychotic, 36
Identity, confusion of, 36
Illinois Test of Psycholinguistic Ability, 111, 148, 151, 158, 182, 203
Immaturity, 23
Inadequacy, personal, 36, 51
Inattention, 55
Individual Education Programs (IEP's), 5, 161
Informal Reading Inventory, 148
Intelligence, superior, 10, 186-196
Interventions, prescriptive, 215-230

**K**

Key Math, 148
Knee jerk, 41
Koppitz scoring system, 32
Kuder Preference Record, 122